Praise for *E-Commerce Security:*

"This is a very important book. It deals with the realistic security problems of electronic commerce, in which the weak links are ubiquitous and the best defenses known today are only partial solutions. It is mandatory reading for anyone thinking about getting into e-commerce, because otherwise you will be enormously at risk."

—Peter G. Neumann, Moderator of the Risks Forum
and author of *Computer-Related Risks.*

"Clear, lucid, right on target, and comprehensive . . . Anup Ghosh covers all major categories of digital risk, including client software, transmissions protocols, web-commerce servers and the operating system. If you manage any part of an organization's Internet connection, you owe it to yourself to read this book."

—Peter Tippett, M.D., Ph.D
President, ICSA (International Computer Security Association)

"Anup Ghosh has produced a comprehensive and balanced treatment of e-commerce security issues that addresses the risks at all points of the link between buyer and seller. His readable and realistic analysis explores, not just the vulnerabilities of the network, but also the loopholes in client and server software and operating systems. In this rapidly changing environment, *E-Commerce Security: Weak Links, Best Defenses* is an up-to-date appraisal; Ghosh goes well beyond the obvious threats to illuminate many issues that deserve the thoughtful attention of corporate e-commerce architects."

—Peter Coffee
Advanced Technologies Analyst, PC Week Labs

"The book is to the point, easy to read, comprehensive, and up to date. It deals with an issue of critical importance to anyone contemplating or involved in business on the Internet. Explanations are exceptionally clear."

—M. E. Kabay, Ph.D
Director of Education
ICSA (International Computer Security Association)

E-Commerce Security
Weak Links, Best Defenses

Anup K. Ghosh

WILEY COMPUTER PUBLISHING

John Wiley & Sons, Inc.
New York • Chichester • Weinheim • Brisbane • Singapore • Toronto

Publisher: Robert Ipsen
Editor: Marjorie Spencer
Managing Editor: Erin Singletary
Text Design & Composition: Benchmark Productions, Inc.

Designations used by companies to distinguish their products are often claimed as trademarks. In all instances where John Wiley & Sons, Inc., is aware of a claim, the product names appear in initial capital or all capital letters. Readers, however, should contact the appropriate companies for more complete information regarding trademarks and registration.

This book is printed on acid-free paper. ∞

This publication is designed to provide accurate and authoritative information in regard to the subject matter covered. It is sold with the understanding that the publisher is not engaged in rendering legal, accounting, or other professional services. If legal advice or other expert assistance is required, the services of a competent professional person should be sought.

Library of Congress Cataloging-in-Publication Data

Ghosh, Anup K.
E-commerce security: weak links, best defenses / Anup Ghosh.
    p.   cm.
Includes bibliographical references.
ISBN 0-471-19223-6 (pbk.: alk. paper)
1. Electronic commerce—Security measures. 2. Business enterprises—Computer networks—Security measures. 3. Internet (Computer network)—Security measures. I. Title.
HF5548.32.G48   1998
658.4'78–dc21   97-38328
                                                                                   CIP

Printed in the United States of America
10 9 8 7 6 5 4 3 2

For my parents

Contents

Preface   xi

Acknowledgments   xv

Chapter 1   **Dangers in a Changing Paradigm of
            Business**   1

Banking on the Internet   3

Investing on the Internet   4

Doing Business on the Internet   6

Threats to E-Commerce   9

Vandalism and Sabotage on the Internet   11
Breach of Privacy or Confidentiality   12
Theft and Fraud on the Internet   17
Violations of Data Integrity   19
Denial of Service   20

E-Commerce Security: A System-Wide Problem   21

Client Security   22
Secure Transport   23
Web Server Security   23
Operating System Security   25
The Future of E-Commerce Security   25

References   26

Referenced Web Sites   28

Chapter 2   **Deadly Content: The Client–Side
            Vulnerabilities**   31

Executing Malware   35

ActiveX (In)security   38

vii

ActiveX Containers	38
ActiveX Scripting	39
Authenticode: Establishing Trust for ActiveX	41
Deadly Controls	63
Java Security	*66*
The Java Sandbox	68
Holes in the Sandbox	72
Signing Applets	72
Desktop Integration Problems	*78*
The Cybersnot Problem	79
The UMD Security Hole	81
The MIT Bug	82
The Other Dirty Dozen	*82*
JavaScript	84
Plug-Ins and Graphic Files	87
Attachments	88
Push Technology and Active Channels	89
References	*92*
Referenced Web Sites	*94*

Chapter 3	**Securing the Data Transaction**	**97**
	Secure Channels	*101*
	Using SSL to Establish Secure Sessions	103
	The Role of Certification Authorities	106
	Web Spoofing	109
	How SSL Works	114
	Securing Web Sessions Using S-HTTP	119
	Stored-Account Payment Systems	*124*
	First Virtual	126
	CyberCash	127
	Secure Electronic Transaction	131
	Stored-Value Payment Systems	*135*
	Pros and Cons	136
	How E-Cash Works	137
	Securing E-Cash	138
	Representing Electronic Cash	140
	E-cash	142
	CyberCoin	146

	Smart Cards	147
	Applications of Smart Cards	148
	Storing Value on Smart Cards	150
	CAFE	151
	Mondex	152
	Visa Cash	153
	Summary	*154*
	References	*155*
	Referenced Web Sites	*156*
Chapter 4	**Securing the Commerce Server**	**157**
	The Web Server	*159*
	The Databases	*160*
	The Server-Side Scripts	*161*
	Web Server Security	*162*
	Installing the Web Server Securely	163
	File Access Permissions	164
	Escalating Client Privilege	165
	Accept These Options at Your Own Risk	166
	Controlling Access to Sensitive Documents	168
	Dangerous CGI Scripts	*179*
	Mitigating the Dangers of CGI Scripts	179
	Database Vulnerabilities	*185*
	Designing More Secure Software	*189*
	Buffer Overflows	191
	Analyzing the Security of Software	*197*
	Summary	*202*
	References	*202*
Chapter 5	**Cracks in the Foundation**	**205**
	Securing the Operating System	*205*
	Minding the Operating System	*206*
	Name Your Poison: Unix or Windows NT	*208*
	Firewall Insecurity	*210*
	Locking Down the Firewall	213
	Data-Driven Attacks	214

The Network Server Vulnerabilities   *216*
     Caveat Emptor   218
     Burying the Deadly Defaults   219
     Flaws in the Web Server   226
     Flaws in CGI Scripts   229
     Networking Software Insecurity   232
     Denial of Service   236
     Weak Authentication   240
     Operating System Holes   244
Defending the Server   *247*
References   *249*
Referenced Web Sites   *250*

Chapter 6   **Securing the Future of E-Commerce**   **253**
Certifying Components for Security   *253*
What Is a Software Component?   *254*
The Status Quo   *257*
     Penetrate-and-Patch   257
     Certifying Identity   260
Certifying Software   *261*
To Be Stamped   *262*
     Java Components   262
     ActiveX Components   264
     The Rest of the Bunch   265
Certifying Technologies   *265*
How Safe Is It?   *270*
References   *273*
Referenced Web Sites   *274*

Index   **275**

Preface

Electronic commerce is a new way of engaging in timeless activities—interacting, bartering, and transacting with people and businesses. In a letter written in 1810, Thomas Jefferson said, "Money, not morality, is the principal commerce of a civilized nation." Today, as we become increasingly dependent on the Internet for our personal and professional interests, Jefferson's maxim remains steadfast. Ultimately, money—not morality—will drive the Internet. In spite of its origins as a DARPA-funded research project and its early adoption in the academic communities, the Internet has proven to be an essential vehicle of commerce today. Although some long for the days when the Internet was used strictly for research and collaboration, the Internet must be recognized for its critical role in business today. As in any other means of business, we cannot assume all players will abide by a code of moral conduct. The mere fact that business is being performed online over an insecure medium is enough to entice criminal activity to the Internet.

To this end, a number of technological solutions have been introduced to assure end users and businesses of privacy and confidentiality in online transactions. This book examines the most critical security concerns for users and businesses engaging in all manner of Internet-based e-commerce. In any online activity, a number of software components from one user's software client to another party's server will execute to handle the online transaction—whether it is mail, file transfer, remote login, Web surfing, or commercial trade. History has shown that a failure in any one of these components may compromise the integrity of the whole transaction. This book starts from the premise that a weak link in the chain of components that handle online sessions can compromise the security of the entire transaction and ultimately undermine the confidence of consumers and businesses in e-commerce.

It is important to emphasize that this book is not intended to scare anyone away from participating in e-commerce. Rather, the point is to remove the hype and hysteria surrounding security concerns in e-commerce and replace them with a discussion based on the relevant risks in the underlying technologies. This book addresses the critical security issues in participating in e-commerce today.

Although human factors are almost always weak points in the security of computer systems, this book focuses on the technological issues in e-commerce security. Without an underlying secure infrastructure, there is little hope of ever achieving secure e-commerce. Four critical software components make up almost any e-commerce transaction: the client-side software, the data transaction protocols, the Web (or commerce) server, and the underlying operating system software. A flaw or failure in any one of these components can result in complete system compromise.

Gene Spafford, a computer security researcher at Purdue University, was recently quoted as saying, "Using encryption on the Internet is the equivalent of arranging an armored car to deliver credit-card information from someone living in a cardboard box to someone living on a park bench." The point of this quote is to mock the disparity in technical solutions currently applied to Internet-based transactions. First, an armored car is not the appropriate level of security for the delivery. Surely, a sealed envelope would have sufficed. In Internet sessions, strong encryption is not essential for most data that is sent. Second, realize that the individuals' own environments are not that secure. A cardboard box will not provide much security against a determined thief. Similarly, today's network servers and client software are not adequately secured to prevent determined Internet criminals (or crackers) from obtaining critical data that was sent with the use of strong encryption methods. Breaking into some servers is as simple as breaking into a cardboard box. Finally, it is important to realize that the security of every link in the chain of software components should be equally strong. If the security of the transport is significantly stronger than the security of the end systems, the end systems become obvious targets for crackers. This book addresses the security concerns in each one of the components involved in Internet-based transactions.

Chapter 1 gives several real-life cases of failures in one or more of these components that ultimately compromised security. These examples underscore the point that e-commerce security problems are not theoretical, but they actually occur in practice. As an example that gives credence to Spafford's analogy, consider the case of Carlos Felipe Salgado Jr., who recently pleaded guilty to the theft of personal information on over 100,000 credit card holders via the Internet. He was caught in an FBI sting in which he purportedly paid $260,000 for a diskette containing this confidential information. Allegedly, someone obtained the data by hacking into company databases through the Internet.

Chapter 2 discusses the many risks inherent in the client-side software, including Web browsers, plug-ins, and active content applications such as Java applets and ActiveX controls. The focus of Chapter 2 is to enlighten the reader about the dangers of active content on the Internet. The significance of active content is that it overcomes the limitations of HTML in surfing the Web to make the Web a viable medium for all ranges of business and entertainment applications. Active content is being embedded in Web pages everywhere, often without the end user's awareness of its presence. What makes active content dangerous is that anyone who puts up a Web page has the ability to run programs on your machine. This means that someone else may be able to access your personal files, corrupt your files, send data back over network connections, or deposit Trojan horses, all without your knowledge. The chapter also discusses other problems with Web clients as evidenced in several release versions of the Netscape Navigator/Communicator and Microsoft's Internet Explorer. In addition, it covers the security ramifications (with real examples) of desktop integration of the Web browser and the operating system, as well as the security issues inherent in push technology.

Although push technology promises to deliver content in new and innovative approaches, it also holds the potential for abuse of end-user security and privacy. Push technology is changing the way we receive our information from the Web. Rather than requesting data from the Web, we have it pushed to our machines. Push technology can be an extremely efficient way of receiving updates from favorite Web sites or channels, customized through personalized filters. The use of push technology to deliver active content and software upgrades (essentially program executables) now makes downloading of potentially malicious programs completely transparent.

Chapter 3 describes several protocols now used to secure the data transaction in e-commerce applications. Currently, end users and merchants have a variety of options to use in securing the data from client to server. An overview of several secure transaction protocols widely used in both personal computers and smart cards is given, along with an assessment of their strengths and weaknesses. What is important to remember is that data transaction security simply protects the data from being observed in transit by unauthorized third parties. That is, the data cannot be read and interpreted by someone who has no business observing the data sent over the Internet. This is important to provide privacy of transactions. But secure transaction protocols will not provide security for the systems on either end of the transaction protocol. The security provided by these protocols can be completely circumvented if either end of the transaction is insecure.

Chapter 4 addresses weaknesses in Web server software used to handle e-commerce transactions. This chapter takes a critical look at an often overlooked aspect of e-commerce: server-side security. Flaws in any one of the three basic components of the commerce server—the Web server, the interface software, and the database—can be sufficient to allow an intruder access to sensitive company and client data. The chapter presents salient vulnerabilities in each of these components and methods for securing them. It highlights the simple problems in configuration of Web servers that have a huge impact on the security of the Web server. In addition, the importance for designing security into software design and the necessity to analyze software for security are underscored.

Chapter 5 addresses the security of the Web server machine itself. The Web server machine is usually, in fact, a network server offering a host of network services to the Internet at large. Vulnerabilities in the network services, including and beyond the Web server itself, can be ports of entry for nefarious Internet users. Underlying the server software is a bunch of supporting operating system software. Vulnerabilities in this software can be used to bypass the secure mechanisms (such as access control in network services) and secure configurations of Web server software to violate the security of the commerce server. In most sites offering commercial transactions over the Web, the valuable data is stored on databases that reside behind the firewalls and the network server machine. Data-driven attacks can exploit weaknesses in the network server software to access the valuable database server machine. Chapter 5 classifies network server machine vulnerabilities into seven broad categories that have been demonstrated in practice. The chapter shows how the two most popular network server platforms found on desktops today, Unix and Windows NT, stacked up against vulnerabilities found in practice according to the seven categories.

Finally, Chapter 6 provides a peek into the future of e-commerce security. Software used in e-commerce applications will likely follow the component-based software paradigm now being actively promoted and developed by software companies. The future of e-commerce applications will be secured more readily when security is considered during development and before release. Chapter 6 discusses techniques for hardening and analyzing the software components that underlie e-commerce transactions against malicious attack. The use of certification of security for software components is discussed as a practical approach for assuring confidence in the security of e-commerce.

Whether you are a computer professional, a business manager, a system administrator, or a Web surfer, this book will explain the relevant risks and provide best defenses for using the Internet today for e-commerce.

Acknowledgments

Writing this book was not an effort of one. It took a great deal of input and support from a large number of people to make *E-Commerce Security: Weak Links, Best Defenses* possible. I would like to give thanks to everyone who helped me along the way to make it as good as it can possibly be. Special thanks to Reliable Software Technologies, the company that gave me the opportunity to investigate e-commerce security. Thanks to my research colleagues at RST, Jeffrey Voas and Gary McGraw, for supporting and pushing the edge in security research. Thanks to Paul Pruitt and Steven Cours of RST, who researched much of the material in Chapter 5. Thanks to Andrew Stauffer, Frank Charron, Scott Marks, Roger Alexander, and Jonathan Beskin for reviewing parts of the manuscript and providing valuable comments. Thanks to Marjorie Spencer at Wiley for recognizing the value of this work and making its publication possible. Thanks to Margaret Hendrey at Wiley for pushing forward the progress of the book and providing helpful feedback throughout the process.

Finally, but most important, this book would not be were it not for the support of those most influential in my life—my family. My wife, Nita, deserves immeasurable credit and appreciation for the support she gave from the start through the end of this book. Thanks to everyone else in my now extended family for your support and patience with my infrequent and short visits.

Chapter 1

Dangers in a Changing
Paradigm of Business

Electronic commerce, or e-commerce, is changing the way in which consumers, merchants, and businesses interact and transact. E-commerce provides consumers the ability to bank, invest, purchase, distribute, communicate, explore, and research from home, work, cafes, bookstores, airports, conferences, hotel rooms, or virtually anywhere an Internet connection can be had. Perhaps more important for consumers is that the dizzying array of products and services offered over the Internet is in a form very close to that of true free market competition. Without the imposition of political boundaries and geographic distances, it is as easy to do business with a remotely located specialty book store as it is with the local superstore bookstore. Retail businesses are able to increase sales with a presence on the Internet. One benefit of e-commerce is that the store is effectively open 24 hours a day, 7 days a week. Furthermore, staff need not be awake and "in the store" to receive orders and process payments. Orders can be processed online in real time, or off-line in batch processes. Since e-commerce is not constrained by geography, local shops can compete with national and multinational companies for consumers located anywhere in the world.

E-commerce is impacting non-retailing businesses in significant but often less visible ways. In spite of the hype surrounding e-commerce for consumer products and services, the market that will have the most significant impact on e-commerce will be the

1

horizontal market for business-to-business commerce. This market includes all aspects of using networked computers for business purposes including office automation, electronic mail, corporate intranets, extranets, and Web and EDI systems for document exchange and purchasing. E-commerce has become synonymous with Internet-based commerce. Before the Internet became a medium for business, Electronic Data Interchange (EDI) systems were purchased at great cost to exchange data over proprietary networks. Barriers erected by expensive proprietary networks known as value added networks (VANs) and one-of-a-kind EDI systems have now fallen to the Internet. Internet based EDI allows small to midsize businesses to compete on equal footing with larger companies.

Three growth areas in e-commerce that will impact anyone curious enough to pick up this book are in banking, investing, and inter-business commerce. The growth potential in these areas is examined next in this chapter. While this book is an advocate for developing e-commerce markets, this book examines the security issues in utilizing the Internet for commercial applications. Security mechanisms currently in place and taken for granted in most forms of commerce are only now being developed for e-commerce. While many forms of commerce use relatively inexpensive security checks to discourage fraud, the technology developed for on-line commerce must be extremely vigilant to prevent and discourage security violations. The very nature of computing has the ability to amplify many fold the effect of a simple error in securing e-commerce software to large-scale fraud, theft, or security intrusions. For example, most diners are not too concerned about the possibility of a waiter keeping an imprint of their credit card number. Similarly, most of us feel comfortable to give our credit card numbers over the phone to a merchant operator when using the phone for commercial transactions. Why should e-commerce be any different? The answer lies in the scale by which fraud or theft can be perpetrated by flaws in the software systems that make e-commerce possible. A simple error in configuring a commerce site's Web server can lead to the compromise of thousands of credit card numbers, which can be quickly distributed widely. Dumpster diving for credit card numbers does not concern banks too much, while large-scale fraud and theft do.

To drive home the seriousness of security issues in Internet commerce, several case studies of real security and privacy intrusions are presented. The point of these case studies is not to cause concern about the problem, but to provide evidence of the seriousness of the situation. Even while this book was being drafted, several new high profile security violations have hit the headlines of major newspapers. Most newspapers carry at least one "failure in e-commerce security" piece a week. As the pace of e-commerce grows and the software used to implement e-commerce functions becomes more complex, the number of expected failures in security will only rise.

To begin to address the problems of e-commerce security, four key areas in securing e-commerce are introduced in the latter portion of this chapter from which the rest of the book is organized. To date, only one component of e-commerce transactions has gained recognition and development: secure transaction protocols. While secure transactions protocols are essential for privacy in transactions, they are not the silver bullet solution for securing e-commerce. If nothing else is gained, the one take home message of this book is that it is not sufficient enough to secure only one component of e-commerce transactions. All software components involved in handling e-commerce transactions over the Internet must be equally secured. This book explains the security issues in each of the four major components of software used to handle e-commerce transactions: the client-side software, the data transaction protocols, the Web server software, and the network server operating system software.

Banking on the Internet

Businesses and consumers are banking on the Internet in more than one sense. Despite the early proliferation of electronic banking applications on private networks through dial-up services, most electronic banking applications have migrated to the Internet. Consumers will not be tied to one particular bank and its software, nor to a single terminal where the bank's own software must be installed. Banking on the Internet provides the flexibility of banking from any Internet access terminal using the now ubiquitous Web browser. Banking on the Internet can reduce the number of staff banks must maintain without having to make the investment in establishing private networks.

The World Wide Web, or the Web, and its user-friendly, graphically rich browsers have made the Internet both friendly and accessible to the common desktop user at home and in the office. The ubiquity of the Web browser has made it the *de facto* vehicle for e-commerce. The limitations of HTML (the language of the Web) are being overcome by active content applications such as Java applets and ActiveX controls. The flip side of the emergence of the Internet as a means for commerce is that companies that ignore or repudiate the Internet as a medium for conducting business stand to lose market share in a changing business landscape. Businesses that use proprietary networks and protocols but are unwilling to support Web protocols stand to be left out of the windfall of e-commerce.

Banking services offered to consumers over the Internet will allow consumers to generate bank statements, check balances, transfer money between accounts, and authorize fund transfers to deposit money, to pay monthly bills, and to write personal checks. The Internet will provide a very competitive medium for banks to woo consumers. Consumers will be able to quickly and easily scan savings and loan rates and banking fees without having to interact with bank personnel. Beyond home banking, consumers will be able to write electronic checks to online merchants that draw value directly from the consumer's own bank account rather than use a line of credit.

The Internet will make banking a much more competitive environment in another critical aspect. Local banks will now be competing with national and international banks whose Internet presence removes barriers of physical distance. In addition, a number of "virtual" banks have now entered the market to compete with traditional banks for clients. The environment created by Internet banking will present the vast array of services currently offered by banks in a form that is very convenient to consumers. In the near future, home banking will include the ability for customers to download e-cash from their bank accounts onto smartcards through peripheral devices, similar to how cash is currently withdrawn from automated teller machines (ATMs). The advantage of using e-cash over electronic checks is that the e-cash transactions may enforce anonymity; checks and credit card transactions won't. These issues are explored in greater depth in Chapter 3.

Investing on the Internet

Firms that offer investment services in stocks, mutual funds, bonds, and other financial instruments also stand to benefit greatly from the emergence of Internet commerce. Electronic ticker tape displaying NYSE and NASDAQ stock quotes appear frequently in Web pages of many interactive newspapers, online service providers, and financial companies. This service is generally provided free of charge and usually delayed several minutes. Even better, many Web pages now offer the ability to customize Web pages based on each individual investor's profile. Dynamic HTML pages are created according to the stocks or mutual funds that a particular investor likes to track.

Dynamic HTMLs are Web pages that are created specifically according to the needs of the individual Web surfer. For example, dynamic HTML pages may update a chart of a particular stock's performance over the last 12 weeks. In addition to tracking investment portfolios, some Web sites will track articles in online newspapers and magazines for specific companies the user likes to monitor. Such software produced by PointCast exploits "push" technology to send this data to the user periodically. The difference between push and "pull" technology is that with push technology, the user no longer must go to a Web site for the information; rather, the desired information is collected and then pushed to the user's machine. Another term coined for push technology is "intelligent agent" applications. This software searches the Internet for information specified *a priori* by consumers of the software. Instead of using standard keyword searches, which can be both ineffective and inefficient, intelligent applications will use neural networks and pattern recognition software to "learn" information from returned Web pages in order to create a useful index for searching for related information. The information retrieved by the intelligent agents is periodically downloaded (or pushed) at predefined intervals to the user's hard drive so that the information is immediately available when the user goes online.

The continuous update of stock prices has allowed investors to track the performance of their stocks and mutual funds throughout the day. This information is critical for those investors daring enough to buy and sell equities based on fluctuations in the market. Perhaps equally important for investors is the ability to browse, compare, and contrast financial prospectuses online so that they can make well-informed investment decisions. Most of the large investment houses have already established an Internet presence in the form of Web pages. Investors can either browse through the vast database of information provided on these pages or make directed searches to particular funds in order to review performance, risk, load fees, and other valuable investing information.

Many financial investment firms are now providing interactive brokerage services through the Web. For example, investor profiles entered in forms on Web pages are used by programs to assess the level of risk for the investor and to recommend the type of funds in which to invest. The Web is being exploited in more powerful ways now for investing. Companies such as E★trade, Accutrade, E-Schwab, E-broker, and several dozen other firms now are providing consumers the ability to buy and sell equities over the Internet. These companies are beginning to compete on the same ground as full-service retail brokerages such as Dean Witter, Morgan Stanley, and Merrill Lynch. What makes the online start-ups particularly competitive is that the cost of executing a transaction online varies from only $12.00 to $29.95. Investors who compare this cost to the $250 per transaction on average with one of the full-service brokers will wonder why they are paying the steep transaction fees associated with full-service brokers.

Investors willing to engage in financial trades over the Internet establish accounts with a brokerage firm through an Internet Web site and access these accounts whenever they want to place an order. Initially, orders were handled by brokers in the traditional way of buying and selling equities. Once the request was received and acknowledged, the broker placed the order on the exchange floor through clearing houses. The electronic submission of the request from the investor simply replaces the process of placing the order over the phone. More recently, however, electronic investing is moving toward bypassing the broker. In this scenario, the investor can place an order through a brokerage house directly to the clearing house, which executes all orders traditionally placed by brokers.

The security and reliability of online brokerages will be selling points to investors. Many investors are still skittish about purchasing or selling stocks over the Internet. The rumor mill is replete with horror stories of inaccurate stock information and misplaced orders. Some online brokers have resorted to scare tactics in advertising campaigns such as declaring electronic investing online with a competitor as "electronic suicide." The reliability of these services is also a big issue. If a brokerage's Web site is down, the ability to retrieve investing information and to place orders will be compromised. Availability of information may be the most critical requirement for brokerages and investors alike.

Doing Business on the Internet

Aside from banking and investing services, e-commerce will grow significantly in the horizontal market of inter-business and intra-business applications. According to a study by the Yankee Group, the horizontal market of e-commerce is expected to surge to $134 billion by the year 2000 [Vinet 1996]. This growth will be fueled by an increase in the number of online businesses from 150,000 in 1995 to approximately 2 million in 2000. Consider that in 1996 Digital Equipment Corporation (DEC) performed over $235 million in Internet transactions alone [Hamilton 1997]. General Electric (GE) is using EDI services to connect suppliers and their customers worldwide over the Internet. In 1996, GE expected to purchase over U.S. $1 billion worth of goods over the Internet [Smart 1996]. By the year 2000, GE projects half of its purchases will be over the Internet [Smart 1996].

Businesses are looking to e-commerce applications to perform intra- and inter-business functions efficiently. Companies currently doing a large volume of business with other companies are seeking more efficient ways to conduct business over the Internet. For several years now, companies have built business-to-business information systems at great expense. The emergence of the Internet as a common medium for commerce is breaking down the prohibitive cost barriers that once allowed access to only the largest of businesses. Using local area networks, the Web, and underlying Internet protocols, corporate intranets are providing the means for back-office automation. Investment banking powerhouse Morgan Stanley has used the Web to publish and disseminate information throughout its organization [Kambil 1997]. Nearly all of the firm's 10,000 employees access the server on a daily or weekly basis for corporate information. The savings over paper-based dissemination processes is estimated to be between $300,000 and $700,000 annually for each process. In the first 18 months the intranet was in service, the company documented savings of over $1 million.

Although replacing the reams of paper work generated every day to support daily business functions is appealing, the real benefit of office automation is the reduction in processing costs and the speed with which forms can be processed. Corporate intranets are now supporting the back-office administrative functions using familiar Web client interfaces that already exist on everyone's desktop machine. Employees who need to fill out an expense form, for example, can simply point their browsers at the appropriate link on a corporate server. Once filled out on screen, the form is sent back to the server and either processed immediately or stored in a database for further processing in batch jobs. This simple idea is being embraced by major corporations that are seeking to reduce the costs of bureaucracy and improve the efficiency of processing forms essential to business functions. The idea has spread outside company intranets into the horizontal market for businesses. There is even a new buzzword for this activity—*extranets*. Extranets are an extension of local area networks (LANs) over the Internet. This permits one company to share its systems over geographically distributed groups or with other companies very cheaply, albeit with some risk. In addition to seeking more efficient ways for conducting business over the Internet, companies that do large volumes of business with other companies are also trying to make the process of finding suppliers of products and services more competitive.

When EDI first emerged, business transactions were conducted on VANs, which connect groups within a company or different companies, in some cases, over a private network. The entry costs for establishing an EDI system over a VAN have been too high for small to midrange businesses. The emergence of EDI over the Internet is now reducing the entry costs significantly and radically affecting the growth of EDI. Using the Internet and the Web as the vehicle of commerce, smaller companies can connect with large companies anywhere and exchange documents electronically. Rather than waiting for overnight delivery of documents, any company can have them delivered in minutes electronically.

Another burgeoning market will be the vertical market that connects businesses to consumers. The vertical market and its infrastructure will enable consumers to purchase products and services from their home computers. Consider Amazon.com (www.amazon.com), an Internet-based company that has captured a large market share of all books being sold on the Internet. Amazon.com offers a catalog of over 2 million books online to buyers anywhere for sale anytime. Amazon.com is able to leverage the Internet's capabilities in reducing or eliminating costs that other "physical" bookstores incur. For example, Amazon.com incurs almost no direct warehousing, sales, or rental costs for books because its automated order processing links the buyer directly to the wholesalers, who ship books from the warehouses directly to the buyers [Kambil 1997]. The savings in warehousing overhead is passed on to consumers, who in turn drive the growth of Amazon's business. Amazon has posted an amazing 35 percent *monthly* sales growth.

Another online success story is Auto-By-Tel (www.autobytel.com). Auto-By-Tel generates roughly $2 billion annually in sales [Kambil 1997]. Auto-By-Tel serves as a hassle-free broker between consumers and dealerships. Consumers are able to specify their desired car in exacting details on a Web-based form. Auto-By-Tel forwards this data on to a dealership near the client. The dealer is able to quote an "aggressive" price over the phone because of the group sales commanded by Auto-By-Tel. The consumer is assured that the dealer will stick to the quoted price, and the purchasing process is therefore simplified. The legwork for researching cars is performed over the Web by consumers, while the negotiation process is also performed on the Web and phone, before the final details are penned in person.

Cyber malls, which are electronic storefronts for businesses that wish to provide their products on the Internet, experienced a brief rise in the media spotlight but have faded into obscurity. Cyber malls were launched by larger organizations such as AT&T to provide the front-end Web and back-end transaction processing infrastructure for smaller companies wishing to participate in e-commerce without dealing with the hassles of setting up a site on the Net. AT&T went as far as to declare that it will indemnify losses to these companies because of potential problems in the infrastructure. Although providing the infrastructure for smaller businesses to get involved is a good idea, the market just was not there in 1996 for the small businesses. Like other fads from the past, this one may well resurrect itself sometime in the near future.

One impetus to drive the vertical market will be the establishment of a system of micro-payments. Micropayments will permit companies to charge small fees for downloading

intellectual property such as documents, news articles, digital images, video clips, and other digital assets. The idea is that with a system for charging small amounts, consumers will be willing to pay for intellectual property, and its owners can earn dividends through volume sales. Cybercash Inc. of Reston, Virginia, (www.cybercash.com) has implemented a micro-payments system for making payments from consumer electronic wallets to businesses on the Internet. In the process of brokering the transaction for the merchant selling, the consumer, and the bank from which the funds are drawn, Cybercash makes a few cents on the dollar for every transaction. As in a credit card transaction, the consumer does not see the charge. Unlike with traditional credit card transactions, the merchant never sees the credit card number, nor does Cybercash, the brokering agent. Ultimately, the growth of e-commerce in both horizontal and vertical markets will be influenced by the standardization of protocols and document formats.

Threats to E-Commerce

The vast growth potential of Internet-based commerce is tempered by legitimate concerns over the security of such a system. Despite the potential rewards of conducting business on the Internet, major corporations have been slow to embrace this technology—and with good reason. The number one rated concern for both businesses and consumers in establishing and participating in e-commerce is the potential for loss of assets and privacy due to breaches in the security of commercial transactions and corporate computer systems. A single publicized security breach can erode confidence in the business and not only damage the reputation of the firm, but also hurt the e-commerce industry as a whole.

Threats to the security of computer systems and commercial transactions can be classified as internal or external. The threat that is most often overlooked, yet is most likely to occur, is the inside threat. Providing internal access to an organization's digital assets can be the Achilles' heel of many security plans through either malicious intention or carelessness. Few modern systems can withstand attacks from users who are logged on to internal machines. A mixture of traditional security practices with the latest in computer security tools can assist security managers in protecting corporate assets. The principles of need-to-know and compartmented information can be useful in determining to whom privileged accounts and passwords should be given. Careful screening of employees trusted not only with company secrets, but also with access to valuable digital assets should be a part of any security plan. Real-time intrusion detection analysis tools that monitor internal networks for unusual activity can be useful for catching a perpetrator in the act of stealing or sabotaging data. Even without these sophisticated tools, regular monitoring of audit logs automatically kept by many computer systems can go a long way to determining if corporate assets are being probed or breached.

The internal threat is clearly a danger, but most companies are concerned about the external threat—the extent of which is unknown. Despite the threat of abuse from employees, many companies feel reasonably safe that the internal threat can be controlled through corporate policies and internal access control. What really scares both system managers and corporate executives is the unknown outside user who may gain unauthorized access to the corporation's sensitive assets. This book addresses this concern specifically for protecting corporate assets against the outside threat. The advantages of capturing a share of the e-commerce market are clear. For businesses that have an e-commerce presence on the Internet, the whole world will be at their door. The upside is that the world consumer market is within easy reach. The downside is that along with legitimate consumers, all kinds of malicious users may be trying the lock on the door, including organized international criminal syndicates, state-sponsored terrorists, former KGB agents well-trained in industrial espionage, and the ever wily hacker looking for a joy ride.

How big are the problems with security in Internet commerce providers? There is no definitive answer to this question—only anecdotal examples and ad hoc surveys, usually published by security consulting firms. A joint survey by the FBI and the Computer Security Institute (CSI) of Fortune 500 companies reported that 42 percent of the respondents had reported unauthorized use of their information systems. Even more astonishing, 32 percent of the respondents reported losing upwards of U.S. $100 million due to security breaches. Dan Farmer, creator of the SATAN network scanning tool and an independent security researcher and consultant, recently published a survey he performed of approximately 2200 computing systems from November through December of 1996. The survey (www.trouble.org/survey) is not intended to be, in Farmer's words, "a serious or definitive statistical survey." However, it does provide some indication of the problems in computer security that many corporations entering the e-commerce arena will face. What makes this survey particularly noteworthy is that the subjects he selected are relatively high-profile and commerce-oriented Web sites. Furthermore, the survey completely side-stepped the issue of which secure payment protocols to use by scanning the host systems themselves. Clearly, if these systems are vulnerable, the choice of which secure payment protocol to use is a moot point. The systems Farmer profiled include Web hosting services for banks, federal institutions, and newspapers, along with a randomly sampled selection of Internet sites for comparison. In summary, using simple, nonintrusive scanning techniques, Farmer found that nearly two-thirds of the hosts had serious potential security vulnerabilities. Furthermore, this number was about twice what he found with the randomly selected hosts. If this survey is an indication of the security problems in Internet commerce, the security of e-commerce systems is indeed in jeopardy.

In addition to serving a purpose in highlighting trends, surveys are also easy to write off without actual anecdotal examples. To illustrate the authenticity of the problem, several case studies of Internet security violations, none earlier than 1996, are presented next. The case studies are grouped by the type of crime that was committed: breach of privacy/confidentiality, sabotage/vandalism, compromise of data integrity, theft, fraud, and denial of service. The case studies were all drawn from the RISKS Digest, an Internet-wide forum for sharing computer risks and war stories. RISKS is a Usenet news group (comp.risks) that is moderated by Peter Neumann of SRI. The RISKS Digest archives can also be found on the Web at http://catless.ncl.ac.uk/Risks. RISKS articles can be reused without explicit authorization under blanket permission granted for all RISKS-Forum Digest materials. The author(s), the RISKS moderator, and the ACM have no connection with this reuse.

Vandalism and Sabotage on the Internet

Web defacing or vandalism has probably received the most coverage in the popular media. Web defacing is the act of rewriting *someone else's* Web page, usually by illegal means, to display a message of the vandal's choice. The messages left on vandalized Web sites can be politically motivated or simply ego driven to loudly illustrate the point that the victim's system is vulnerable. A number of high-profile acts of Web vandalism occurred in 1996, including Web pages representing the CIA, the Department of Justice, the U.S. Air Force, and NASA.

In August of 1996, the Department of Justice's (DOJ's) Web site (www.usdoj.gov) was vandalized by crackers who broke into the DOJ's Web host machine [Edupage Editors 1996]. The crackers took the opportunity to place swastikas, obscene pictures, and criticism of the Communications Decency Act. The penetration resulted in the temporary shutdown of the site until the damage could be assessed and the Web site restored. A month later, the CIA Web site (www.odci.gov/cia) was cracked by a group of Swedish hackers who were protesting a Swedish court case against a group of youths arrested for computer security crimes in 1991 [Neumann 1996]. The vandalized Web page read "Welcome to the Central Stupidity Agency." Links to the Playboy Web site, hacker Web sites, and broken links were also placed on the page. Coincidentally, the day the CIA Web site was hacked also marked the day the DOJ put its Web site back on the Net.

December of 1996 witnessed the falling of another government Web site. The U.S. Air Force's Web site (www.af.mil) was vandalized by hackers [Neumann 1997]. The altered title of the Web page read, "Welcome to the Truth" above graphics of dripping blood and a pair of red eyeballs. Text added to the page included, "You can learn all about gov't corruption here. Learn the secrets that they don't want you to know." Graphics included an X-rated picture with the caption, "This is what your gov't is doing to you every day."

In yet another government Web site hack, NASA's Web page (www.nasa.gov) was defaced in March of 1997 [Kennedy 1997]. The text left on this page was a reference to the Internet Liberation Front (ILF), which attacked GE and others in December of 1994. The crackers promised to continue where the ILF left off.

The extent of the damage done by the Web vandalism cases is a matter of dispute. The government will almost always claim that the extent of the damage is limited strictly to the Web hosting machine. Crackers who have broken into the Web servers have claimed to have been able to access sensitive e-mail and classified files of the sites they have broken into. Either case is plausible. If the Web site is hosted by another organization, wherein the Web host machine is completely isolated from the government agency's networks, it is unlikely that breaking into the Web hosting machine will compromise the agency's other computers. On the other hand, if the machine is an integral part of the agency's local computer systems, breaking into the Web host machine may result in the compromise of other assets. Beyond the loss of assets, vandalizing an organization's Web page can be extremely damaging to the organization's public relations. The Web page is the organization's interface to the world. If a Web page is vandalized, the organization itself appears vulnerable. Vandalizing government agencies' Web pages can be politically motivated; vandalizing a financial concern can undermine a company's business. In many financial concerns, reputation and consumer confidence of integrity and security are the most important intangibles, which once lost are hard to regain.

Breach of Privacy or Confidentiality

When engaging in transactions or simply communicating over the Internet, most people naively assume that their messages remain private. In fact, it is quite easy for an interested party to eavesdrop on other people's Internet conversations. While the electronic age has made communicating arguably easier, it has also made intercepting communications easier for unknown third parties. While this book deals with Internet-based communications, the same privacy issues hold true for other electronic means, such as cell phones and pagers. The White House Communications Agency was embarrassed when hackers managed to intercept and publish on the Web transcripts from pager messages sent while the President was visiting Philadelphia in September 1997 [Wagner 1997]. While the messages were not of national security significance, they did update the President's travel schedule and unearthed romantic affairs among the White House staff. Since pager messages are broadcast, anyone who can tune into the right frequency can pick up confidential communications. In fact, a New Jersey based company, Breaking News Network, did exactly this for its news agency clients. The company intercepted sensitive communications between the New York police department, the fire department, and even the mayor's office and sold the messages to news organizations. The company is being prosecuted for illegal interception of pages [Bellovin 1997].

Other broadcast media such as cell phones suffer from the same vulnerability to interception of confidential messages. A more famous example came to light in January of 1997. Newt Gingrich, Speaker of the House, had a conversation over a cell phone recorded by an amateur voyeur who used a radio scanner to pick up phone conversations [Koball 1997]. The conversation involved a plotting strategy with senior members of the Republican party on how to deal with Gingrich's ethics investigation problems and his popularity crisis in the U.S. These case studies illustrate that most communications today are not private unless explicitly protected by encryption mechanisms. The message is not that the new technologies for communicating are bad, but that the users should not assume that the communications are private. In other words, you should not say anything over the Internet, pagers, cordless phones, and cell phones that you wouldn't say in a crowded elevator.

In Internet-based sessions, messages are transmitted through a number of middlemen before reaching their final destinations. These middlemen are Internet routers for the messages and include the mail servers on either end of the connection. Any one of these routers may copy, modify, or even delete the messages. Providers of e-commerce systems are acutely aware of the high value placed on privacy and confidentiality of Internet transactions. One of the biggest fears that consumers have in online commerce is sending their credit card numbers over the Internet. To this end, a number of secure payment transaction systems have been developed to protect the privacy of transactions and the confidentiality of sensitive data such as credit card numbers. The cases presented in this section illustrate how confidentiality and privacy can be violated, sometimes in seemingly secure transactions.

In January of 1997, RSA Data Security Corp. issued a challenge to decipher a message encrypted using a 40-bit key, which is the most secure level of encryption that the U.S. government allows for export. The challenge offered a $1000 reward to anyone who could correctly decipher the message. The goal of the challenge was to promote research and practical experience using today's encryption technology. It is well known in the security community that 40-bit ciphers cannot protect a secret for very long against a sophisticated attack. The challenge produced a tangible example for all to witness of how vulnerable 40-bit encryption is. Ian Goldberg, a student at the University of California at Berkeley, took only three and a half hours to crack the cipher [Stangenberger 1997]. The unscrambled message suited the occasion: "This is why you should use a longer key." The 40-bit key length is at the center of a controversy over U.S. export restrictions on encryption technology. Goldberg was able to crack the cipher using a brute force approach. He harnessed idle CPU cycles from 250 machines in Berkeley's Network of Workstations environment that allowed him to test 100 billion possible keys per hour. This is analogous to a safe cracker trying every possible combination at an extremely high speed. The key that deciphered the message was found after 30 percent of the keyspace was exhausted. In 1995, the ISAAC computer group at Berkeley, which Goldberg helped found, discovered a flaw in the Netscape Web browser software that made cracking SSL encryption possible without requiring a brute force approach.

The RC5 encryption algorithm from RSA provides the ability to provide increasing levels of security from 40-bit encryption to 2048-bit encryption. Each additional bit of security doubles the search space of keys, thus doubling the amount of effort needed to crack the encrypted message using brute force techniques. The second challenge by RSA Data Security to crack an RC5 48-bit cipher was broken February 10, 1997 [Neumann 1997]. This time Germano Caronni, a student at the Swiss Federal Institute of Technology, managed to crack the cipher with a lot of help from fellow enthusiasts. Germano enlisted the aid of 3500 networked computers to attain a rate of 1.5 trillion keys searched per hour. The code was cracked after about 57 percent of the key space was exhausted—about the median expected effort.

These two cases illustrate how the effort to launch a brute force attack against a cipher can be distributed over a large number of computers that can be collectively used to crack ciphers. The important lesson to be learned from these cases is not that encryption is insecure, but rather that it is not impregnable. As in most areas of computer security, the level of protection provided should be commensurate with the value of what is being protected. The effective security of an asset is judged by the level of effort required to compromise it. To obtain greater assurance of message confidentiality, higher levels of encryption should be used. For most e-mail or Web communications, 40-bit encryption may be sufficient for the data sent. For particularly sensitive information, encryption keys of lengths greater than 128 bits may be desirable.

Bruce Schneier, a well-known cryptoanalyst of Counterpane Systems (www.counterpane.com) and author of *Applied Cryptography* (Wiley 1996), has made it easier to crack messages encrypted using S/MIME. Both Netscape's Communicator 4.0 Composer and Microsoft's Outlook Express use S/MIME to encrypt messages. Schneier created a Windows 95 screen saver that uses the machine's idle cycles to crack e-mail messages encrypted using S/MIME 40-bit encryption keys [Garfinkel 1997]. On a single 166 MHz computer, the screen saver takes on average of about 35 days to crack. Using the power of networked computers can reduce this time significantly. The screen saver is designed to exploit networked computers to simultaneously search the key space to find the "right" 40-bit key. According to Schneier, a dozen computers can crack an encrypted e-mail message in under 3 days, while a thousand computers can crack the code in less than 50 minutes. So is Schneier a renegade hacker who aims to terrorize privacy? Not exactly. The point of Schneier's screen saver is to send a message to people, business, and the U.S. government, in particular, that 40-bit encryption is simply inadequate for securing data. Remember that each additional bit doubles the amount of work necessary to crack ciphertext. Current U.S. laws prevent U.S. companies from exporting encryption software that uses keys greater than 40-bits in length unless the keys are "recoverable." The U.S. software industry claims that these export laws, which consider encryption as munitions, are hurting their global competitiveness against foreign companies that do not have such restrictions. Privacy advocates such as Schneier believe that 40-bit encryption is too weak to be considered secure.

Breaking ciphers may actually be the most difficult way to compromise individual user security. A number of privacy issues are raised by client-side active content—programs that automatically download from the Internet and execute on the user's machine when a user hits a Web site with embedded active content. Examples of executable content include JavaScripts, VBScripts, Java Applets, ActiveX controls, and multimedia presentation files that are executed via browser "plug-ins." Plug-ins are software applications that execute when a file of a particular format is downloaded from a Web site by a Web browser. Plug-ins may be installed with the Web browser or they can be downloaded from the vendor's Internet site and plugged into the Web browser. In March of 1997, a flaw in a well-known browser plug-in, Shockwave, was demonstrated to violate the e-mail privacy of those using the Netscape Navigator for Web browsing and the Netscape mailer for e-mail [Markowitz 1997]. Shockwave's vendor, Macromedia, claims that the free software is installed in over 20 million desktop machines. Users at risk are those that are running a Windows 95 or Windows NT platform with Netscape Navigator 3.0 with Macromedia's Shockwave plug-in installed. For the attack to work, the user must also use the Netscape mailer.

Shockwave is a plug-in that allows users to download and view movies played over the Internet. David de Vitry, an application developer, discovered the flaw when examining how the Netscape mailer handles addressing mail. To implement the attack, a Web master need only put up a Web page with a malicious Shockwave "movie." The movie is actually malicious active content that is automatically downloaded to the user's machine and executed by the Shockwave plug-in without requiring any links or forms to be selected. The Shockwave movie can read the user's e-mail inbox, or any other mail folders—including those messages the user deleted. With a few commands, the movie can save the e-mail text to a data variable and send the data back to the Web server from which the Shockwave movie originated. The flaw has even broader security implications. A Shockwave movie can potentially access any local file on the client's machine and send this data back to the malicious Web site. Furthermore, a Shockwave movie can execute from the user's desktop to access "secure" corporate intranets behind firewalls that prevent external access and send this data back to the malicious Web site. Only knowledge of the secure intranet's Web address is needed. The dangers of active content executing in client applications are discussed in Chapter 2.

A final anecdote concerns most consumers' worst fear: the loss of confidentiality of credit card numbers used in Internet-based transactions. In November of 1996, an error in using an e-commerce product called SoftCart resulted in consumer credit card numbers collected for purchase orders being exposed to the Internet-at-large [Edupage Editors 1996]. The order forms, which contained sensitive information such as credit card numbers, were stored in a directory on the Web server that was accessible to any Web browser that was pointed in the right direction. The vendor of the software, Mercantec, explained that the problem was due to human error. That is, when the merchant installed the software, the file with the credit card numbers was improperly placed in a directory completely accessible to the Web. Mercantec claimed that the documentation for the product clearly explained how to avoid these types of security hazards. In practice, security features are often defeated by flawed software configurations that are often the default configuration. This issue is explored in depth in Chapter 4.

Theft and Fraud on the Internet

Much as in the physical world in which we live, the types of people who exist on the Internet are quite diverse, from scientists to business professionals to children to criminals (note that these categories are not exclusive). As with the physical world, the places we visit on the Web can vary from wild and wacky to academic to detestable. For these reasons, it is important that we treat the people we deal with and the places we go on the Internet with caution. Much as we put up our guard with people we don't know or trust in the physical world, we should also practice such prudence with people we deal with on the Internet. In the physical world, we are cautious when we visit unfamiliar sections of a city. Similarly, we need to exercise caution when we visit unfamiliar Web sites or sites with which we have had no prior relationship. Theft and fraud on the Internet are made possible when people are duped into trusting the Web site and its operators, with whom no prior relationship exists.

A study by Deloitte & Touche on behalf of the European Commission recently reported that citizens and businesses in the European Union have lost anywhere from 6 billion to 60 billion European Currency Units—much of it apparently because of fraud over the Internet [Edupage Editors 1997]. The study notes that much of the fraud is a result of criminals setting up a site on the Web that appears to be a legitimate business, when in fact it is a facade for a criminal enterprise. Consumers are duped into giving their credit card numbers for products or services that are never delivered.

The study also claims that one major international bank has fallen victim to this type of fraud. Whether the bank was impersonated by an impostor or lost money to a scam is unknown. The study reveals the double-edged sword of encryption. Although necessary to secure privacy and confidentiality on the Internet, encryption also serves to shield criminal activities from law enforcement scrutiny. In Chapter 3, the trade-off between accountability and privacy in e-cash protocols that offer a balance of both is discussed.

Where common duplicity may fail, technical wizardry can succeed in fraud and theft on the Internet. A couple of anecdotal examples illustrate this wizardry well. The infamous German cracker group, Chaos Computer Club, demonstrated in February of 1997 how money can be stolen electronically over the Internet [Brunnstein 1997]. The group demonstrated on a German television program how an ActiveX control can be used to schedule a transaction of money from the victim's online bank account to a numbered bank account belonging to the hackers. The group designed a Web page that attracted Internet surfers with the slogan, "Becoming a millionaire in 5 minutes." To implement the attack, they placed an ActiveX control (a form of active content invented by Microsoft Corp.) on the Web page. Once users point their Internet Explorer at the Web page, the ActiveX control downloads and then begins the attack. The attack uses Quicken to schedule a transaction at some point in the future to transfer funds between the user's account and an account specified by the ActiveX control. The victim does not find out that the transaction occurred until after the statement of account activity is received and the account activities are reconciled (if at all). One saving grace is that the account number to where the money is transferred will be known. By the time the illegal transfer is noticed, the money may well have been moved yet again to another bank account, possibly in a country with strict bank secrecy laws.

Several preconditions are necessary for the attack to work. First, the victim must be running a Windows 95 or Windows NT platform. Second, the victim must point an Internet Explorer browser (or another browser that executes ActiveX controls) at a Web page that has this hostile ActiveX control embedded in it. When the ActiveX control downloads, the client's browser must accept it. Finally, the client in this case must be running the European version of Quicken with electronic funds transfer (EFT) set up. Although the requirements are many, they are far from implausible. Internet Explorer is currently installed on millions of Windows desktops throughout the world, and a user can be lured into hitting a Web page with an ActiveX control without too much difficulty. Getting a user to accept an ActiveX control is also easy if the user thinks the ActiveX control is doing one thing (such as playing a game) while it is secretly doing something else (such as scheduling a Quicken transaction). Programs that perform this kind of bait-and-switch are called Trojan horses after their infamous Greek predecessor. The final requirement that the user has electronic funds transfer set up through Quicken is not as likely as that a user will be running Windows, but as home banking and e-commerce become more ubiquitous, the chances improve. Even if EFT and Quicken are not installed, the user will not notice that a hostile ActiveX control has executed, but may instead be paying attention to, for example, a game display.

Another example of fraud that gained notoriety in the Internet security community involves pornography and phone bills. This combination is another case of tried-and-true scandals that have now infiltrated the Internet, with a twist of technical innovation. Web surfers were unpleasantly surprised with phone bills in the hundreds and even thousands of dollars that resulted from visiting a pornographic Web site [Uphoff 1997]. The Web site promised *free* pornographic images to surfers. The catch, though, was that the users must download special software to view the images. Although this tactic may sound like an obvious ruse, in many Web applications, "special" software, such as plug-ins and helper applications, must be downloaded before the user can actually experience multimedia formatted files. In any case, the victims fell for this line of reasoning. To download the special viewer, the user needed to only click on a link from the Web page. The link did download special software, although the software in this case was a Trojan horse program. When the Trojan horse executed, it disconnected the modem from the user's Internet service provider (ISP), lowered the volume, then dialed a number directly to a server in Moldova, a former Republic of the Soviet Union. The server in Moldova then routed the connection to an Internet site in North America where pornographic pictures were indeed stored. Although the Web site did deliver on its promise, it did so by forcing remote users to make a long distance phone call through Moldova. The server in Moldova essentially served as the user's ISP. This means that the scam could continue even after the user leaves the pornographic Web page. In fact, as long as the user maintains the connection, the phone bill would rack up connection time charges.

Violations of Data Integrity

Data integrity attacks are not often discussed in the context of Internet sessions, but they are a concern for e-commerce types of transactions. Violations in the integrity of data sent over networks are often incidental and unintentional, but the potential to maliciously alter data in order to affect some outcome exists. Two cases illustrate how problems in data integrity can have financial consequences. In January 1997, a program error in discount brokerage Charles Schwab's Telebroker system resulted in incorrect information conveyed to investors that queried account information over the phone [deCarteret 1997]. The program error resulted in a number of mutual funds being excluded from the accounting of investors' assets. Therefore, when investors used Telebroker to determine the value of their holdings in Schwab, the response from Telebroker was a value less than their actual holdings, if one or more of their holdings included one of the excluded mutual funds. Among the excluded funds were Janus, Putnam, and Schwab's own. The result was panic among scores of investors who believed that the market value of their holdings must have dropped significantly in a very short period of time. Schwab promised to "make whole" any investors who made buying or selling decisions based on the incorrect information. According to Schwab, a system upgrade or modification precipitated the resulting error.

The second case of data integrity problems occurred in another financial application. In March of 1997, America Online (AOL) acknowledged that it posted inaccurate stock information about a particular company, Ezra Weinstein & Co. [Edupage Editors 1997]. AOL, however, blames Standard & Poor (S&P), its stock information provider, for the bad information. AOL suggests the bad information originated from S&P because AOL doesn't "make up" stock prices. An AOL spokesperson was quoted saying that the data is computer-translated and that occasionally the information AOL receives is wrong. Whether the information that originated from S&P was inaccurate or the computer translation processes mutated the data is unknown. A malicious attack against data such as stock information at key distribution points, such as AOL, can certainly affect the outcome of investment decisions made by investors everywhere. The incorporation of data integrity checks can detect data that has been tampered with or incidentally corrupted with near certainty. Given the popularity of push technology in broadcasting financial information, such as stock quotes and quarterly performance, a single corruption of data can affect scores of investors who make decisions based on the integrity of the data. Fortunately, good data integrity techniques exist to detect the corruption of data. Much like encryption, the technology exists but is often not implemented as widely as it should be. Data integrity techniques are discussed in Chapter 3.

Denial of Service

Denial of service attacks have been called the ultimate Internet security nemesis. A denial of service attack is aimed solely at making services unavailable. The attacks are particularly difficult to defend against, because they exploit infrastructural weaknesses or flaws in widely used protocols, such as the Internet protocol (IP). For example, information warfare doomsayers have been warning about the vulnerability of our critical infrastructures—telecommunications, transportation, electric power, banking, financial, government, and defense—to denial of service attacks. The reason for all this foreboding is that strategically pinpointed attacks can bring down entire systems critical to the nation. In the United States, for example, defense communications leverage heavily off of the commercial telecommunications backbones. Mapping the telecommunications as well as the electric power grids of the United States identifies specific points of convergence where a well-placed attack would have the ability to bring down entire geographic sections of the country and industrial sectors. Furthermore, because the telecommunications infrastructure is global, attacks launched in foreign sites have the potential to bring down service in the United States. Sovereignty rights may prevent the United States from defending its national interests against these types of attacks. An attack against the commercial telecommunications infrastructure would not only weaken consumers and businesses, but also adversely affect the defense of the nation. A Presidential commission, the

President's Commission on Critical Infrastructure Protection (www.pccip.gov), was created specifically to study this problem in 1997.

The problem is further exacerbated by the rapid advances in technology. In the past, the telecommunications infrastructure consisted of copper lines that by necessity were widely distributed to homes and businesses. Today, much of the telecommunications backbone is made up of fiber optic cable that has the ability to carry data in capacities much greater than the copper wire it replaced. As a result, many diversely routed copper cables have been replaced with a single fiber optic cable (often shared by different companies serving different customers and applications). The upshot of this is that in spite of advances in technology, a single backhoe attack today can take out a much greater number of services and consumers than it could have in the past! Incidents of denial of service accidents due to backhoes have been documented in the RISKS archive (catless.ncl.ac.uk/Risks/VL.IS.html). In Chapter 5, Internet-based denial of service attacks are covered in some depth along with two cases that illustrate the vulnerability of Internet-based services to these pernicious attacks.

The anecdotal examples of Internet-related crimes in the preceding sections have set the stage for Internet security issues. If the system of e-commerce is not adequately secured, big business and consumers will not enter the market for fear of the types of violations described here. Notice that many of the incidents related to computer security could not be prevented strictly through the use of one of the secure payment protocols. Client and server security in e-commerce systems is as important as the data transaction security.

E-Commerce Security: A System-Wide Problem

The security of an e-commerce system must be ensured on the four fronts by which this book is organized: Web client security, data transport security, Web server security, and operating system security. Most people consider only the data transport protocols when considering e-commerce security. Securing data during transport is important to preventing unauthorized parties from capturing transaction data, but it is only one part of the solution in securing e-commerce. The primary goal of this book is to provide both consumers and providers of e-commerce services a system-wide perspective of the risks inherent in the technology used in e-commerce. The client- and server-side security risks are equally important to understand and address. In fact, history has shown that if the security of one part of a system is significantly weaker than other parts in the system, the weaker part is most likely to be attacked first. This book lays out the risks present in the critical software components that are involved in most forms of e-commerce today. It does not, however, pretend to cover all facets of security. The focus of this book is on the risks present in the technology used by e-commerce components. Operational procedures, personnel issues, and physical security all play important roles but are not covered here.

Client Security

A topic that has received attention in the popular press is also salient to e-commerce—Web browser security. Viewed differently, the vulnerability of Web client software used to browse Web pages or to perform commercial transactions can impact the security of corporate systems. Two main risks have emerged in using Web clients for e-commerce: vulnerabilities in browser software and the risks of active content on the Web. The latter concern is growing larger with the popularity of Java applets, ActiveX controls, and push technology; the former remains an obscure but relevant danger to corporate systems.

Chapter 2 first describes the hazards of active content for anybody who surfs the Net, including application programs such as Java applets, ActiveX controls, and Word macros, as well as the hazards of downloading/viewing different file formats such as Postscript, JPEG, and GIF. Corporations involved in e-commerce must be at least as concerned about the hazards of active content on the Web as must their clients. Even with rigorous security measures in place to protect both the data in transit and network servers, vulnerabilities in Web client software can compromise the security of the corporate systems. Employees who use browsers to "surf the Net" may potentially compromise the security of corporate systems. Most popular browsers provide the option to install plug-ins that will automatically execute files viewed from remote Web sites. Certainly, this provision makes surfing the Web interesting as far as multimedia presentations go; however, executing an untrusted application opens the door for malicious attack.

Companies must also decide whether to trust the Web browser itself or perhaps to restrict its use. Most browsers are given the privilege to execute programs locally, to write to user disks, to upload and download files and programs from the Internet. Because the browser source code is generally not distributed with the browser, the consumer must trust that the browser is not vulnerable to exploitation, that back doors for entry to a system are not present, and that the browser is not performing any malicious actions. This issue takes on increased importance if employees are permitted to download browser software from untrusted sites and to install the software themselves. Chapter 2 describes the dangers of both active content applications and untrusted browsers.

Secure Transport

To date, resources in securing e-commerce have been heavily focused on data transaction security. Chapter 3 presents two broad classifications of data transaction protocols: stored-account and stored-value systems. The methods by which these two systems of exchanging value and the resulting security implications of each are quite different. In addition to the secure payment systems, Chapter 3 presents two protocols that provide a secure channel for communication: Secure Sockets Layer (SSL) and Secure HTTP (S-HTTP). The implementations and security characteristics of the two protocols will be of interest to anyone who uses either method for secure Web sessions.

Smartcards have been widely used in Europe for a number of years for a range of applications from transportation to telecommunication. Now smartcards are finding their utility in e-commerce applications. Smartcards have been widely touted for integrating the functions of a number of different cards we all currently carry, such as identification, credit, debit, cash, and loyalty plans. One invaluable function smartcards serve is in securing the private keys used for encryption. Keeping private keys stored on computer systems can sometimes compromise their integrity. Because file systems are often shared, it may be possible for secret keys to be snared when they are stored on computer systems. Keeping secret keys on smartcards can provide physical security as well as portability for using private keys anywhere.

Chapter 3 examines the use of smartcards in one of the most controversial uses of e-commerce: storing and exchanging e-cash. Several protocols for e-cash are emerging with different approaches to security. Chapter 3 outlines the competing protocols and their security attributes and risks.

Web Server Security

Although much attention has been focused on securing the data transport, the security of the e-commerce servers has been inadequately addressed. It is important to remember a tenet of security that will often be repeated in this book: *the security of the system is only as strong as its weakest link.* The security of the commerce server is of critical importance to both Internet commerce providers and consumers. Vulnerabilities in the server may expose e-commerce providers to malicious attacks from anywhere on the Internet. Security breaches that are exposed in the media will shake consumer confidence and result in potentially devastating financial losses. Clearly, e-commerce is an enterprise-critical operation. Given the prevalence of commercial protocols and emerging standards for data transport security, one area left for e-commerce providers to install, maintain, and secure is the e-commerce server system. E-commerce servers typically include a front-end Web servers, back-end databases, and interface software for handling Web requests and updating back-end databases.

The Web server runs continuously and waits for requests from other Internet sites including home and office. When a request is received (in the form of a page hit over the Internet), the server will typically call an interface software program. The interface software programs are generally known as Common Gateway Interface (CGI) scripts. These programs perform some action based on the request received by the Web server. The responsibilities of these programs include storing and retrieving information to and from back-end databases in order to serve requests from the Internet. The back-end databases are usually relational or object-oriented databases that store the information required for commercial transactions. For example, when accessing credit card purchase transactions via the Web, your account number is used as a key to look up your account activity that is stored in online databases. The request is handled by interface programs that will encrypt the information before returning it to you over the Internet. Online databases typically store transaction records, account balances, inventory, and statistics.

Flaws in any one of the three software pieces of e-commerce servers can be a serious vulnerability in the security of the corporate systems. In spite of the plethora of secure protocols developed for data transactions, little progress has been made in the way of providing secure e-commerce servers. One reason for the complacency might be the false sense of security engendered by encryption protocols and firewalls. Encryption is used to provide confidentiality of data from the point of leaving the end user's software client to the point of being decrypted on the server system. Once the data is stored "in the clear" on the server, data confidentiality is no longer ensured. Data confidentiality aside, encryption will not prevent malicious attackers from breaking into the server systems and destroying data and records of transactions.

Firewalls have been used to protect internal computer systems from outside attacks as well as from unauthorized inside users. The effectiveness of a firewall is usually in providing a deterrent from would-be attackers. However, most determined attackers can breach a firewall. One widely quoted statistic from a company that is successful in network penetration studies is that it can break through as many as 75 percent of all firewalls of clients who hired them to attempt to do so. Even firewalls that are well configured and relatively secure can provide only trivial security assurance against attacks that originate through Web requests, unless, of course, Web service is not provided.

Chapter 4 addresses the vulnerabilities in Web commerce servers and describes methods for assessing and improving the security of the server systems. The chapter shows how simple errors in configuring the servers can have severe security consequences. Methods for properly configuring servers as well as testing the servers are presented. Two of the most difficult problems in dealing with server-side security are vulnerabilities in the network server programs and CGI software. Chapter 4 discusses how flaws or even "features" in the software implementations can be exploited by malicious users. Techniques for mitigating the dangers of flawed server programs and CGI programs are presented.

Operating System Security

The last security topic area to be discussed—certainly not the least in importance—is the security of the operating system of the network server. Most organizations rely heavily on firewalls to prevent vulnerabilities in the host operating systems from being exploited by Internet-based crackers. Chapter 5 discusses the role of firewalls in ensuring host security and their limitations in e-commerce applications. The second thrust of Chapter 5 is in framing the importance of the operating system in the security of network servers used for e-commerce applications. The operating system is the foundation on which commercial online applications are built. Weakness in the foundation can be exploited to compromise the server regardless of the security attributes of the applications. For this reason, it is insufficient to simply use secure transaction protocols because this data is often stored in plaintext on the network server. If the network server host is vulnerable to attacks, then this data might be compromised. To this end, the chapter presents a taxonomy of seven different types of network operating system vulnerabilities and contrasts and compares Windows NT and Unix platforms against these vulnerability categories. While the individual vulnerabilities listed will be rectified, the vulnerability categories will not be in the near future. Rather, new vulnerabilities will be found particularly as new operating systems are developed and used in new application areas.

The Future of E-Commerce Security

The state of the art in e-commerce is advancing so quickly that the information in this book only provides a snapshot in time. The risks, though, have been prevalent in computer systems for decades. The difference, however, is the way in which we are using computer systems in our daily lives. This book presents the important risks in the technology that underlies e-commerce activities. To provide a glimpse of what the future holds in e-commerce, Chapter 6 looks at component-based software and its role in creating and securing e-commerce systems.

Component-based software will attempt to bring software into its industrial age, where systems will be built from prefabricated components, much as electronic systems are today. We are still in an age of master craftsmanship in software where every craftsman is still custom-building his or her own software with little software reuse. Component-based software provides a framework by which software objects can be designed, interfaced, and reused in different systems. Some frameworks even provide economic models by which the designers of components reused in different systems are rewarded on a per-use basis.

The chapter also introduces the concept of certification of software components for security. Today, certification is provided for electric devices by the Underwriters Laboratory (UL) to maintain electrical safety standards. Tomorrow, we expect that software components will benefit similarly from certifying their use as safe for e-commerce applications. Because most security violations are made possible by flaws in software, certifying components for security *before* releasing them provides a viable economic model by which e-commerce systems can be safely deployed.

It is clear that e-commerce is a reality of today. The question that looms large is the *extent* of the success of e-commerce in transforming the current model of business and the rewards of such a system for businesses and consumers alike. The largest barrier to the growth of e-commerce today is in the uncertainty of the security of e-commerce systems. This book lays out the security risks in the technology on which e-commerce systems are built. By learning to manage the risks effectively, consumers, businesses, and the e-commerce industry as a whole will benefit.

References

Bellovin, S. "Prosecution for Pager Interceptions." *RISKS Digest*, 19:35, August 19, 1997.

Brunnstein, K. "Hostile ActiveX Control Demonstrated." *RISKS Digest*, 18:82, February 14, 1997.

deCarteret, N. "Computer Glitch Gives Investors Instant Loss of Balance at Schwab." *RISKS Digest*, January 28, 1997.

Edupage Editors. "AOL Says It Got Incorrect Stock Info from S&P." *RISKS Digest*, 18:90, March 14, 1997.

Edupage Editors. "EC Study Cites Fraud on the Internet." *RISKS Digest*, 19:13, May 9, 1997.

Edupage Editors. "Justice's Web Site Is Infiltrated." *RISKS Digest*, 18:35, August 19, 1996.

Edupage Editors. "Revealing Software Glitch Bares Credit Card Info on the Web." *RISKS Digest*, 18:61, November 15, 1996.

Garfinkel, S. "S/MIME Cracked by a Screensaver," Online. WIREDnews, September 26, 1997. Available: www.wired.com/news/news/technology/story/7220.html.

Hamilton, S. "E-Commerce for the 21st Century." *IEEE Computer*, Vol. 30, No. 5, May 1997, 44–47.

Kambil, A. "Doing Business in the Wired World." *IEEE Computer*, Vol. 30, No. 5, May 1997, 56-61.

Kennedy, D. "NASA: Another Website Bites the Dust." *RISKS Digest*, 18:88, March 7, 1997.

Koball, B. "Newt Gingrich's Confidential Teleconference Compromised by Cell Phone," *RISKS Digest*, 18:75, January 10, 1997.

Markowitz, S. "Shockwave Security Hole Exposes E-Mail." *RISKS Digest*, 18:91, March 17, 1997.

Neumann, P.G. "48-Bit RC5 Bites the Dust." *RISKS Digest*, February 14, 1997, 18:82.

Neumann, P.G. "CIA Disconnects Home Page after Being Hacked." *RISKS Digest*, 18:49, September 25, 1996.

Neumann, P.G. "U.S. Air Force Webpage Hacked." *RISKS Digest*, 18:74, January 7, 1997.

Schneier, B. *Applied Cryptography*. John Wiley & Sons, 1996.

Smart, T. "Jack Welch's Cyber Czar." *Business Week*, August 5, 1996, 82–83.

Stangenberger, A. "Berkeley Student Ian Goldberg Takes 3.5 Hours to Crack RC5 40-Bit Key." *RISKS Digest*, 18:80, February 1, 1997.

Uphoff, J. "Malicious Net Software Leads to Big Telephone Bills." *RISKS Digest*, 18:80, February 1, 1997.

Vinet, R. "Business-to-Business E.Commerce to Lead the Way." *E. Commerce Today*, Vol. 96.11.29, November 29, 1996.

Wagner, D. "Eagle (the President) and the Eagle Beagle: pager intercepts." *RISKS Digest*, 19:39, September 22, 1997.

Referenced Web Sites

Amazon.com	www.amazon.com	Still the most popular on-line bookseller.
Auto-By-Tel	www.autobytel.com	The hassle-free way to buy a car on the Net.
Counterpane Systems	www.counterpane.com	Bruce Schneier's company. They have released a Windows 95 screen saver that will brute force crack S/MIME encrypted e-mail messages.
Cybercash	www.cybercash.com	Developers of electronic wallets for secure credit card transactions on the Net and micropayments for small value purchases.
Dan Farmer	www.trouble.org/survey	Survey of computer security for e-commerce sites.
NASA	www.nasa.gov	NASA's site was hacked as recently as March of 1997.
PCCIP	www.pccip.gov	The President's Commission on Critical Infrastructure Protection.
RISKS	catless.ncl.ac.uk/Risks	The RISKS Digest archives. Moderated forum on risks to the public in computers and related systems. Peter G. Neumann is the group moderator.

U.S. Air Force	www.af.mil	Another victim of cracker angst in December 1996.
U.S. Central Intelligence Agency	www.odci.gov/cia	Its Web site was hacked in September 1996.
U.S. Department of Justice	www.usdoj.gov	Its Web site was hacked in August 1996.

Chapter 2

Deadly Content:
The Client-Side Vulnerabilities

Executable content applications make the Web an exciting and interactive medium for Internet surfers. Before executable content, Web pages were mainly static displays of information coded in the Hyper Text Markup Language (HTML). Most Web pages using simply HTML serve the function of billboards, with Web forms, search engines, and graphic animation sometimes breaking up the monotony. Animation of graphic images has made some Web pages more dynamic, but only in the sense of a passive activity like watching TV. That is, the information presented changes with time, but the session still consists of the user watching the screen. Executable content, on the other hand, provides the ability for users to interact during Web sessions. Executable content refers to a program or programs that are embedded in Web pages. When users point their Web browsers at a Web site that has an embedded executable content program, the program will typically automatically download to the users' machines and begin executing locally.

Executable content, also called active content and mobile code, exists in many forms. ActiveX controls and Java applets are some of the best known forms of active content. But so are scripts such as JavaScript and VBScript, which are commonly sent from Web sites. Even files that we commonly consider data, such as digital images, can be classified as executable content. These files execute on plug-ins—special-purpose interpreters. Browser plug-ins are software modules that can be integrated with the Web browser.

When the Web browser begins to download a file of the plug-in's format, the plug-in will execute the set of instructions included in the file. Plug-ins are often required to view graphic file formats or to play audio files. The capability to execute instructions embedded in Web pages and mail attachments has blurred the distinction between data and programs. Although graphic files may be considered input data to a plug-in, many graphic files constitute programs unto themselves. For example, a PostScript file is actually a set of instructions to a PostScript interpreter that renders the specified image. This topic is discussed in The Other Dirty Dozen section later in this chapter.

It is the interactive nature of active content that makes it particularly appealing for commercial applications. For example, car buyers can use a loan calculator program attached to a Web page to determine the monthly payments on a new car based on interest rates, loan amount, and the duration of the loan. Web publishers who have reached the limitations of HTML are beginning to embrace active content programming languages such as Java, ActiveX, JavaScript, and VBScript to provide Web surfers a "rich computing" experience. Many commercial applications require programming language support well beyond the capabilities of HTML to meet user requirements. For example, some businesses prefer to provide a client application that presents a user-friendly graphical interface complete with buttons and pull-down menus customized for that particular business or type of transaction. Providing spreadsheets, text editors, or word processors can make business-to-business e-commerce more meaningful than simple Web-based forms. Full-featured languages such as Java, C, and C++ can be used to implement these functions and others. The technology to provide these functions is now available through the use of active content models such as Java applets and ActiveX controls. The important issue to be resolved is to be able to provide these functions in a full-featured language without potentially violating the security or privacy of end users. Because e-commerce applications are increasingly leveraging active content, this chapter is dedicated to addressing the dangers of active content for end users. By knowing the risks of active content, users can decide when best to execute active content and how to avoid its hazards.

The limitations of HTML that Web publishers are bumping into is the lack of computing capabilities on the client side of the Web session. Currently, Web clients simply display HTML data sent from a server in a formatted output. In addition, Web forms can be used to send raw data entered by users to the Web server. This kind of client/server computing is an incremental advance from the days when dumb terminals were served by big mainframes. Aside from the obvious improvement in the graphical user interface, the real difference between today's Web sessions and the old client/server computing days has been in applying this model to the Internet to achieve wide-scale distribution of information. Active content technologies such as ActiveX and Java now provide the ability to not only widely distribute software but also to make a significant advancement in client/server computing by placing intelligence in the client. An intelligent client provides the ability to process data locally on the client host machine to the greatest extent possible. Because commercial Web sites may serve a great number of requests, the more processing that can be off-loaded to the client machines, the faster the response times will be and the greater the number of requests that can be served per unit time.

Intelligent clients can also exploit "push" technology to reduce the end users' effort to effectively utilize the Web. Today's model of Web sessions consists of users actively surfing the Internet to retrieve or "pull" data to their local machines. Users must either know which Web sites to go to or use Web search engines to find relevant data. Both approaches have problems. Users who are restricted to particular Web sites lose the advantage of the vast information provided on the Internet, and they will be provided with a limited and possibly narrow range of data. Using Web search engines tends to yield too much information with a low "signal-to-noise" ratio. That is, the useful data retrieved by the incredibly comprehensive Web search engines is drowned out by the amount of irrelevant or poor content that is also returned by the search.

The fact that the Web is an open forum to publish information by anyone is both virtue and vice. The Web empowers individuals to publish thoughts, art, software, pictures, essays, and papers anytime for wide-scale dissemination. However, without a moderator or peer review, the quality of Web content can sink to incredible lows. The point is not that Web content should be universally moderated, but that Web search engines pick up the rough with the diamonds, and the rough tends to obscure the diamonds. As an alternative, the push model is addressing the problem of retrieving useful information from the Web by turning the pull model upside down. Rather than actively searching the Web for information, users subscribe to services such as news distributors that filter data from premium sources according to individual preferences. The services push relevant data at predefined time intervals to subscribers' Web clients. Products such as PointCast Network (www.pointcast.com) are exploiting push technology to bring filtered information to consumers through surf-free premium channels such as periodic updates of news, particular stocks, sport scores, and entertainment. Both the Microsoft Internet Explorer 4.x (MSIE 4.x) and the Netscape Communicator 4.x have integrated push technology into their browsers (and, in some cases, in your desktop). In subscribing to these services, consumers should be aware of the security risks they are incurring. The consumer is effectively giving permission for these services to write information to the user's disk. Doing so opens a window of opportunity for violations of security and privacy. Exploiting push channels for security and privacy breaches has not been seen in practice—at least not yet. Push technology security concerns are covered in The Other Dirty Dozen section.

A third capability of Web clients is to use the pull model, but in a more intelligent fashion. Rather than have a user interactively trolling the Web for useful information, an intelligent agent acts on behalf of the user to periodically scan relevant information from Web sites. The agent is a Web client that can be programmed to learn the preferences of its end user. The agent will then search Web sites based on highly customized individual preferences and return the information to the user. Although the concept is not that different from Web searches, the intelligence is placed on the client, not the Web server; the client maintains the customized user preferences and can be scheduled for periodic updates for dynamic information.

A limitation of HTTP—the Web protocol—that impacts e-commerce applications is the inability to maintain state between successive operations. Web sessions are considered *connectionless* because every subsequent request to a Web server has no memory of the last request (including the data sent and the state of the transaction) sent to that server. For Web applications that require a series of data exchanges to constitute a single transaction, the stateless protocol is a problem. One solution that some call a kludge is to use "cookies"—data that represents the current state of the session. Cookies are sent with each HTTP request and read and processed by the server to determine the current and next state. Cookies are stored on the user's local disk to maintain state between server requests. Cookies are commonly used in practice by Web sites to collect Web site usage information. For example, the Web site can determine if a user has visited before, which pages the user visited, and from which site the user jumped to the current site. Cookies are also used to maintain authentication information during a Web session, so that users do not have to re-authenticate themselves for each subsequent access. Cookies work in simple applications, but they can be clumsy to program in server-side applications.

Even worse, cookies pose privacy and security concerns for end users. Collecting Web usage data for individuals and using this data for profiling Web visitors may constitute a breach of privacy depending on who you ask—those who stand to gain and those who stand to lose from profiling. Because cookies are stored on the user's local disk at the behest of the Web server, it is also possible that the Web server may be able to read and write files on the user's disk that are beyond of the purpose of maintaining state between Web requests.

Another good use of active content applications involves distributing work on a very large scale. One can more efficiently perform extremely computation-intensive functions (such as weather forecasting and life simulation models) by delegating pieces of them out to many computers that all share the computational load. Algorithms have been designed to use idle CPU cycles on inter-networked machines just for this purpose. In the past, distributing the computational workload required participants to download code and data, compile the code, execute the application, and then upload results back to the managing site. Obviously, this requires a fair amount of user participation, baby-sitting, and active interest. Active content is now being exploited to automate this process worldwide over thousands of computers. To participate in a large-scale distributed computation project, users need only point their browsers at the central management Web site for the project that contains an active content application, such as a Java applet. The applet automatically downloads to the user's machine, executes during idle CPU cycles, then reports the results back to the managing Web site. Given enough participants, computationally hard problems can be solved in a reasonable amount of time. Recall from Chapter 1 the Swiss student who was able to crack the RSA 48-bit cipher using 3500 computers to attain a rate of 1.5 trillion keys searched per hour. Active content can be used to automate cracking of ciphertext over thousands of computers. Although the point of the Swiss student's experiment was to demonstrate how easily the RC5 48-bit ciphertext can be cracked given Internet resources, this type of technology can also be leveraged by criminal elements to crack government or corporate secrets.

Executing Malware

As the last hypothetical example illustrated, active content can be a useful accessory for nefarious purposes. Consider an organization that places a cipher-cracking Java applet on its Web page while disguising its true purpose. Either the organization can hide the applet so that it does not appear in a Web browser, or the applet may appear to perform some other function (e.g., a game) when in fact it runs the cipher-cracking code. Every Web surfer who hits the Web page will download the Java applet and surreptitiously begin executing the code-cracking applet (if Java is enabled in the browser). Unless the users are savvy enough to realize that an extra process is running on their machines during idle cycles, the applet will run to completion and return results to the Web site. This scenario was postulated in the McGraw-Felten book, *Java Security: Hostile Applets, Holes, and Antidotes* (Wiley, 1996). Casual Web surfers will unknowingly have become accessories to a malicious and potentially criminal act.

The cipher-cracking example is just one potential misuse of active content. Active content can pose a number of different hazards to anybody with a Web browser and an inclination to surf. Surprisingly, many consumers are oblivious to the dangers of active content in violating both the privacy of their personal data and the security of their machines. According to popular sentiment, most consumers are fearful of having their credit card numbers stolen during an e-commerce transaction. Fortunately, several secure Internet protocols presented in Chapter 3 ensure confidentiality in e-commerce transactions by encrypting the credit card number during transmission between the client machine and the server host machine. Some protocols even keep the credit card number encrypted on the merchant server so that even an ill-intentioned merchant cannot read the credit card number. Although these protocols provide a high level of assurance during transmission, vulnerabilities on either end of the transaction—the commerce server or the client machine—can compromise sensitive data. Vulnerabilities in *server-side* applications that can compromise sensitive data are presented in Chapter 4. For example, Web servers that use the HTTP GET method to retrieve sensitive data from Web clients can cause the leakage of that data to other sites—even if a secure protocol is used in the transaction. Server-side programs such as CGI scripts that fail to correctly remove malicious commands from Web server requests may end up compromising sensitive data residing on the commerce server's database. Later, in The Other Dirty Dozen section, a JavaScript attack is described that can capture contextual Web client information—even confidential information sent in a secured Web session.

As the example illustrates, the risks of client-side vulnerabilities are equally concerning. Flaws in a Web browser may compromise sensitive data residing on a user's home personal computer. A flaw found by a Danish company in Netscape's Navigator browser versions 2.x, 3.x, and 4.0 allows a Web site to potentially view files stored on the user's computer, even if the machine is behind a firewall [Young 1997]. The Web site master needs to know only the name of a file on the user's computer in order to view it. Realize, though, that some personal files such as mail folders have standard names and reside in standard locations. The Web site can use knowledge of the user's Web browser (available from most Web page requests) to infer the likely location of these files. This means that a Web site can potentially retrieve personal mail when a user connects to the Web site.

Because browsers have permission to read from and write to the user's local file system, the potential also exists for a malicious browser to corrupt files or send local files to a Web site using the HTTP protocol. The latter type of attack is a form of information warfare that could be targeted to specific people or organizations to steal sensitive data. What makes this scenario unlikely, though, is that most commercial browsers are produced by major software development corporations, usually distributed widely, both over the Internet and in retail outlets. Deliberately writing and distributing malicious software (*malware* for short) would be tantamount to a major pharmaceutical producing and distributing tainted over-the-counter drugs.

The emergence of the Internet for commercial applications and, to a greater extent, the proliferation of active content on the Web, have made the potential for executing malware a real possibility warranting concern for end users everywhere. The Web has made it possible for anyone, from major corporations to students, to develop and distribute software programs while bypassing the normal retail distribution channels. The ease with which software can be distributed and executed over the Web is a double-edged sword. On one edge, the time-to-market to develop and distribute software is reduced significantly for commercial organizations. For individual developers, barriers of entry to the market are broken down by publishing software on the Web. For end users, purchasing shrink-wrapped software involves the time and expense of obtaining the software, installing it correctly, and executing the application. With active content on the Web, executing software placed on Web pages is as effortless as pointing a Web browser at a Web page and is still mostly free of charge.

On the close edge of the sword, the ease of publishing and distributing software over the Web can make it exceedingly easy for rogue developers to anonymously place malware on the Web without having to go through the normal checks and controls associated with retail distribution. Producing shrink-wrapped software requires a software development team with the backing and resources of a commercial organization to press CDs, produce manuals, provide technical support, provide patches and upgrades, and set up the distribution through retail outlets. Along the way, several parties are involved, from banks to distributors to retailers to consumers. Each additional step imposes expense and a check on the authenticity of the developer and product [Leichter 1997]. Although these checks are taken for granted by consumers, the difficulty and expense of producing commercial software can weed out rogue developers who lack assets or financial backing. As active content proliferates on the Web, the barriers to bringing software to the market are effectively removed, allowing almost anyone to develop, publish, and distribute home-grown software on the Web. Even well-intentioned individuals or development teams can place flawed software on the Web that can be exploited to violate end users' security and privacy. In the rest of this chapter, the security models (if any) and hazards associated with the execution of different types of active content are presented for applications as diverse as ActiveX, Java, scripts, browser plug-ins, e-mail attachments, and push technology.

ActiveX (In)security

ActiveX is a framework for Microsoft's software component technology that allows programs encapsulated in units called controls to be embedded in Web pages. A programmer can develop a program, wrap it in an ActiveX interface, compile it, and place it on a Web page. When end users point their Web browsers (that support ActiveX) at the Web page, the ActiveX control will download and attempt to execute on their machine. Because ActiveX controls are simply programs that download and execute on a user's system, they can do absolutely anything they are programmed to do—including damage your system by removing critical files. Security measures designed to prevent untrusted ActiveX controls from executing on users' local machines are presented in the next section. Security measures designed to prevent *trusted* ActiveX controls from damaging a system do not exist. ActiveX controls form the basic component technology of the ActiveX framework. Other ActiveX technologies such as ActiveX containers and scripts also pose security risks to the end user. In this section, the roles of each of these technologies are summarized along with their associated security risks.

ActiveX is language independent, but platform specific. This means that although ActiveX controls can be written in several different languages including C, C++, VisualBasic, Delphi, and even Java, ActiveX controls can be executed only on a 32-bit Windows platform. Web browsers that support ActiveX do not care what language the control is written in so long as the object code is accessible through an ActiveX interface. Unlike with Java, ActiveX controls are not portable to different machine architectures. In fact, even Java applets wrapped in an ActiveX control will execute only on Win32 machines (sometimes called Wintel machines) because the ActiveX wrapper is machine-specific object code. This limitation has not been the downfall of ActiveX, however, because Microsoft has captured the desktop market.

ActiveX Containers

A technology used in many ActiveX applications is an ActiveX *container*. ActiveX controls can be embedded in an ActiveX container, which is an ActiveX application composed of one or more ActiveX controls. An ActiveX document (sometimes called a compound document) is one kind of container. Documents allow the functionality of controls to be extended. For example, think of a desktop publishing application as a container that can hold multiple types of components: a text editor, a spreadsheet, and a graphics plotter. Each of the components serves its own function in isolation, but in combination with other components, it serves a larger application function.

Providing sophisticated processing functions such as a spreadsheet and text editor can be particularly useful in e-commerce applications, in which rich client computing functions can overcome the limitations of HTML. A rich client computing experience offers users the ability to interactively engage with a Web software application with the full capabilities now available to shrink-wrapped software. In Web applications, containers support interactive execution of ActiveX controls. An ActiveX container can work much like a browser plug-in. Once installed in the browser, the container can subsequently execute controls downloaded from one or more Web sites into the container. Of course, containers are not necessary to execute ActiveX controls, but they can extend functionality. A simple example is allowing a marquee control to be customized on the fly with user-inputted text.

One potential danger of interactive execution of multiple ActiveX controls is unintended consequences [Laminack 1997]. Unintended consequences can result from interactive complexity—that is, when two or more programs interact and display behavior that neither one was programmed to do. For example, consider two ActiveX controls embedded in the Web pages of an online bookstore. When a shopper hits the bookstore's Web site, both ActiveX controls download to the user's browser in an ActiveX container. One control is responsible for appending selected books into a "shopping cart" that resides on the user's local disk. The other control is responsible for executing a batch file also downloaded to the user's disk. The batch file consists of commands for preprocessing the orders in the shopping cart before sending the order to the bookstore. Each control is benign by itself; however, with a little manipulation, the ActiveX container can be made to turn against the consumer. Instead of appending a book to the shopping cart, a malicious attack may manipulate the shopping cart control to append a command such as DEL C:* to the batch file. (The ways this may occur are covered in the next section.) When the preprocessing control executes, it will execute the commands in the batch file in sequence, until it reaches the delete command, at which point the contents of the hard drive on the computer will be erased. Although neither control was programmed for this kind of malicious behavior, it is possible that the interaction of the two, coupled with malicious input from a Web site, can damage users' systems.

ActiveX Scripting

The third ActiveX technology of concern is ActiveX *scripting*. ActiveX scripting provides the ability to interactively send commands to an ActiveX control using scripting languages such as VBScript, JavaScript, or Microsoft's version of JavaScript called JScript. Scripting commands to ActiveX controls can come from within the container itself or from a server. Used in the client/server paradigm, ActiveX scripting allows a Web site to interactively send commands to an ActiveX control running on an end user's machine. Scripting languages such as VisualBasic and Perl provide a rich set of features, comparable to most programming languages, and their predefined functions can make writing scripts easier and sometimes more powerful than with a comparably sized program.

Unlike many programming languages, scripting does not require a compilation step. Rather, execution of scripts is interactive through the use of command interpreters. The implication for ActiveX controls is that arbitrary commands or programs can be sent from any Web site and executed by an ActiveX control running on users' desktops. ActiveX controls that accept scripting commands either from other controls or from Web servers can pose a great amount of harm to the end user's computer. Regarding the two ActiveX controls used to shop at the online bookstore, ActiveX scripting could facilitate this attack from potentially any site that knows these controls are on a machine. Realizing that the controls can be scripted, a malicious Web site can send interactive commands to the ActiveX controls for a user it knows has visited the online bookstore. This is a case in which the referer log (a log of the sites Web clients jump from) kept by a Web site could be used against a Web surfer in an insidious way. The shopping cart control can be scripted to append to the batch file a set of malicious system commands. The preprocessing control will execute the malicious file with devastating results, without knowing that the file has been corrupted by another Web site.

Another interesting facet of ActiveX scripting is that any ActiveX control can be marked as safe for scripting at the developer's discretion. That is, at the developer's discretion, the control can be marked as safe for scripting so that when it downloads to users' machines, the ActiveX control will accept scripting commands *from any Web page*— without the knowledge of the end user. The end user can only hope that the developer has adequately tested the control to ensure that the control will not respond maliciously to any commands sent from any Web page. However, be forewarned: The end user has no assurance that an ActiveX control marked safe for scripting will not respond maliciously to remote invocations. Remote invocations can initialize the control with any desired settings, can make calls to the control's methods in any order, using any parameters, and can manipulate the properties of the control. Even if the developer of the control has no malicious intentions, errors in coding the control can result in subverting the behavior of the control against the end user's machine. For example, the control can accept scripting commands to manipulate the system registry, to read or write to the file system, to overrun buffers in the memory, or to misuse data entered by end users. Even if end users know and trust the developer or company that wrote the ActiveX control that they are accepting, they have no way of knowing whether the ActiveX control was adequately tested to ensure that the ActiveX control will not respond maliciously to scripted commands sent from any Web site.

All three ActiveX technologies described pose serious security concerns for the end user. Users must be aware of these risks before downloading and executing ActiveX executable content. With any active content application, the proper security stance to assume will depend on the risk to assets that the active content poses. In the case of ActiveX controls, the assets at risk include all files on the client machine's local hard drive, as well as potentially any file systems shared over networked computers. Since ActiveX controls have the ability to execute much like any other program on a computer, ActiveX controls may be used to forge e-mail, to monitor Web usage, to send files back over the Internet, to write files, and to interact with other programs. To illustrate some real dangers of ActiveX, two case studies of ActiveX exploits are presented later in this chapter. To assess your risk in using ActiveX and other forms of active content downloaded from the Internet, first determine what assets are at risk. If the computer you are using to surf the Internet and download ActiveX controls is a stand-alone computer that serves no critical functions, it may be possible to execute active content without fear. On the other hand, if you are surfing the Net from work on an enterprise-critical machine, you should rethink executing active content applications whose behavior you do not know or trust. Microsoft's response to addressing security problems in using ActiveX technology is Authenticode. Authenticode does not prevent ActiveX controls from behaving maliciously, but it can be used to prevent automatic execution of untrusted ActiveX controls.

Authenticode: Establishing Trust for ActiveX

Authenticode is Microsoft's technology for thwarting malicious code from executing on users' Windows platforms. Authenticode can provide two checks before executing ActiveX controls:

- It can verify who signs the code.
- It can verify if the code has been altered since it was signed.

It is important to make a distinction between the author of the code and the person who signs the code because they may not be the same person. A digital signature merely represents an endorsement of the code rather than ownership or authorship. Before an individual or commercial firm can sign code, each needs to apply for and receive a Software Publisher Certificate (SPC) from one of several Certification Authorities (CAs) that serve this function. VeriSign is perhaps the best known example of a CA that provides SPCs.

The process requires the software publisher to generate a public/private key pair that is used to sign software. The private key remains secret to the publisher; the public key is distributed with each certificate. The role of the CA is to bridge the trust gap between the end user and the software publisher. Anyone can generate a public/private key pair and can assume any identity, so simply verifying that a document has been signed does not provide any assurance as to the identity of the publisher. The CA provides the identity checking for end users and will verify the individual or commercial firm's identities. In the case of commercial firms, Dun & Bradstreet, TRW, or other credit checking firms will perform a background check. Provided that the checks are approved, the CA will sign the public key of the software publisher and return a copy of it to the publisher in the form of the Software Publisher Certificate. The SPC conforms to industry-standard X.509 certificates. By signing the SPC, the CA is endorsing the identity of the software publisher that is bound to the public key. The mechanics and theoretical underpinnings of digital signatures are discussed in Chapter 3.

Once the software publisher receives the certificate from the CA, the software publisher can use its private key to sign any software code that it will distribute, regardless of who wrote it. Here is how it works. To provide integrity checks of the software, the software publisher generates a one-way hash of the code, which cannot be reversed. That is, the code cannot be regenerated from the resulting hash, known as the digest. Another property of the hash function is that it is repeatable. As long as none of the bits in the code are altered, running the same code through the same hash function will always generate the same digest. This property is used to check the code for corruption when it is received by the end user. Once the digest is created, the software publisher can digitally sign the digest generated for a particular program.

Digital signing tools are available in the ActiveX Software Developer Kit (SDK) and are compliant with the industry-standard X.509 certificates and PKCS#7 signed data standards. Signing the digest is much like signing a check—it provides the bearer some way to determine the authenticity of the document. In the case of publishing software, the signature is the individual's or company's endorsement that the code was written and approved by that individual or organization. In the absence of shrink-wrap, it is the brand mark of the software publisher. The signed digest is combined with the SPC into a signature block that is attached to the software.

How Authenticode Works Assuming that a software publisher has created a signature block attached to the software component as described here, the end user of the software component can verify the identity of the publisher and the integrity of the component when it is downloaded. When the software is downloaded to the end user's machine, the browser can detach the signature block and perform the checks using Authenticode. To determine the identity of the signer, the browser goes through a two-step process. First, the browser will examine the attached SPC to determine if it has been signed by a trusted Certification Authority. The browsers have a list of "trusted" CAs built into them. If the signature matches the corresponding CA public key signature stored in the browser, then the browser will accept the public key in the SPC as belonging to the identity labeled in the certificate.

The second step uses the public key of the software publisher to check the signed digest to determine with certainty whether the software publisher signed the downloaded code. Provided that the check was successful, the browser will display the equivalent SPC as shown in Figure 2.1. This display provides the end user positive assurance that the publisher did indeed endorse the code.

Figure 2.1 Software Publisher Certificate displayed to end user.

The other check provided by Authenticode determines whether the active content was altered in transit. The browser will regenerate the digest of the mobile code using the same hash algorithm. If the regenerated digest matches the signed digest sent with the code, the end user will have positive assurance that the code was not tampered with from the time it is signed until it is executed on the end user's machine. This whole process is akin to checking the seal on a sealed letter envelope to ensure it hasn't been tampered with during transit and then checking the signature on the letter to verify who sent it.

Authenticode 2.0 provides two new features to provide additional end-user protection. First, software publisher signatures will be timestamped so that end users can determine if the signatures were made while the SPC was still valid. Since SPCs require renewal, typically on an annual basis, the timestamping feature can be used to enforce renewal. Aside from sustaining a revenue stream for CAs, the idea is to require software publishers to meet the minimum requirements to be granted the SPC every year. If after being granted a certificate, a software publisher is known to distribute malicious code, the CA that certified the publisher has the right not to renew the certificate. Thereafter, any component that the software publisher signs will contain a timestamp that will be invalid according to the expired certificate. The end user's browser will note the invalid time stamp and warn the user to think twice before executing the software (see Those Annoying Dialog Boxes). This is the model, after all, that is used by many different licensing schemes in other industries, such as in the medical and legal professions. The key difference is that only the identity of the publisher is verified rather than their competence.

Of course, if the software publisher has a history of distributing malicious code, that will be reason enough not to reissue the certificate. This is also the model used by U.S. citizens who continue to renew their state drivers' licenses every few years. Of course, in the United States, the states cooperate to ensure that a driver's license rejected in one state for a criminal offense will not be accepted in another state. Currently, it is unknown if CAs will share data to prevent one rejected software publisher from obtaining a certificate from another CA.

The second new feature that Authenticode 2.0 provides (over Authenticode 1.0) is the ability to revoke certificates. A Software Publisher Certificate can be revoked by the granting CA, if the publisher violates the code-signing agreement it made with the CA. Most agreements require the software publishers not to deliberately distribute malicious code. If it becomes known that a software publisher has deliberately distributed malicious code, the CA can not only refuse to renew the certificate, but also immediately revoke it. The Internet Explorer 4.0 will check the certificate before downloading the content to ensure that it has not been revoked. If a publisher believes that its private key has been compromised, the publisher can request that its certificate be revoked as well. This revocation of a certificate must be widely disseminated to users' browsers. The CAs can serve the role of disseminating this information that it receives either from end users or publishers for certificates that should be revoked. As long as the browsers are configured to periodically update their lists of revoked certificates, the end user will be protected against software components signed by developers that have had their certificates revoked.

Where Authenticode Falls Short of Security The sum and substance of what Authenticode provides is verification of the identity of the person who signed the control and integrity checks of the software to ensure it has not been altered since it was signed. So what do these two checks provide and where do they fall short? If the ActiveX component publisher signs the component, the end user will know who that person is and if the component has been tampered with after it was signed. However, the signature provides no assurance that the control will not behave maliciously. The Authenticode technology works solely on a trust model. That is, if you trust the one who signs the code, then for better or for worse, you give rights to the control to do anything to your machine. If you do not trust the publisher of the control, you reject its execution outright. Unfortunately, there is no middle ground to let the control execute in a constrained environment where it can be observed first before granting it full access. Once you trust the control to run on your machine, it has free reign to do any number of malicious activities such as erase your hard drive or send copies of your files out to different Web sites. Unlike untrusted Java applets, which are constrained to a "sandbox," ActiveX controls have all the power and privilege of any program running on your machine.

The Java applet sandbox constrains applets from accessing resources outside a particular section of memory, called the sandbox. This means that Java applets cannot access parts of the memory outside their classes, read or write to the disk, or even make arbitrary network connections. Cracks in the sandbox described in the Java Security section have permitted hostile applet exploits. The key difference in security between ActiveX controls and Java applets is that ActiveX security is based wholly on the trust placed in the code signer, and Java applet security is based on restricting the behavior of the applet. One is a human judgment-based approach to security, while the other is a technology-based approach to security [Princeton SIP April 28, 1997]. This distinction is changing with code signing of Java applets. Rather than being constrained in a sandbox, signed Java applets will have the ability to access system resources based on trust, similar to the ActiveX security model. One key difference is that untrusted applets can still be executed within the sandbox. In addition, future releases of Java will incorporate fine-grained access control to system resources based on varying levels of trust, checked by digital signatures. This move is sure to complicate the already difficult process of establishing security policies.

Manipulating Trust The problem with the trust-based model of security that Authenticode employs is that it is vulnerable to simple malicious attacks that manipulate this trust. Two scenarios in the upcoming Deadly Controls section illustrate this vulnerability in no uncertain terms. One fundamental problem is that it is exceedingly easy to obtain a certificate from a Certification Authority to publish and distribute "trusted" software. Because obtaining a certificate requires only supporting evidence of identity rather than competence in designing software, literally anyone can obtain a Software Publisher Certificate. Individuals can currently obtain a Class 2 certificate from VeriSign to sign software for the cost of U.S. $20. The only pieces of information required to obtain the certificate are name, address, e-mail address, date of birth, and social security number. VeriSign simply verifies the authenticity of this information. If the information proves to be correct, a certificate is issued.

Obtaining a certificate to distribute software is not an inherently bad idea. In today's technocracy, everyone deserves the right to develop and publish software. The Internet provides a global forum for sharing software cheaply and easily. Publisher certificates give end users a high level of confidence in those who endorse the software that is being run on their systems. However, the use of this certificate to evoke feelings of security assurance in the end user misrepresents the checks that Authenticode actually provides. Because the certificate provides no assurance of the secure behavior of the software, approving ActiveX controls for execution based on the certificate should be construed as a decision based not on security, but rather on trust.

Flawed Software The problem with permitting ActiveX controls to execute with full privileges based on trust is the same problem one encounters when trusting flawed software that pervades the industry today. A vast majority of the vulnerabilities found in software that have been exploited for malicious gain were not deliberately placed in the software. A look at the incident response notices from organizations such as the CERT Coordination Center (www.cert.org) shows that many of the notices are initiated by the software vendors themselves. Either the vendors discovered the vulnerabilities after the software was released or their end users reported problems to the vendors, which in turn notified the incident response teams.

Before installing or patching software from a vendor, end users or administrators need to trust that the software was delivered from the genuine vendor. To this end, most incident response notices pointing to vendor patches are now accompanied by message digests for the patches themselves. When the system administrators download the patch, they can regenerate the message digest and compare it to the expected digest. A miscompare points to a problem in the downloaded patch (or potentially a malicious substitution of the patch). A stronger form of assurance is for the vendor to digitally sign the message digest so that the end user will have positive assurance that the patch originated from the vendor and not from a rogue organization impersonating the vendor.

Signing the message digest of the code is exactly what Authenticode requires and checks. The fallacy of associating a genuine signature with security is that the signature confers no meaning on the security of the signed code. Signing code will not make it any more resistant to malicious attack. Even the best-intentioned software publisher can release software that may turn against the end user's machine. Therefore, we can expect to see many of the same types of vulnerabilities in ActiveX controls that we see in other software running on machines today.

The problem is more acute with ActiveX controls than with the vast majority of other software running on machines today. First, users who check signatures may get a false sense of security that the code is secure. Second, since ActiveX controls can communicate via distributed processes over the Internet, they are inherently vulnerable to network-based attacks. Unlike much of the application software running on desktop machines today, ActiveX controls can be easily exploited even when executing behind firewalls. Firewalls are a good at preventing vulnerabilities in software running inside the firewall from being exposed to the Internet-at-large. However, firewalls by design permit Internet requests to certain software running on machines inside the firewall. For example, most firewalls let mail and Web requests through to internal machines. Some let FTP and telnet sessions through, using special software called proxies to handle the requests. The problem with trusted ActiveX controls is that an ActiveX control can easily open a hole in the firewall that allows the control to make connections back to a Web server (a standard practice both for the controls and the firewall). This means that the ActiveX control can behave maliciously by design or through manipulation by a malicious server. The ability for ActiveX controls to accept scripting commands makes them vulnerable to manipulation from malicious servers. This point is underscored by the fact that many ActiveX controls are marked safe for initializing and scripting.

Scripting ActiveX Controls As mentioned earlier, ActiveX controls can be marked as safe for initializing and scripting. In fact there is a great deal of incentive for developers to mark their controls as safe for initializing and scripting, even if they have not adequately tested it to see if it is [Johns 1996]. The motivation is to provide a seamless Web browsing experience for users. Recall that when the user downloads an ActiveX control, the browser will check the signatures to ensure that the control has a valid signature block.

The signature block reveals the identity of the publisher and is used to determine if the code has been altered.

A more obscure check that is performed by the browser is to determine if the control has been marked as safe for initializing and safe for scripting. If it has been so marked (with two distinct checks), the user will have to encounter the nominal set of dialog boxes when downloading ActiveX controls, depending on the safety level selected (see Those Annoying Dialog Boxes). On the other hand, if the control has not been marked safe for initializing and safe for scripting, a whole host of dialog boxes will be presented to the user with myriad choices for dealing with the control. For example, in the IE 3.x, if the safety level is set to high and one of the two checks fails, any scripting commands sent to the control will result in a dialog box similar to that shown in Figure 2.2.

If the safety level is set to medium in the IE 3.x and the control has not been marked and signed as safe for initializing, a dialog box similar to the one in Figure 2.3 is presented to the user.

The user must decide if it is acceptable that this control has not been marked safe for initializing and determine whether to accept all controls on this page even if they are not marked safe for scripting or to decline this and all other controls that are not marked safe for scripting. The upshot is a difficult browsing experience with a complex set of choices that will ultimately affect the security of the user's machine. The IE 4.x preconfigures

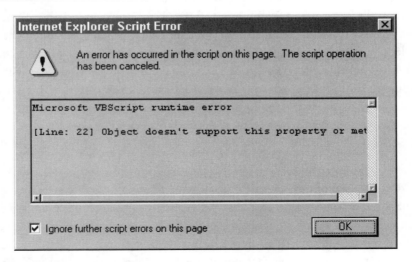

Figure 2.2   Dialog box appears when scripting is not permitted.

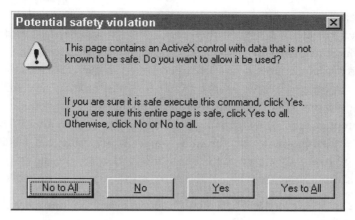

Figure 2.3   Dialog box that appears when control has not been marked as safe for initializing.

most of the safety levels to minimize the decisions required by end users. The default settings are configured for convenience, not security. The end user or system administrator should set the safety levels in each browser according to the organization's defined security policy. From a software publisher's point of view and perhaps the end user's, it is better to not have the user deal with these complex decisions. The simple way to prevent the dialog boxes from showing up in the first place is to mark the controls safe for initializing and scripting.

What does it mean to mark the control safe for initializing and scripting? If the control is marked safe for initializing, *any* Web site that knows of the control's existence in the browser can initialize the control with the parameters of its own choosing. This means that the control can be configured by another Web site with different parameters that can certainly alter its behavior—possibly in malicious ways. The problem is even more critical with scripting. If the component is marked safe for scripting by the component's publisher, any Web site can send commands in scripting languages such as VBScript or JavaScript to interactively control the component.

To ensure that the component truly is safe, the component's developer must ensure that no matter what values are sent to initialize the control from any Web site (malicious or not), the control cannot compromise the user's privacy or violate the machine's security. Similarly, a control marked safe for scripting must not act maliciously, despite any commands that can be sent from any Web site (malicious or not). It is far from trivial to verify that the control will remain safe when it is initialized or scripted from any Web page [Johns 1996]. In fact, the technology and methods for verifying benign component behavior in the face of clever malicious input are not well understood. It is currently the subject of active research. In essence, the burden of responsibility for certifying the safety of ActiveX components has been leveled on the component developer's shoulders until a suitable certifying technology is developed that can be employed by Certification Authorities. This topic is addressed in Chapter 6. Unfortunately, the component developers have little motivation to ensure safe behavior on the part of their components in the face of potentially malicious initialization and scripting from other Web sites. Because not marking the component safe for initializing and scripting can result in a host of warning dialog boxes to the user, the primary motivation for the developer is to mark it safe to make it more user friendly—without regard for the consequences.

Good Controls, Dangerous Methods   The Deadly Controls section describes real attacks from malicious ActiveX controls. To give some context to this discussion about manipulating ActiveX controls, consider an ActiveX control that is *not* known to be malicious. The ByteCatcherX control (www.save-it.com/byteftpx.htm), for instance, is purported to assist in downloading software over the Internet. A Web site that is interested in having its software downloaded to the end user's disk may post this control on its Web page. This control lets users stop the downloading of a file and resume later with no loss of data. Anyone who has ever downloaded a multimegabyte file from a Web site over a 28.8K modem knows why this is a useful feature. Downloading a file that large can tie up a phone line for a period of hours. Users may want to use the phone line for, say, a conversation.

Another common problem is a disconnected modem session as a result of difficulty with a user's Internet service provider (ISP). If the session is disconnected, the data already downloaded will be useless; a new connection will need to be made and will start the download over from scratch. This is a very painful process for end users. Certainly having a program or ActiveX control that is intelligent enough to realize that the full download did not occur and that it can be resumed without loss of data would be beneficial to users.

Enter ByteCatcherX. Two features of this control make it fairly interesting from both end-user and security analyst points of view. First, the control can detect modem disconnections from the Internet; after a certain timeout period, it reconnects, reestablishes the session with the Web site, and resumes a download from the point where the download was interrupted. The second interesting feature is the control's ability to automatically shut the machine down after the file has been downloaded (on request). End users may indeed find these two features useful for downloading software. Web sites attempting to accommodate home users may place this control on their Web pages to support automatic downloading and reconnection in the event of Internet connection downtime. From a security analyst's perspective, the control seems to provide two features that have been exploited for malicious purposes in other applications.

Recall from Chapter 1 the Moldova pornographic scam that ran up huge phone charges for unsuspecting Web surfers. A Trojan horse program was downloaded by visitors to a certain Web site promising pornographic pictures. The program disconnected the modem from the user's ISP, lowered the volume, then dialed a number directly to an ISP in the former Soviet Republic of Moldova. The ISP then routed the Web session to an Internet site in North America where pornographic pictures were stored. So the end user did indeed see the pornographic pictures, but only after unknowingly dialing Moldova and racking up huge phone charges. Although the Trojan horse program was unspecified, there is no reason that it could not have been a signed ActiveX control. Referring to the ByteCatcherX control, we see the capability for an ActiveX control not only to detect an Internet disconnection, but also to dial an ISP and reestablish the connection to the Web page. Of course, the same ActiveX control could have been written to disconnect an ongoing Internet connection and redial an ISP in a foreign land.

The second feature of the control that allows a user to configure the control to shut down the machine is strikingly similar to the malicious ActiveX Exploder Control discussed in the Deadly Controls section. The essence of the Exploder Control was a demonstration that a signed control can shut down a Wintel machine even without the user's knowledge. Clearly, the ByteCatcherX control demonstrates the same capability, although unlike the author of the Exploder Control, the author of the ByteCatcherX control probably did not receive threats for legal action if the signed control was left up on the author's Web page. Both features of the ByteCatcherX control demonstrate the broad capabilities that any ActiveX control can bring to bear on users' machines. If a misguided developer were to use these capabilities in an unfriendly manner, the result could be grave security violations. If this control can be manipulated from other Web sites, it may be possible to turn its features against the end user. Again, it is important to stress that this control is not known to be malicious, nor has it been known to be manipulated maliciously. Since the authors of the ByteCatcherX and the Exploder controls were equally successful in obtaining certificates from CAs, and end users have no way of assessing whether one developer is more trustworthy than another, the difference is fully at the discretion of the developer—not of the end user or the client browser.

Security Zones Recent changes implemented in the Internet Explorer 4.x Web browser have attempted to repackage Authenticode "security." Microsoft's Internet Explorer 4.0 browser incorporates the concept of security zones for handling active content, based on the same trust model that permits signed ActiveX controls to execute on the desktop. The security zone merely organizes Web sites into different categories. Figure 2.4 shows the security options window of IE 4.0 that allows the user to configure Web sites into different zones.

The idea is to divide the Internet up into zones of trust. Four basic zones of trust are local, trusted, the Internet, and restricted Web sites. The level of trust for each zone is indicated by a check in the high, medium, low, or custom configuration box. The point of setting up zones is to categorize Web sites according to varying levels of trust. Despite the seeming fine-grained ability to specify level of trust for a Web site, it is important to realize

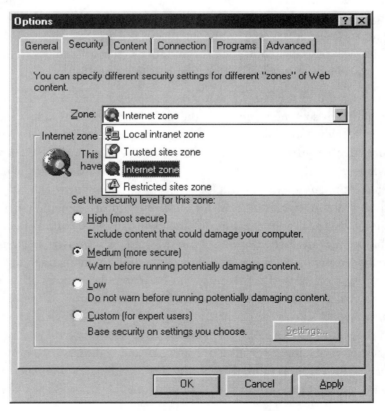

Figure 2.4   Security options window of Internet Explorer 4.0.

that the trust policy is still binary. Either you trust the site or you do not. The particular zone of trust from which an active content component is downloaded will influence which dialog box, if any, will be displayed to the user before the active content is executed (see Those Annoying Dialog Boxes). For example, downloading an active content component from a Web site in the untrusted zone will pop up a dialog box similar to the one now popped up when one downloads content in an IE 3.x browser configured with the high level of safety, as shown in Figure 2.5.

If the component is signed by a publisher whose identity is vouched for by a trusted CA, the component can be permitted to execute. If the component from the untrusted zone is not signed, it will not be permitted to execute. On the other hand, downloading an active content component from the local zone will result in the automatic execution of a component without any dialog box interference. As far as the security policy of executing ActiveX controls, there is essentially no change in the trust-based model of permitting these components to execute on users' machines. The fundamental flaw of this approach is the use of human judgment rather than a technology for determining what is secure.

The major changes in the use of security zones is in the management of the security zones. IE 4.0 still allows the user to set the security policy through menu-driven options, as with the security options in IE 3.0 (see Setting the Security Policy for a discussion). Perhaps the most significant change is that the system administrator for a local area network (LAN) can now set the policy for IE 4.0 users. Administrators can determine which components are allowed to execute on users' machines based on who signed the components. Using the Microsoft Internet Explorer Administration Kit (IEAK), the administrator can preinstall permitted certificates on users' individual browsers and block other

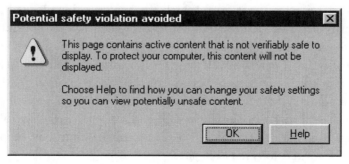

Figure 2.5 Dialog box that pops up when one is downloading content in the IE 3.x configured with the high level of safety.

certificates from being downloaded, thereby preventing other signed components from being executed. The result is a centralized security policy that the administrator can remotely manage by adding new certificates for permitted controls and even removing certificates from the list of permitted certificates if given due cause. This is a step in the right direction for setting and enforcing corporate security policies. The important point is that the security policy makes decisions on which components to execute—not on the secure behavior of the control—but rather on the identity of the publisher.

The second major change in the use of security zones will be the execution of signed Java applets, which is supported in JDK 1.1. (This topic is discussed in more detail in the Signing Applets section.) Authenticode 2.0 will support signed applets that can be released from their sandbox selectively, depending on the zone from which they are downloaded and the freedom they require [Microsoft Internet Security White Paper 1997]. This security policy is called fine-grained access control. The Java sandbox security model that prevents applets from behaving maliciously (regardless of who signs the applet) will still be enforced if the applet is downloaded from an "untrusted" zone. On the other hand, if the applet is downloaded from the trusted intranet, the applet may be given free reign to perform destructive operations such as reading and writing to files on the hard drive or networked drives, accessing other programs on the desktop, as would a Java application running locally. Unlike ActiveX controls, Java applets can be signed with information that states what level of system resources are necessary for the applet to execute. Signing an applet with its required resources is called *capabilities* signing. Authenticode 2.0 purports to support capabilities signing [Microsoft Internet Security White Paper 1997].

Netscape's Communicator 4.x also supports access control of signed applets via capabilities. For example, the signature block of a Java applet may contain the requirement that the Java applet be able to read from the disk and write to a network socket. Depending on the zone of trust from which the applet is downloaded and the corresponding security policy coded for that zone, the applet may be permitted to perform these otherwise sandboxed functions. A compromise zone of trust may be the "trusted" zone. Sites in this zone may be well known and visited often by users. Java applets downloaded from this zone may be let out of the sandbox on a tight leash to allow them to access some system resources but prevent them from accessing other system resources. For example, an applet downloaded from the well-known Gamelan site (www.gamelan.com) may be permitted to read local files, but may be prevented from opening network sockets to other Web sites.

Setting the Security Policy The problem with the trust-based model for ActiveX is made worse by several different factors: the ability to set the security policy on each browser to essentially none, on-the-fly security policy decisions, the ability to accept all code from a particular vendor, and the ability for unintentional flaws in program code to be exploited. The ability to prevent most active content from executing on your machine is configurable in most browsers. By default, most browsers enable the execution of active content. Figure 2.4 shows the configuration options in IE 4.0 for downloading active content from different zones. These configuration settings simply determine which dialog boxes, if any, are displayed to the user before active content is executed. As discussed in the Security Zones section, the security policy for ActiveX controls is binary. The use of the preconfigured security zone settings tends to obscure this binary security policy.

The real choice is made when one selects the custom configuration settings button shown in Figure 2.4. Doing so brings up the window in Figure 2.6. Unfortunately, both the label on the button in Figure 2.4 ("for expert users") and the long list of options to

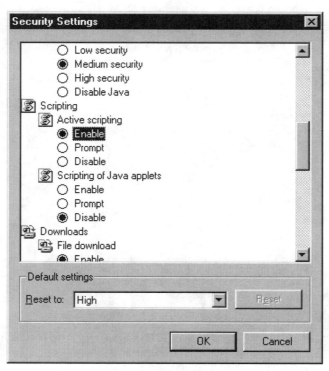

Figure 2.6 Custom configurations window for "expert users."

check as shown in Figure 2.6 make this option more difficult for users to specify. In a sense, these options obscure the real security policy decision a user must make.

The ability to prevent active content from executing on a machine is less obscured in IE 3.0. In the IE 3.x for Windows 95, the Options, Security window (shown in Figure 2.7) allows the end user to set the security policy of executing active content applications.

This window turns out to be the most critical for determining how vulnerable a machine is to malicious active content. The first thing to note is that all the options to download active content are enabled by default. Therefore, the default security policy that comes with the browser out of the box is to allow any active content application to download. If any information on the machine is too critical to lose, every box in this window should be unchecked. Although the first option appears to disallow the execution of active code, do not be misled into believing that simply unchecking this box will prevent active

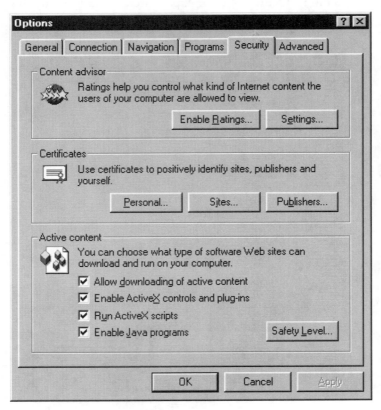

Figure 2.7 The IE 3.x security options window.

content applications from downloading and executing. To prevent ActiveX controls and Java applets from downloading and executing, uncheck *all* of the boxes.

A similar option appears in versions of Netscape Navigator. The Options, Network Preferences window shown in Figure 2.8 from Netscape Navigator 3.01 allows the user to disable downloading of Java and JavaScript programs.

Finding these options in Netscape's Communicator 4.01 is a little more difficult. Go to the Edit, Preferences menu, and select Advanced. The window shown in Figure 2.9 displays a safe setting for active content. The user can elect to enable Java or JavaScript from this window.

ActiveX controls are not supported in Netscape's Navigator 3.* and Communicator 4.01. Again, by unchecking these boxes, users can prevent active content from harming their machines. This stance is the safest position to take in preventing malicious behavior

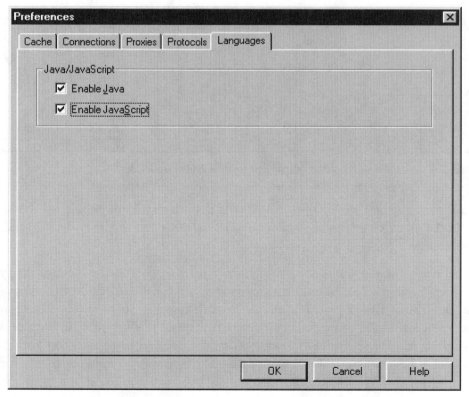

Figure 2.8   Security options window in the Netscape Navigator 3.x.

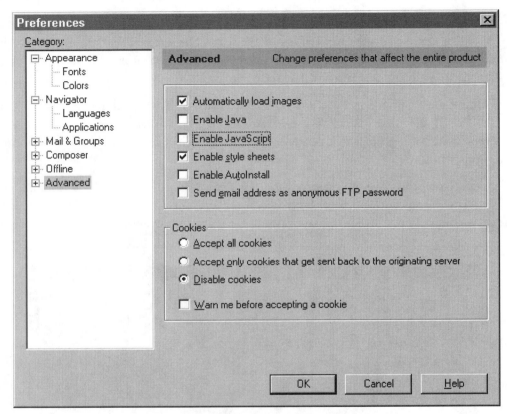

Figure 2.9 A safe setting for active content in Netscape 4.x.

from active content. The downside, however, is that users will not be able to take advantage of the useful or interesting Java applets or ActiveX controls if they decide to disable active content.

The active content options effectively allow users to control the security policy for their own machines. That is, end users can choose to incur the risk of downloading active content or protect their machines simply by disabling these options. The choice made should reflect the risks of executing active content versus the lost utility of not executing active content applications. The browser allows this decision to be made on a machine-by-machine basis, which makes sense for individually owned computers. In a corporate environment, however, the security policy should be set according to the organization's best interests. If an individual chooses to allow ActiveX controls to download and execute on a machine holding enterprise-critical data, the user may be posing a risk to the organization. For example, a battle commander that uses a Win32 machine to connect with other field units would be best advised not to surf the Web with active content enabled. Active content may not only introduce viruses and Trojan horses, but may also copy data from the commander's classified hard drive and send data back over the network.

It is not feasible to enforce organization-wide security policies from each and every browser running on the organization's networks. To deal with these issues at the corporate or group level, the security policy for active content must be determined beforehand and dealt with at the appropriate system points. The IE Administrators Kit for IE 4.0 is a step in the right direction to enforce system-wide active content policies. Another potential solution is to filter active content at routers and concentrators before requested code reaches users' machines. The downside of organization-wide decisions is that every user may be denied access to some of the more interesting and innovative technologies on the Internet today. Once again, the appropriate assessments must be made to decide which machines are most at risk and which machines can incur the associated risk.

Those Annoying Dialog Boxes For anyone who has ever surfed the Net using one of the two popular Web browsers, encountering dialog boxes is a common event. For example, the Netscape Navigator will pop up a dialog box when users are leaving an SSL-secured Web session, just to let them know that the next Web page they see will not be transmitted over a secure connection (the IE can be configured to do the same). A good idea, seemingly, but what effect does it have on the end user? For the genuinely interested end user, this information is valuable. Most users tire of these dialog boxes quickly, though. Fortunately or not, most dialog boxes provide the option not to see them again under the same circumstance. For example, the dialog box just mentioned provides users with the option not to see the warning when they are leaving a secure session. Or this option can be preconfigured in the browser's security options menu. Although it might be nice not to have to see the box when moving between secure and insecure Web sessions, those who think they are still in a secured session after they have moved to a Web page not secured by SSL run the risk of sending confidential data without realizing that it can be potentially captured by Internet eavesdroppers.

The annoying dialog problem also exists in the Internet Explorer, and it is pervasive when users are downloading active content. In Figure 2.4, notice that the user can select one of three levels of safety: high, medium, or low (or none) in the IE 4.0. Users have similar options in the IE 3.x that they can reach by pressing the "Safety" button shown in Figure 2.7. The safety level selected by the user determines what kind of dialog box, if any, will be displayed when the user is downloading ActiveX controls. If the highest safety level is selected, the user will be prompted with a dialog box anytime an ActiveX control is downloaded. If the code has a valid signature, a certificate dialog box similar to the one shown in Figure 2.10 will appear in the browser.

The certificate shows the name of the control, the publisher of the control, and the expiration date of the certificate, in addition to hot links to Web pages relating to the publisher and the particular control. If the control has not been signed and the safety level is set to high, a warning dialog box similar to that shown in Figure 2.11 will pop up.

This warning provides the user notification that an unsigned ActiveX control attempted to download, but was averted. If you ever installed this component before, however, this warning has no impact at all on the fact that the component you previously installed *will be executed*. So, although you may think that the warning prevented

Figure 2.10   IE Certificate dialog box.

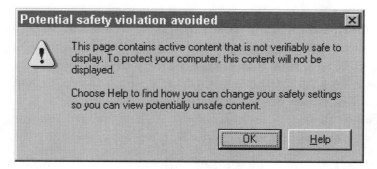

Figure 2.11 IE Unsigned control warning dialog box.

the execution of the control, if it has already been installed, the control is trusted, and the control will execute.

The other levels of safety that can be selected simply provide more freedom for software components to execute on users' machines without any intervention via dialog boxes. If the medium safety level is selected, a pop-up dialog box similar to the one in Figure 2.12 will appear when the user downloads unsigned software or components whose signatures have expired.

Unlike the dialog box in Figure 2.11, this dialog box permits the user to execute the unsigned control directly. Selecting the lowest level, none, provides no protection from executing unsigned ActiveX controls. Clearly, this option is not advised. By selecting the safety level options, users are taking matters into their own hands. The browser will not prevent an ActiveX control from behaving maliciously if the user grants the privilege for

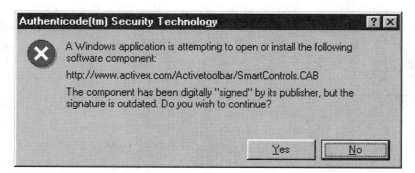

Figure 2.12 Warning dialog box in the MSIE that pops up for unsigned controls.

the ActiveX control to execute, regardless of who publishes it or which Certification Authority signs the certificate. The safety levels appear to provide some level of granularity beyond accept and reject to executing ActiveX controls. In reality, the decision of whether to execute ActiveX controls is made in the security options window of Figure 2.7 in IE 3.0, Figure 2.6 in IE 4.0, Figure 2.8 for Navigator 3.x, or Figure 2.9 for Communicator 4.01. The safest stance is to simply prohibit active content from executing on a machine. If users do permit active content to execute, the safety levels either defer the decision to an on-the-fly decision or remove the decision from users' hands altogether by allowing all active content to execute.

Making Security Decisions on the Fly Setting the security options windows is one way of setting the security policy for which active content applications are permitted to execute on users' machines. If the active content is enabled, the annoying dialog boxes will be displayed in the user's browser every time an ActiveX control is downloaded—depending on which safety level is chosen. Assuming that the user does enable ActiveX controls and select the high level of safety, the user now has the ability to make security decisions on the fly. That is, while surfing the Net, the user will have the option of installing and executing ActiveX controls or rejecting them as they are downloaded.

Making security decisions on the fly is generally a bad idea. Using the argument made in the Setting the Security Policy section, users should not be making decisions at an individual level that influence the security of the entire organization's networked system. For the home user, it sounds appealing to make judgments on which ActiveX controls to download and which to reject. However, as discussed in the section called Those Annoying Dialog Boxes, after a while, it is simply human nature to either consistently accept or consistently reject controls. Users who consistently accept or reject controls might as well code the security policy accordingly. The browser vendors realize this tendency, and as a result, they have placed checkboxes in the dialog boxes to bypass them altogether. Notice the checkboxes in the bottom of the dialog box in Figure 2.10. These checkboxes allow the user to completely bypass the Authenticode mechanisms (and dialog box) for all software components downloaded from a particular vendor, signed by a particular Certification Authority, or both. End users have the option to accept all components ever signed by Microsoft or all components whose certificates are signed by VeriSign. This blind acceptance of controls based on the publisher's name brings up the second problem for making security decisions on the fly.

The second problem with using the dialog boxes to make on-the-fly security decisions is related to the criteria by which the security-critical decisions are made. Remember, Authenticode tells only the software publisher's name and whether the component has been altered. The dialog boxes give no information about the quality of the software component. The certificate provides no assurance about a given component's security. There is no guarantee, either expressed or implied, that the component users are about to accept will not damage their system, corrupt their data, or steal their work. By permitting an ActiveX control to download and execute, users give the control full access to all their files and resources on their machine.

A better model for preventing security violations on home users' machines and corporate networks is to establish *a priori* a security policy for active content that is enforced on the fly. Again, in a corporate environment, this enforcement is better performed at the system level than the individual user level. An alternative is to *certify the security* of active content rather than just the identity of the publisher. Certifying security can provide assurance that the control has been tested to determine if it can cause harm to client machines, whether through deliberate programmed function or through unintended error. It is important to realize that an ActiveX control can behave maliciously even if it was not intentionally programmed for malicious behavior.

Because some ActiveX controls can respond to interactive commands through scripting, it is possible to manipulate a control to behave maliciously on behalf of any untrusted user, in spite of the best intentions of the software publisher. Two scenarios can always defeat any certification scheme based on the developer's identity. First, the developer covertly inserts malicious code in a control that erases all traces of its origin while wreaking its damage. In the second scenario, unintended consequences of a control through interactions with other controls or scripts violate system security despite the best intentions of the control's developer. The technology to implement security certification is still being researched and developed. Chapter 6 introduces security certification for software components.

Perhaps the best known and understood method for preventing security violations from active content applications is confining them in a security sandbox during execution. This is the model under which untrusted Java applets execute. The object of the sandbox is to strictly limit the resources that a component can access and manipulate when they are downloaded over the Internet. With some notable exceptions covered in the Java Security section later in this chapter, this model of security has served well in practice to limit the potential damage that Java applets can wreak on any client machine.

Deadly Controls

It should be clear by now that an ActiveX control can execute any function that a Windows program can. To illustrate this point by example, two well-known deadly controls were published on the Web for demonstration purposes: the ActiveX Exploder Control and the CCC ActiveX control.

ActiveX Exploder Control

The ActiveX Exploder Control was written by Fred McLain and placed on his Web page at www.halcyon.com/mclain/ActiveX. The purpose for writing this control was to demonstrate how simple it is for an ActiveX control to perform a potentially malicious operation such as shutting down a user's computer while the user is surfing the Web. The control performs a clean shutdown of Windows 95 systems when it is downloaded and executed, as with other ActiveX controls. On some machines, particularly laptops that employ power conservative features, the control will also turn off the power to the machine after it shuts down Windows 95. The control makes a call to Windows API functions that are equivalent to selecting the shut down menu item from the Windows Task bar, but with a power-off feature added.

What makes this control even more interesting is that McLain signed the control with the Software Publisher Certificate he obtained from VeriSign. Thereafter, when a user downloaded his control, the user was presented with the friendly certificate identifying Fred. Then, even if the user set the safety level to high on an Internet Explorer browser, the end user could still download and execute the control, which subsequently shuts down the machine. After the press got wind of this Web page, a controversy erupted that put McLain at the center of the debate over signed controls. Threatened by lawsuits, McLain removed the control from his page. The control is back up on the page in fine form as of this writing (it shut down the computer used to write this book); however, it is no longer signed. Because the Internet Explorer can be configured to different safety levels, it is still easy to download and execute his control. One need only set the safety level to medium or none to execute the control. If the safety level is set to medium, Authenticode will display the dialog box shown in Figure 2.13 when the control is downloaded.

Simply pressing OK is sufficient to execute the control. Even though the control is not signed, it does not mean it can't be. McLain provides the source package for the Exploder control so that users can download it, sign it, and place it on their own Web pages. Once it is signed, the control will download and execute like any other signed control. This is a stark reminder that the signature does not provide assurance of who wrote the code—only endorsement of the code.

McLain warns us that it is easy to write a control to erase a whole hard drive, to scan the hard drive for tax records, and mail these files and others to anyone who might be

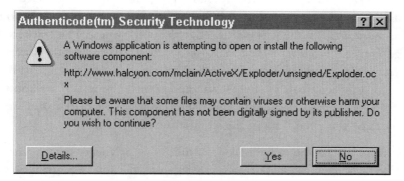

Figure 2.13   ActiveX Exploder control warning box.

interested. To provide more proof, McLain wrote the Runner control that when downloaded will run any program on a machine. The control works by starting the program COMMAND.COM. The COMMAND.COM program can be instructed to execute any program or DOS command on your system, including erasing a whole hard drive. To make the leap to the malicious realm, these types of controls can masquerade as Trojan horses such as animated graphics or games, while doing something more insidious in the background.

Consider a two-pronged attack by ActiveX controls [Garfinkel 1996]. The first attack begins when a signed control that allows the user to play a networked game such as Quake is permitted. In fact, though, the control is actually a Trojan horse. That is, while allowing the user to play Quake, it also has changed the Internet Explorer's ActiveX security level so that any unsigned ActiveX control will be executed when it is downloaded. This control has now opened the door for any malicious ActiveX control to execute on the user's desktop without knowledge or approval. For example, when the game is over, the next unsigned ActiveX control placed on a Web page will execute on the user's machine without any constraints. A malicious ActiveX control can format the hard drive, can post documents from the hard drive back to a Web site, and may allow arbitrary commands from remote users to be executed on the user's machine at someone else's behest. Game Over may in fact be the last prophetic message the user sees before the damage is done.

The Computer Chaos Club ActiveX Control

In late January of 1997, the infamous German Computer Chaos Club (CCC) demonstrated in dramatic fashion the fundamental security problems with ActiveX controls

[Brunnstein 1997]. On a German television program, three East German crackers demonstrated how electronic funds can be transferred from a user's account to an unnamed account without the user's knowledge or authorization. The crackers developed a Web page entitled *Becoming a Millionaire in 5 Minutes* to attract the interest of Web surfers. An ActiveX control was placed on this Web page so that when it was visited, the control would download to the client's disk and launch the attack surreptitiously. It is unknown from news reports whether this control was signed or not. But since anyone can sign a control, this issue is moot for all intents and purposes.

The control, which when downloaded has full access privileges of any other Windows program, initially checks to determine if a version of Quicken financial software is installed on the machine. Apparently, only the European version of the Quicken software was susceptible to this attack. Provided that Quicken is installed, the control will generate a transaction form scheduled to transfer some specified amount of funds (perhaps an initialization parameter) from the user's account to the account named by the control using the electronic cheque feature of Quicken. This transaction form is saved by Quicken in a file of pending electronic cheques without requiring the personal identification number (PIN) of the account holder [Weber-Wulff 1997]. The next time the user sends the scheduled electronic cheques, the transfer will automatically be performed without the user's knowledge. The CCC demonstration clearly shows the hazards of surfing the Web when malicious content can download and have unrestricted access to your system resources.

Java Security

Java has captured the imagination of programmers, Web surfers, and the business community. From a programmer's perspective, Java offers true object-oriented (OO) programming, rather than OO extensions to a procedural language. To the Web surfer, pages embedded with Java applets come alive when viewed. Java applets make the Web an interactive experience rather than a channel surfing pastime.

Businesses are adopting Java quickly for several reasons. First, it is a true multi-platform language. This means that Java programs written on one platform (e.g., Unix) will run on another (e.g., Windows). Second, the ability to run Java applets on client machines adds new layers of functionality to the Web. Practical business applications, such as transaction processing, can be programmed once and run on client machines anywhere, regardless of the client platform. In contrast, ActiveX controls will run on only Win32 machines. This strategy is survivable for ActiveX as long as Windows maintains a tight grip on the desktop.

Businesses and end users that run all variants of Unix and Macintosh machines will not be able to run ActiveX controls embedded on Web pages. From a business perspective, it makes more sense to develop Web applications that can run anywhere on the user's choice of the desktop machine.

Third, Java was originally designed to be a full-featured language to run in embedded systems. Unlike general-purpose PCs, embedded systems are application specific. For example, most consumer devices—including TVs, VCRs, refrigerators, microwaves, and CD players—are all embedded systems running software. Currently, most of the software is one of a kind, developed for specific processor chips in low-level languages such as assembly. This means that the code will be very difficult to reuse and maintain over successive generations of the devices. In addition, without a full-featured language, programming complex tasks in assembly language becomes an art that only a few old-time hacks have mastered. Providing the capability to run Java in embedded devices will make consumer devices even more intelligent and open the door for intelligent homes, where consumer devices are networked via wireless LANs and customized to suit each homeowner's needs. The incorporation of CardJava (a subset of the Java language) on smartcards is a major step towards integrating all the cards in your wallet into a single multiuse card. It is this kind of cross-platform portability that is making Java such an attractive development language for businesses.

The rush to develop and run Java has been jump-started by the Web. JavaSoft, the Sun Microsystems division that created and supports Java, has been quick to capitalize on the Web. Because Java programs are, according to JavaSoft, "write once, run anywhere," the Web became an ideal environment to distribute Java programs, called Java applets, and fundamentally change the nature of HTML documents. Although running full-featured programs distributed over the Web is an appealing idea, the creators of Java realized the security problems inherent in distributing mobile code.

To address these security concerns, they created a security model, sometimes called the Java sandbox, by which any untrusted Java applet must abide. The sandbox prevents untrusted Java applets from accessing sensitive system resources. Java is a full-featured language, so a distinction was made between full-featured Java programs, called Java applications, and Web-based Java programs, called Java applets. Like any other program, Java applications have unrestricted access to system resources. Java applications do not abide by the Java sandbox. As a result, Java applications can be written to perform any number of functions relegated to traditional software development. In this respect, Java applications are like C and C++ programs and even ActiveX controls. They are given full reign to perform any programmed function. Java applets, on the other hand, are embedded in HTML documents, will execute only from Web browsers, and must execute within the confines of the Java sandbox. The emergence of applet signing has changed the restrictions imposed on signed Java applets. This topic is discussed in the Signing Applets section.

The JavaSoft team did well to design a security model for Java applets, but flaws found in the security model have resulted in widely publicized security holes. Although a whole book [McGraw, Felten 1996] could be dedicated to explaining the security problems of Java, this section offers an overview of the Java Sandbox, some of the holes found in the sandbox, and the next incarnation of Java security: code signing.

The Java Sandbox

The Java sandbox is the Java security model. The term "sandbox" is used by JavaSoft to represent an area in which a Java applet can play but not escape. For example, the sandbox prevents applets from executing any file input/output functions such as reading from or writing to the file system. In addition, many network operations are prohibited, such as listening to network connections on the client machine's ports. The only network connection allowed for Java applets is the connection back to the host machine from which the applet originated. As discussed earlier in this chapter, the Java sandbox represents a technological solution to preventing malicious code behavior while Authenticode relies on human judgment.

The Java sandbox is enforced by three technologies: the bytecode verifier, the applet class loader, and the security manager [McGraw, Felten 1996]. The three technologies work in concert to prevent an applet from abusing its restricted privileges. Because each provides a different function (to be described next), a flaw in one can break the whole sandbox. For this reason, not only must their design be solid, but their implementations must not be flawed. The complexity of the functions that each technology provides makes a correct implementation a difficult goal to attain. The Java security problems found to date have been a direct result of flaws in the implementation of these functions.

The Bytecode Verifier

The bytecode verifier performs a number of *static* checks when the applets are downloaded from Web sites. The checks are called static because they can be performed without executing the applet. Static checks study the *structure* of the code rather than its *behavior*. Applets are downloaded as a series of class files in a platform-independent form called *bytecode*. Bytecode is generated for each class file by a compilation of the class file's Java source code. The bytecode that results is a binary representation of the applet's classes written in the instruction set of the virtual machine [Yellin 1997]. The Java Virtual

Machine (JVM), which is compiled for each particular platform, executes the Java byte-code, but not before the bytecode is verified. A basic but essential check is to ensure that the bytecode is of proper format. The bytecode verifier scans the downloaded code before it is executed and verifies that it conforms to the specifications of the JVM through four different passes [Yellin 1997]. For example, the first pass through the byte-code ensures that the class files have the proper class file format. These checks made during the first pass ensure that the class files:

- Begin with the right "magic number"—an attribute of all Java class files
- Are not truncated and do not have extra bytes appended to the end
- Have recognized attributes of proper length
- Do not contain any unrecognized information

If bytecode is generated from a non-Java compiler, chances are the bytecode will not make the first pass of the bytecode verifier. The three other passes at the bytecode delve increasingly deeper into the bytecode to ensure that it conforms to the JVM. A theorem prover is used to verify that the bytecodes meet a set of structural constraints before being executed by the JVM. For example, the bytecode verifier ensures that no internal registers are accessed unless they are known to hold the correct data type. All opcodes are checked to ensure that they have the correct type arguments in registers and on the stack.

Unlike other languages wherein instructions can take operands of generic types, every Java instruction will execute only on an argument of a specific type. Because Java is a type-safe language, these checks can be performed statically before the code is allowed to execute. A simpler method to enforce type checking is to perform it *dynamically*. That is, before any operation is performed, the JVM would verify that the operand to the operation is of correct type. The problem with dynamic type checking is that it is very expensive in terms of the cost on performance. Programs that are type-checked during run time run too slowly to be practical. The trade-off in going to static type check is in theoretical complexity. Using a theorem prover to statically type check Java bytecode is a clever use of Java's type-safe design. However, static type checking is difficult to implement and even more difficult to provide any guarantee of correctness. Flaws in the implementation of static type checking can be exploited for malicious gain by accessing objects that would otherwise be prohibited.

From a security point of view, a "hostile" compiler may introduce some instructions that the processor could execute but that a Java compiler could not generate. If the byte-code verifier is robust enough, it can detect any nonstandard bytecode that may result from non-Java-compliant compilers. How effective the bytecode verifier is in detecting nonstandard bytecode is still an open research question. Research conducted at the University of Washington under a project code-named Kimera discovered a bytecode verifier flaw that could potentially allow a manufactured Java class file to slip through the bytecode verifier undetected and crash the virtual machine [Sirer, McDirmid, Bershad April 23, 1997]. The Kimera project attempted to ascertain the rejection rate of millions of known bad class files through different JVMs. It found 24 potential flaws in the Sun JVM and 17 potential flaws in the Microsoft JVM. Although the potential flaws found do not pose an immediate security threat, it is possible that unless otherwise patched, the flaws may be exploited by malicious bytecodes in the future.

The Applet Class Loader

The Applet Class Loader is responsible for downloading each of the classes necessary for a Java applet to run that do not exist on the client machine already. One attack that a hostile applet may attempt is to replace one of the classes existing locally on the client machine with its own code. One of the Applet Class Loader's most important security functions is to ensure that fundamental parts of the Java environment are not replaced by any classes that the applet may reference remotely [McGraw, Felten 1996]. For example, if an applet were allowed to replace the security manager, it might be able to get away with executing dangerous methods. The JVM has a way to keep track of which classes are downloaded from the network and which are loaded from the local file system. Applets downloaded from the network are untrusted, but those loaded from the local file system are completely trusted. Each class is loaded by its own class loader. Class loaders for built-in classes are specially marked as trusted. Each class is tagged with a reference to the class loader that installed it. Whenever a class attempts to access memory or invoke a method, the JVM, and by extension, the security manager, uses the class loader tag to determine the privilege level of the class.

When an applet is downloaded, the Applet Class Loader will create its own namespace. Defining a namespace unique to each applet is important to separate untrusted classes downloaded from the network from local classes that reside on the client's machine. This separation prevents untrusted applets from replacing trusted classes that are part of the standard Java library. In addition, classes belonging to one applet are prevented from referencing classes belonging to another applet's namespace. Each applet can see only its own classes (instantiated in its own namespace) and the classes belonging to the standard Java library. When a class references another, the class loader follows a predefined search order. First, the built-in classes are searched. If the referenced class is not found among the built-in classes, the applet's own namespace is searched for the referenced class. Searching the built-in classes first prevents an applet from redefining a standard class with its own definition. This kind of an attack would be an instance of spoofing a trusted class.

The bytecode verifier and the applet class loader together provide a baseline security for each applet that is downloaded, before it is interpreted by the JVM. Once the applet executes, the security manager is consulted for possible privilege access violations.

The Security Manager

After the bytecode verifier and applet class loader have had their crack at the applet classes, the only remaining technology to prevent security violations is the security manager. The security manager provides dynamic checks while the applet is executing. It is able to enforce abstraction boundaries between classes to prevent one class from accessing private variables and methods outside its class [Wallach et al. 1997]. The security manager is consulted by code in the Java library before any potentially dangerous method is attempted. All access requests by Java classes are referred to the security manager. These requests may be made to running threads, the operating system, the network, or other classes. The security manager will permit or deny the operation based on the class requesting the method. Recall that each class is tagged with the class loader that installs it. This label tells the JVM whether the class code currently on the call stack is an untrusted class downloaded over the network or a trusted built-in class. Built-in classes are given higher privileges than classes loaded remotely. If an untrusted class attempts to perform a dangerous operation, the security manager will throw a security exception.

The security manager has the lion's share of the work in enforcing the Java security model. Fortunately or not, the security manager is completely customizable. Each different browser vendor may implement a different security policy for Java applets. JavaSoft provides a default template for the security manager. The template is a boilerplate security policy that must be customized for each Java-enabled application. Currently, the Netscape Navigator and Microsoft Internet Explorer implement the same security policy for Java applets. However, there is no reason to believe that these security policies might not diverge. Changes in the security manager will largely be responsible for new or different Java security policies. The upcoming section on Signing Applets discusses a different security model for Java applets that will provide access privilege based on trust.

The three technologies described in this section are highly interdependent and non-overlapping. It is important to remember that a flaw in any one of them may result in a security hole in your system. The next section describes well-known flaws already uncovered in the security model.

Holes in the Sandbox

Despite the best efforts of Sun—and subsequently, JavaSoft—the Java security model has been broken on more than one occasion. The holes in the sandbox have been widely reported in national newspapers such as *USA Today* and the *Wall Street Journal* and in television programming such as MSNBC. Although many of the holes found are of a serious nature, the only attack applets known to exploit them exist in laboratories—in particular, the Princeton University Safe Internet Programming team's laboratory. Of course, this is subject to change at any time. To date, the CERT Coordination Center has not reported receiving any security incidents "in the wild" related to Java security holes. However, the potential for violations in the Java security model has prompted CERT to release two advisories (CA-96.05, CA-96.07).

What is remarkable about the attention Java security has received is the disproportionate amount of press covering the risks that users assume when they surf the Web with Java enabled. Compared with other forms of active content, such as ActiveX controls, JavaScript, e-mail attachments, and plug-ins, Java applets have a sound security model to prevent malicious behavior. The key difference between the security model for Java applets, in its current form, and other forms of active content is that Java applets implement a security policy based on a technological solution—the sandbox. With all other forms of active content, the security policy is "user beware." That is, the user must trust the source of the active content and assume the risk in case the active content causes harm, whether through malicious intention or through inadvertent flaws in the code.

Table 2.1 chronologically lists well-documented holes found in the Java security model. The source for most of these holes is in the McGraw and Felten book [McGraw, Felten 1996], unless otherwise referenced. See browser vendor Web sites for the particular details and patches.

Signing Applets

The security model described for untrusted Java applets in the section The Java Sandbox very simply and strictly prevents Java applets downloaded from the network from using sensitive system services. The security policy for untrusted applets is black-and-white: if applets are downloaded across a network connection, they must abide by the strict constraints of the sandbox; if applets are loaded from the local file system, they are completely trusted and given free rein of the system, as with Java applications. The limitations on system services that networked Java applets can use also limit the applications that Java applets can be programmed to perform. For example, any application such as a word

Table 2.1 Chronology of Known Java Security Flaws

Date	Java Security Flaw	Description
February 1996	DNS flaw in JDK 1.0.1	Princeton SIP team discovered a flaw in the Java Applet Security Manager. The bug can be used to bypass the requirement that an applet only connect back to its originating Web server.
March 1996	Path name bug	David Hopwood of Oxford University discovered a flaw in JDK 1.0.1 that allows attack code to be loaded from a local disk as trusted code.
March 1996	Princeton Class Loader bug	Princeton team discovered flaws in the Byte Code Verifier and Class Loader that provides a hostile applet full system access.
May 1996	Type casting attack	Tom Cargill and the Princeton team found a flaw in the Java interpreter that allows an applet to call private methods that can leverage a full system penetration.
June 1996	Type confusion attack	David Hopwood found another error in the Java interpreter that allows colluding attack applets to cause type confusion in order to leverage full system penetration.
June 1996	Array implementation error	Princeton team found an array implementation error that allowed a type confusion attack to be leveraged into full system penetration.

Continued

Table 2.1 *Continued*

Date	Java Security Flaw	Description
July 1996	More type casting problems	Cargill and Princeton team discovered another implementation error in the Java interpreter similar to the May 1996 attack, with similar results.
August 1996	Flaw in Microsoft's Java implementation	Princeton team found a flaw in Microsoft's IE 3.0 Security Manager that allows an untrusted attack applet to be trusted as part of the Java package.
February 1997	Privacy attack applets★	Major Malfunction and Ben Laurie found two flaws enabling privacy violations through Java applets. A flaw in Netscape 3.0, 3.01, and 4.0 allows the client machine's IP address to be captured. The MS IE 3.0 and 3.01 browser is susceptible to a more serious attack that could allow a Java applet to portscan the client machine.
April 1997	Code signing flaw in JDK 1.1.1★★	The Princeton team found a flaw in the JDK 1.1.1 and HotJava 1.0 that gives an unprivileged but signed applet the ability to take on a signed privileged applet's identity and assume the impersonated applet's privileges.
April 1997	Verifier problems discovered in many JVMs★★★	The Kimera group at the University of Washington found 24 potential flaws in the Sun JVM and 17 potential flaws in the MS IE 3.0 JVM.

Table 2.1 *Continued*

Date	Java Security Flaw	Description
June 1997	Vacuum bug security flaw in JDK 1.1★★★★	The Kimera group found a flaw in JDK 1.1.2 and the HotJava browser that enables a malicious applet to read private information such as user's password, browser history, and private security keys, among other information. This information can be sent back over the network to the hostile site.
August 1997	Server redirect flaw★★★★★	Ben Mesander of Creative Concepts, Boulder, CO, found a flaw in the JVMs of the MSIE 3.x and 4.0 that allows a Java applet to open a network connection to a server other than the one it came from. A CGI script on the applet's Web server can redirect the applet to make a network connection to another server in violation of the Java security model.

★ McGraw 1997
★★ Princeton SIP April 29, 1997
★★★ Sirer, McDirmid, and Bershad April 23, 1997
★★★★ Sirer, McDirmid, and Bershad June 23, 1997
★★★★★ Lash 1997

processor that requires file I/O cannot be programmed in a Java applet. The security policy for networked applets applies equally to all applets, regardless of the source. So an applet downloaded from a corporate intranet system is given no more file access privileges than an applet downloaded from an untrusted Internet source. Although this is indeed a conservative security policy, many Java developers have become disconcerted with the inability to program applets to perform useful operations because of the binary security policy.

To provide greater flexibility to run Java applets in a trusted environment, JavaSoft has provided the ability to sign applets using the Crypto API released with the Java Developers Kit version 1.1 (JDK 1.1). The Crypto API provides classes to generate and check digital signatures, message digests, and a set of abstractions for managing people's or organization's keys and certificates. The Crypto API provides the ability to digitally sign applets with unforgeable proof of identity, much as ActiveX controls can be signed. The idea is to be able to allow applets access to system resources based on who signs them. For example, applets distributed by a corporate intranet could be signed by the corporate signature authority responsible for approving internal applet development. Browsers for the company's users would then be configured to accept, execute, and possibly provide full system resources to any applet signed by the designated signature authority. On the other hand, applets downloaded from untrusted sites may either be executed in the sandbox or not executed at all.

This method of implementing a security policy is similar to the Microsoft Authenticode security enforcement. It is a policy based on trust and human judgment. There are important differences, however, between the security policy enforcement provided by Authenticode and JavaSoft's applet signing. First, the Java security model described in the Java Sandbox section is still valid. That is, untrusted applets downloaded from the network still must abide by the constraints of the sandbox. Unlike under the ActiveX security model, untrusted applets can still execute, albeit with the limitations of the sandbox. Second, the applet signing model is expected to migrate toward a shades-of-gray security policy rather than the existing black-and-white security policy for trusted or untrusted applets.

In JDK 1.1, the security policy for executing applets, is black and white. That is, Java applets that are retrieved from the built-in classes are given free rein of the system, while untrusted Java applets downloaded over the network are kept on a tight leash within the sandbox. This black-and-white policy will change with newer versions of the JDK that support fine-grained access control. Applet signing in JDK 1.1 gives the ability to cut the leash on networked applets and let them out of the sandbox. However, this does not change the black-and-white model of security. That is, once an applet's signature is verified and trusted, the applet is given full rein of the system resources. This policy is similar to the Authenticode security policy of giving full rein to trusted controls, with one key distinction: an untrusted Java applet can still execute without breaching the sandbox. An untrusted ActiveX control, on the other hand, can execute if it is permitted to, but there is no sandbox or other mechanism to prevent the untrusted control from wreaking havoc on a machine. A nice feature of the sandbox is that you can at least preview the applet in the confines of the sandbox where it can do no harm to your machine.

Like our complex world, the black–and–white model of applet security is changing to shades of gray. Applet signing will be used to grant access to system resources in varying degrees of privilege. The idea is similar to that for multilevel secure systems often used in classified defense projects. For example, a single database may contain unclassified, secret, or top secret data. The data that is served up to a requesting client will depend on the security clearance of the client. Similarly, depending on the level of trust assigned to an applet, different levels of access to the system resources will be granted. The examples of the intranet applet and the untrusted networked applet still apply. That is, an applet downloaded from the corporate intranet may be given full privileges to perform functions on a local machine. On the other hand, an untrusted applet from an unknown source can either run within the sandbox or not be run at all.

Sound like the IE 4.0 security zones? Not quite. The IE security zones do define different zones of trust. The IE 4.0 browser divides the network into local, trusted, the Internet, and restricted sites. Controls downloaded from restricted sites (or known bad sites) are not executed, but controls downloaded from local are always executed. The other two zones provide the flexibility of running a control, depending on the level of trust the individual (or system administrator) places in particular sites within the zones. Incidentally, none of these security policies are written in stone. That is, they are completely configurable either by the user or more globally by a system administrator. Despite the cosmetic similarities, it is important to realize that the security policy of Authenticode is still black and white. Users can either execute an ActiveX control or not execute it. ActiveX controls are either given full rein of your system or not allowed to execute at all. All the security zones do is determine to what extent dialog boxes are displayed in the user interface before executing (or not executing) an ActiveX control.

Is a shades–of–gray model better than the black–and–white model? Not necessarily. One problem with the shades–of–gray model is that it loosens the reins on Java applets. Even worse, it adopts the trust-based model of security policies. It now becomes an individual decision whether to give an applet increasing levels of access to system resources based on signature endorsement rather than an attribute (such as security) of the applet. Adopting the trust-based model might be a necessary evil to develop the applications that users and developers are demanding. The other disadvantage of the shades–of–gray model is complexity. From a user interface standpoint, having to make more decisions makes life more difficult. Users would rather not have to worry about whether letting an applet have network socket access instead of file I/O access compromises the integrity of their files. From a development standpoint, the additional complexity necessary to implement the shades–of–gray policy could lead to more errors with security-critical consequences. Certainly, the code-signing flaw found by Princeton's team (in Table 2.1) is evidence of this danger.

Desktop Integration Problems

With the introduction of Internet Explorer (IE) 4.0 and the Netscape Communicator 4.0 packages, the battle for integrating the Web with the desktop has begun in earnest. The Active Desktop, a feature of IE 4.x that can be enabled when it is downloaded with shell integration, essentially integrates the Web with the desktop. The Active Desktop replaces the desktop interface with the ubiquitous Web browser interface. Users will browse through their local file systems much as they currently surf through the Internet. The Internet and the desktop will be merged in one seamless interface. The distinction between the end of the Internet and the beginning of the desktop (i.e., local files) will be blurred. Integration of the browser with the desktop means that the browser and its active content applications could have the capability to make fundamental operating system calls that can potentially compromise users' local systems. Desktop integration may open the door for active content applications and even server-side programs to manipulate files and data on client-side systems—capabilities heretofore unrealized with the isolation of Web applications from desktop resources. The forthcoming Memphis operating system from Microsoft completes the integration of the Web browser with the operating system. Does this sound like a fantasy or a nightmare? The answer may depend on your perspective. From a user standpoint, having a single, well-recognized interface from which to perform all computing functions is an appealing idea. From a security standpoint, the integration of the Internet with the user desktop can open new security holes.

In addition to bringing the Web browser closer to the operating system, desktop integration means bundling multiple desktop applications using a similar code base. For example, both Netscape and Microsoft's Web browsers are bundled with mail and news reading agents. Previously, users would have to call up separate applications, often written by separate vendors, to read mail, surf the Web, and read news. Although the integration of these applications makes running Internet applications a one-stop-shopping experience, the repercussions in the security of this integration are only now being understood. For example, if a Web site containing malicious content wanted to target specific users, rather than waiting to see if the victims will surf to the Web site, the Web site master can proactively send the Web page to the targeted user as an attachment to an e-mail message. If the victim is using the Netscape mail agent, for example, the Web page will be retrieved automatically and displayed to the victim when the victim opens the mail. Malicious content from the retrieved Web site will be executed, possibly with damaging results. Links embedded in Microsoft Mail or News can potentially compromise the security of the user's system if they are opened [Microsoft Internet Mail 1997].

Microsoft has already discovered that URL links embedded in Office 97 documents can potentially compromise the security of users' systems [Office 97 Links 1997]. Users of IE 3.0 and 3.01 were vulnerable to both of these integration problems. Both security holes have been fixed in IE 3.02 and later release versions. Although only time will tell what new security holes these software packages will introduce, we can infer from past behavior the risks of desktop integration.

In the span of one week in late February and early March of 1997, three security holes in the IE 3.0 were found in rapid succession and widely publicized in the media. One common characteristic of the holes is that all resulted from side effects of desktop integration features already present in IE 3.0. Understanding the nature of these security holes may provide some insight into the types of security holes we may see in future versions of browsers that fully integrate the Web with the desktop. Certainly, if these holes had not been discovered by these "cybersleuths," these problems could have persisted in the Active Desktop version of IE and in the forthcoming Memphis operating system [Haney and Brickman 1997]. The question that remains is, with the integration of the desktop and the Internet, what future security holes will be found with ramifications similar to those for the holes already found?

The Cybersnot Problem

Three students from Worcester Polytechnic Institute, who collectively call themselves Cybersnot Industries (www.cybersnot.com), found a bug in the Internet Explorer versions 2.x, 3.0, and 3.01 that allows Web page developers to run programs on remote users' machines. The bug allows a Web page developer to create links to programs existing on the Web surfer's desktop machine. This bug exploits a feature of IE 3.0 desktop integration in which .LNK and .URL files placed in Web pages actually link to files on the desktop (i.e., the user's hard drive). Although this feature is convenient for calling programs directly from the browser, it can prove to be quite dangerous if remote Web sites are able to arbitrarily call any programs on the user's desktop. Cybersnot Industries provides a simple demonstration of this ability from its Web page (www.cybersnot.com/iebug.html).

The first demonstration provides two links to the desktop Calculator program that most users have installed with their Windows 95 and Windows NT systems. Simply clicking either link will start the desktop Calculator. One link is a .LNK file that works on just Windows 95 systems; the other link is a .URL file that works in both Windows 95 and Windows NT. As long as the user installs Windows in the C:\Windows directory (the default installation), these demonstrations will work. And in general, as long as the Web site knows where key programs on the hard drive are located, these attacks will work. In the overwhelming majority of Wintel machines, most Windows installations occur in the standard C:\Windows directory, making this requirement a trivial precondition.

Bringing up the calculator sounds innocuous enough. However, the .LNK and .URL link files can also be made to execute shell programs, which allow system commands to be executed. On Wintel machines, the COMMAND.COM program is an example of a shell program that will execute DOS commands. For example, using the DOS command DEL, it is easy to erase files on your hard drive. Cybersnot gives an example of linking to these shell programs. The example has three links to programs on your desktop. The first links to COMMAND.COM to create a directory called C:\HAHAHA. The next link file opens the Explorer program to view the contents of this directory. Finally, the third link runs the deltree.exe program to remove the directory and its contents, if any. The link files first made calls to the program start.exe before executing the DOS commands. Running start.exe opens a DOS window on the Windows desktop and shows the user which DOS command is being executed. However, this step is not necessary. These commands could have been run surreptitiously in the background. The deltree.exe command executed also used a flag to automatically erase the directory without requiring user approval. To make matters even worse, the Web surfer does not even have to click on the link for this kind of attack to run. Simple programming techniques can make merely viewing the Web page sufficient to execute the link program. Since this bug does not involve downloading ActiveX controls, setting the safety level to high in the IE will not prevent the attack from occurring.

With some more server-side programming, the bug can be made even worse. Other active content applications such as Java, JavaScript, and VBScript can be used in collusion with the link files to download to the user's IE 3.0 browser a file that contains a series of malicious commands. The active content can use the Explorer object to download a batch file from the Web server. This file could contain a series of predefined commands designed to compromise the user's system. The Web page can cause the browser to meta refresh to execute the batch file. Cybersnot provides a demonstration that illustrates the power this attack. A BAT file is downloaded to the user's IE 3.0 cache. When executed from the cache, the .BAT file will alter the system registry to include a new key. The critical system files AUTOEXEC.BAT and CONFIG.SYS files are opened in the notepad application. Finally, the REGEDIT program is started so that the new key is displayed. Any program that modifies your system registry can be considered malicious.

As a footnote to this discussion, Microsoft released a patch in short order that fixed the problem. The hole was subsequently fixed for IE release versions 3.02 and 4.0. Now when a user attempts to execute a .LNK or .URL file, a pop-up dialog box asks the user whether the file should be downloaded. Figure 2.14 shows the dialog box that pops up when the .LNK file to the calculator is selected from the IE 3.02 browser.

Although a dialog box is not an ideal solution, it at least provides the user the chance to stop the download or inspect the file before executing it. Most users will not decompile programs and inspect program code before executing it. Therefore, the user simply must make a judgment on trusting the downloaded program. As with Authenticode, this is a human-factor solution rather than a technology-based solution that prevents malicious code from executing on a desktop machine.

The UMD Security Hole

Later in the same week that the Cybersnot security hole was found, another trio of undergraduate students, this time from the University of Maryland, discovered a different security hole in IE 3.0 with equally deadly consequences. The attack exploits a hole in the floating frame feature of the IE 3.0. A Web site developer can create an icon or graphic link to a file or program residing on end users' machines. Because the icon resides

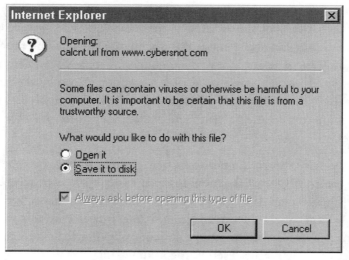

Figure 2.14 Dialog box that appears when a .LNK is selected using the IE 3.02 browser.

in a Web page—not on the Windows desktop—end users would not suspect that the icon is a link to a local file. Simply double-clicking on the link can open, execute, copy, or delete the file. If the file is a malicious program (such as a batch file loaded in the user's cache), the link could potentially cause the execution of commands that could damage Web surfers' machines. The hole was fixed in IE 3.02 and later releases.

The MIT Bug

Not to be outdone by their peers in Worcester and College Park, two students from the Massachusetts Institute of Technology (MIT) reported another security hole in the IE 3.0 during the same week of February/March 1997. The bug is believed to be a variation on the Cybersnot bug. The key distinction is the file type that can be used to link to local programs. The MIT group found that files of type *.ISP can be used to execute programs resident on Windows desktops. If an end user downloads a *.ISP file, this file can have complete access to desktop programs such as COMMAND.COM. This problem has been fixed in IE 3.02 and later release versions.

The Other Dirty Dozen

As if ActiveX controls and Java applets were not enough to worry about, there are several other kinds of active content now being distributed over the Web that can be equally, if not more, hazardous to your machine's health. The fundamental security problem with active content is that the content is actually programs that, when given the privilege to run on users' machines, can also damage the machines. Downloading programs from the Net and executing them is not a new phenomenon. People have been using BBSs for years to retrieve and install programs on their computers. So why the sudden concern about security over active content applications? The answer probably lies in the number of users now connected to the Internet and the seamless integration of active content with Web pages.

Several surveys have shown the near exponential growth in the number of users connecting to the Internet. One of the more interesting surveys was conducted by MIDS of Austin, Texas [Quarterman 1997]. The survey, which reports on data through January 1997, divides Internet users into three groups: core Internet users, consumer Internet users, and e-mail users. The three groups are concentric in that the set of e-mail users includes the set of core Internet users and consumer Internet users. Likewise, the set of consumer Internet users includes the set of core Internet users. The set of core Internet users consists of those users who can *distribute* information using any of the common

Internet services such as the Web, e-mail, telnet, and FTP. The consumer Internet users are those who can *access* information using Internet services. The e-mail users use the Internet mostly for e-mail. Figure 2.15 shows the growth rate projected for Internet usage of the three concentric groups of users over an 11-year period. Because the growth rates are exponential, a logarithmic chart would serve this data better. However, this chart illustrates the dramatic growth in projected Internet usage. The 1990 data is completely washed out by the levels of usage projected in subsequent years.

An estimated 57 million consumer Internet users surf the Web in 1997. By the year 2001, the number of users expected to be fluent in surfing the Net is expected to be 707 million. The upshot of this growth is that more people are downloading and executing active content without even knowing it, simply by surfing the Web. This point goes to the heart of the matter for why active content is so security critical. Before the emergence of the Web, people who downloaded software knew the risks and could manage them appropriately. For example, downloading software from BBSs on corporate machines is considered a taboo practice. Instead, users would go home and download the software on their own PCs.

The ubiquity of active content on the Web has changed this paradigm. Rather than going to special sites to download software, users can now find software programs seamlessly attached to Web pages on many sites. For example, it is hard to surf through Microsoft's Web pages without being barraged by ActiveX controls and VBScripts trying

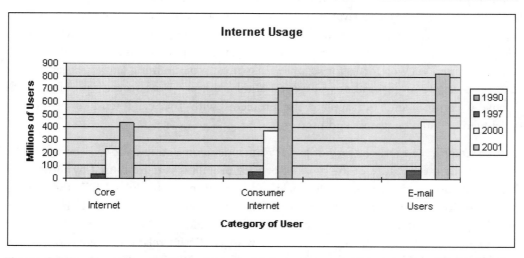

Figure 2.15 Dramatic growth in projected Internet usage. The data is available for the Internet-at-large and can be given to anyone as long as the source is cited: MIDS, Austin, Texas (www.mids.org).

to download and run in your browser. The risks of downloading software have greatly risen, not only because the number of users is growing dramatically, but also because users are downloading active content without realizing it and without realizing the dangers of executing active content. The seamless integration of active content in Web pages now makes downloading Java applets, ActiveX controls, JavaScript, and VBScripts automatic. Providing a seamless Web surfing experience is more enjoyable for end users, but end users are also assuming risks without even knowing it and without consenting to it.

This section provides a brief overview of other forms of active content that you may be downloading and executing without even knowing it. The most popular Web browsers are installed out of the box with the default configuration for executing active content enabled. This means that unless you actively reconfigure your Web browser, you will probably be executing the active content described here, possibly without realizing it. This section discusses the risks in executing JavaScript, installing plug-ins, viewing graphic files, and executing e-mail attachments, and it reveals the risks inherent in push technology and active channels.

JavaScript

JavaScript is a scripting language that can be distributed over the Web through use of the familiar client/server paradigm. Microsoft's version of JavaScript is called JScript. When a user connects to a Web page that has JavaScript embedded, the user's browser will automatically download and execute the JavaScript code, unless this browser option has been disabled by the user. Most JavaScript is used to enhance the appearance of the browser interface and Web page. For example, JavaScript tickers are popular for displaying a running electronic ticker of news or stock quotes. JavaScript is also used to check fields of data submitted via Web forms for accuracy. Like most programming languages, JavaScripts can be used for more insidious purposes. Unlike the potential security problems with ActiveX controls and Java applets, the problems with JavaScript tend to be privacy infringement attacks against end users.

JavaScript has a spotty history of privacy infringements dating back to February 1996. To understand the nature of the types of privacy problems that are caused by active content, the spotty history of JavaScript is recounted here. In July 1997, the CERT Coordination Center released CERT Advisory CA-97.20, which describes a new JavaScript vulnerability with problems familiar to people who have followed JavaScript's history. The most common problems found with JavaScript relate to usage monitoring. In 1996, John Robert LoVerso of the Open Group Research Institute (www.opengroup.org) found several bugs in JavaScript that enabled malicious Web sites to violate the privacy and potentially the security of Netscape and Internet Explorer users. (See his Web site at www.opengroup.org/~loverso/javascript/ to get the full description.) Perhaps the most serious security concern that affected Netscape 2.0 and 2.01 users was one that allows Web sites to upload files from a user's disk. The user must click a button for the file upload to occur, but the button can easily be labeled as something more innocent, such as a link to another page. Figure 2.16 shows the Web page that LoVerso put up to demonstrate this exploit.

A single push of the button could upload the system password file to a malicious site. Unfortunately, the user has no warning that a file is being uploaded before, during, or after the upload has occurred. This hole was fixed in Netscape version 2.02 and later release versions of the Netscape Navigator.

Three other privacy problems dating back to 1996 were also found by LoVerso. These have all been fixed in Netscape 3.0 and subsequent release versions. They are presented here for historical perspective on JavaScript vulnerabilities. One JavaScript LoVerso wrote allowed a Web site to obtain a directory listing of the user's disk. Not only is providing people you don't know or trust with a listing of your files an infringement of privacy, but the information could be leveraged into a security violation. Another JavaScript allowed monitoring of Web usage activities. This JavaScript essentially tracked every Web site the user visited and sent this information back to the malicious Web site. The third JavaScript vulnerability he discovered could fire off e-mail messages using the Navigator's mail agent

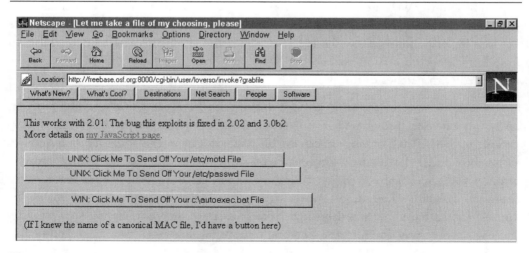

Figure 2.16 The LoVerso JavaScript Problems Web page. Reproduced with permission from John Robert LoVerso.

without the user's knowledge. This hole was closed off in Navigator version 2.02, but it reappeared in version 3.0. Navigator version 3.01 addressed this problem by offering users an option to respond to a dialog box anytime the Navigator is about to send e-mail in their name [Stein 1997].

The most recent JavaScript vulnerability affects Netscape Navigator versions 2.x, 3.x, and 4.0 and Microsoft IE versions 3.x and 4.0. The problem is one of privacy infringement. JavaScript is supposed to operate within the context of the Web page in which it was downloaded. Vinod Anupam of Bell Labs, Lucent Technologies, identified a flaw in JavaScript that allows a Web site to monitor a user's activity in the browser after downloading the JavaScript exploit. The JavaScript can potentially observe what other Web pages are visited and what data (potentially confidential) is filled into Web forms sent to other sites, as well as capture information sent in cookies such as authentication passwords. This information can be sent to a host anywhere on the Internet. The JavaScript must be able to open up a hidden window on the user's browser in order to continue to monitor the user's activities, even after the user has left the malicious Web site. As with the file upload vulnerability previously discovered by LoVerso, the final step of uploading the file must be performed by the end user, but an upload button can be easily disguised as something more innocent, such as a link.

What makes this vulnerability ever more dangerous is that users are not protected even when behind firewalls or even when initiating secure connections with other sites. This means that confidential data entered in a supposedly "secure" session can still be intercepted by another Web site without your knowledge. A different attack with similar consequences is presented in Chapter 3. The "How Confidential Data Can Leak from Secure Sessions" sidebar explains how the HTTP GET method could allow confidential data to leak from a secure session to another Web site. Both Netscape and Microsoft have responded with patches to this problem.★

The safest course of action is to disable JavaScript from executing on your browser, and both browsers provide such an option. Both browsers also enable JavaScript by default. In the IE 3.0 browser, you can disable JavaScript by unchecking the Run ActiveX scripts box under the Security Options menu shown in Figure 2.7. The IE 4.0 browser requires you to configure each zone using the expert customization feature. Rather than using the default configuration security settings for each zone, you must first enable the custom configuration settings (labeled for expert users) as shown in Figure 2.4. Then, you must work your way down to the scripting options (as shown in Figure 2.6) and disable

---

★ Microsoft's security update Web page is at www.microsoft.com/ie/security/update.htm. Netscape's security update page is at www.netscape.com/flash4/assist/security/index.html.

the ActiveX scripting option (which is enabled by default). The means to disable JavaScript in Netscape's browsers was described in Setting the Security Policy.

Interactions between different forms of active content can create security holes that would otherwise not be possible with either form. A vulnerability announced by Netscape on July 25, 1997, illustrates this case well. The Singapore Privacy Bug exploited through LiveConnect provided the same privacy violations as the most recent JavaScript bug described here [Singapore Privacy Bug 1997]. That is, a Web site exploiting this bug can observe the Web sites users visit and capture data entered in forms and sent via cookies. LiveConnect is a software package that enables JavaScript and Java applets to interoperate. As Web content technologies mature, end users will see more and more types of active content interoperating. Without a security model to rein in the activities active content can engage in, the end user assumes all the risk associated with malicious active content.

Plug-Ins and Graphic Files

Plug-ins are special software programs that are integrated with Web browsers. The main purpose of installing plug-ins is to execute data of special formats that are downloaded via the Web or even attached to e-mail. For a user to view the content embedded in certain Web pages, plug-ins for the content type must either be downloaded and installed or preinstalled with the browser. A popular plug-in is the RealAudio plug-in that allows streaming audio files to be downloaded over the Internet. This plug-in allows events to be broadcast and played in users' browsers over the Internet in real time. This impressive feature allows users to hear important talks or programs that may not be otherwise broadcast on a radio station in their vicinity.

When one is considering installing a plug-in, it is important to realize that many plug-ins are special-purpose interpreters. This means that they will execute commands embedded in the special format files that they read. This also implies that the special format files are programs unto themselves that provide both instructions and data to the plug-in. A good example is graphic file viewers. Consider ghostview, a Unix utility that displays PostScript files. Many word processing programs output their documents in a file format called PostScript. PostScript files are actually sets of instructions that instruct the PostScript interpreter (e.g., ghostview) to display the image in the format and fonts specified in the file. PostScript is a language unto itself. This means that instructions can be embedded in PostScript files that can perform system operations without your knowledge as you are viewing a file. PostScript operators include renamefile, createfile, and deletefile [McCurley 1994]. Most ghostscript users are protected from these types of operators because they are disabled by default. What is not known is to what extent other active content interpreters will not execute potentially dangerous commands.

It is possible, and has indeed been found in practice, that program instructions can be coded in a graphical file format that performs other functions in addition to rendering graphics. To the casual observer, the graphic file simply renders an image when it is executed by a plug-in or other viewer. In fact, the graphic file may contain instructions that, when executed, covertly perform other operations. The theory and practice of covertly shipping code in digital images with little or no visible change in the perceived image is called steganography [Currie and Irvine 1996]. Steganography provides a way of covertly distributing viruses, secrets, and other sensitive information. One innovative use of steganography involves embedding illegal software in a digital image, such as a JPEG graphic file. Some countries have banned the use of encryption software because individual privacy is not a high priority of the government. Hiding publicly available encryption software such as PGP in digital images sent over the Internet is one way of attempting to fool "Big Brother."

The best known example of a plug-in vulnerability is the case of the Shockwave flaw. This case study was described in Chapter 1. Shockwave is a plug-in that allows users to download and view movies played over the Internet. The flaw in the Shockwave plug-in allows a Web site to read a user's private e-mail if the user is using Netscape Navigator to view the malicious Web page and Netscape Mailer to read and send e-mail. The malicious Web site could implement this attack by putting a "movie" on its Web page that surreptitiously reads e-mail. This works because Shockwave movies are essentially programs that instruct the Shockwave interpreter to display the digital images, or in this case, to perform other activities. Other implications of this attack are covered in Chapter 1.

Attachments

Related to browser plug-ins and graphic files are e-mail attachments. Most people using the popular mailer packages from Netscape and Microsoft have received at one time or another an e-mail attachment. For people who use the good old fashioned ASCII mail readers such as Berkeley mail, these attachments can be the bane of reading e-mail. However, an e-mail attachment is an easy and cheap way to send a document, image, or presentation to anyone else on the Internet. Viewing an e-mail attachment is not without danger, however. Today's Web browsers make attaching Web pages to e-mail simple and viewing attached Web pages a seamless experience. When receiving an e-mail with a Web page attached, the Netscape Mailer will automatically load the attached Web page into the mailer. While convenient for the user, this feature also makes the mailer a Web browser. All the concerns with viewing active content from within Web browsers now apply to reading mail.

A second concern with e-mail attachments is the ability to execute them directly. Desktop integration with Web browsers and mailers has enabled users to call desktop applications directly from an e-mail attachment, simply by clicking on the attachment. This feature enables an e-mail recipient to view a Word document, for example, attached to an e-mail. It also makes it fairly simple to distribute viruses. Viruses written as Word macros are popularly distributed through exchanged Word documents. Once the infected Word document is opened, the Word macro is executed, infecting the Word application. Any Word document subsequently opened or created from the infected application will also be infected with the Word macro, thus propagating the virus. Therefore, before viewing attachments, it is best to take the protective measure of running a virus scanner on the attachment.

As mentioned, the relationship between graphic files and e-mail attachments is strong; it is simple to attach digital images to e-mail. Mail readers will automatically display such graphics when they are received. In order to display the graphics, the browser executes the graphical file interpreter. The risks of viewing graphic files in Web browsers described in the preceding section also apply to e-mail attachments. For example, consider the potential consequences of viewing PostScript files from a Web browser as described in the last section. Some anecdotal evidence exists of how PostScript files have been used to transmit viruses via e-mail. An article in the *RISKS Digest* from November 1994 describes a PostScript virus that was activated when viewed with NeXTStep's mail application, NeXTmail [Benson 1994]. The author of the referenced article describes several "prank" viruses included in PostScript files that are launched when the files are viewed with the NeXTmail. The examples given are humorous. One caused a bunch of spiders to scurry across the desktop. The user had to squash each spider with the mouse to regain control of the desktop. Another caused all open windows to fall off the edge of the desktop. The final anecdotal example given causes the desktop to shake as if an earthquake hit the user's machine. If these anecdotal examples are based in reality, they show how clever some of the early hackers were in exploiting active content for laughs.

The take-home message from this section is to be vigilant when opening e-mail attachments. As a general policy never open an e-mail attachment from someone you do not know. E-mail bombs are at least as common as real mail bombs. Would you open a package you did not ask for from someone you do not know?

Push Technology and Active Channels

The final type of active content to be considered here is known as push technology. Push technology turns the Web client/server paradigm on its head. Web surfers are used to finding a Web site and requesting information. The information is *pulled* into the user's browser. With push technology, users still have to determine which Web sites they want information from, but once selected, the Web sites take matters into their own hands and *push* information to the browser without the user's prodding. Web sites that push active content are similar to their counterparts in the TV and radio industry. Essentially, these sites broadcast their content. Users need only "tune" their browsers to their channel, hence the concept of active channels, now being pushed by Microsoft in the Internet Explorer 4.0. The idea is to get the latest updates on information without having to request it, because presumably, the user will not know when to request updated information.

The first well-known adopters of push technology came from PointCast and Marimba. PointCast Network is a program that exploits push technology to distribute news over the Internet. PointCast broadcasts news, stock updates, sports scores, weather, and other dynamic content on a seemingly continuous basis.

Users schedule the frequency of their updates in the configuration file. At the lowest resolution, users can have their PointCast client updated hourly. The power of computing is exploited in this application in ways that television and printed content have not been able to deliver. PointCast allows its clients to customize pushed information in order to filter the information they receive. A popular customization is to track all news relating to a particular company to be delivered to the user's Web browser. Similar controls can be applied to track sports teams. The immense popularity of PointCast on users' desktops has to a large extent validated the push technology.

One of the industry concerns with push technology is the amount of network bandwidth consumed by these "broadcasts" to the millions of users who subscribe to active channels. The heavy emphasis on Active Channels in Microsoft's IE 4.0 and the integration of push technology and Marimba's Castanet channels in Netscape's Communicator suite will significantly jump-start the demand for push technology. As push technology catches on more and more, the bandwidth concerns may take on some urgency, particularly within corporate environments with limited bandwidth.

The bandwidth consumed by Internet broadcasts is reason enough for business managers and system administrators to be concerned; the security issues of push technology might give these same people restless nights. Unlike the prevalent pull paradigm of the Web, push technology works on the principle of passive acceptance of data. That is, the client always accepts data pushed from the content provider, without control over what data is being sent. In the pull model, a client actively requests data from a Web site. As annoying as those dialog boxes can be, they at least provide the user a forewarning of the content being downloaded and the ability to stop the download. Push technology, on the other hand, requires this decision to be made once. That is, users subscribe to a channel (Web site) once, and from that point on, any and all content that matches the personal filter is downloaded. Using push technology, Java applets, ActiveX controls, and scripts can all be pushed to your desktop without your knowledge or approval, and without warning.

Bear in mind, the customizations are not geared around filtering out viruses. The subscribed sites therefore have a great deal of leverage to send any data of their choosing. For example, a Web site can send not only updates of news, but also active content, digital images, plug-ins, and even software patches to update the network client on the fly. Because the software client often belongs to one of the subscribers (e.g., PointCast and Microsoft), the client can be programmed to serve any number of functions. It can be an interpreter to execute commands sent from broadcasters. For the more paranoid, the network client can be used to spy on user's networked drives and send this data back over a network socket. How difficult would such an attack be? Remember the network client will have the same system privileges as any other program running on your desktop. Also remember that client approval is granted *a priori* via the subscription for downloading content over an active channel. Consider that the client (e.g., the IE 4.0) can download, install, and execute active content such as ActiveX controls at any point in the future. This means that it is possible to write an ActiveX control, or even a trusted Java applet, to download to targeted clients (subscribers) and perform nefarious functions such as spying on their hard drives or even deleting files. Is this a stretch of the imagination? Perhaps. But the mechanism will be technologically built into the desktop machine.

More realistic security concerns over push technology center on the updates of software. Network clients that support push technology can immediately update themselves with each new patch or each new release version of the software. Marimba (www.marimba.com) is exploiting push technology to automatically provide software updates to installed software on users' desktop machines. Castanet is Marimba's application that pushes software updates to users' desktops. It is intelligent enough to update only the portions of the executable that need updating, rather than the whole software executable. Currently, updating software is a time-consuming and difficult process for the average user. It involves knowing when to update software, going to the vendor's site, finding the executable, downloading it, and installing it. Furthermore, as long as the software appears to work, there is often little incentive for end users to upgrade software, even though most upgrades fix software flaws (which may, in fact, fix security holes). This technique by itself can go a long way toward making networked machines more secure.

Every time a software flaw is found in a software product, the network client (such as the Castanet client) can reach back to the vendor, download the patch, install it, and fortify itself against known attacks. One downside of the technique is that the network client is downloading executables that can alter its own functionality. How safe are these executables? Is it possible that they could be downloaded from a rogue organization posing as the vendor? The answer is *yes*.

Domain name spoofing is a well-known Internet attack. The attack works by fooling a DNS server to resolve a network address to an incorrect IP address belonging to the perpetrator. The perpetrator could then download its own version of the software modified to perform its objectives, such as spying on a user's hard drive. Can this attack be prevented? Yes. Through digital signatures, all executables can be signed to provide proof positive of the identity of the software publisher and to determine if the software has been corrupted in transit. This system is not perfect, however. The system is based on trust, so users must trust their content providers to not download any malicious content. Even with digital signatures, a "trusted" organization can still exploit the push technology for its own gain at the expense of selected targets. Because downloading of content occurs at scheduled intervals rather than at the behest of the end user, this malicious content can be downloaded and executed while the user is asleep at night or on a coffee break. As a result, the end user is unaware of what happened, and the content can erase all traces of any nefarious activity because it has been given full access to the system.

Are these reasons enough to not use push technology? Not unless you are using it on an enterprise-critical or mission-critical machine on which the compromise of your digital assets could result in severe consequences. It is important to note that at the time of this writing, no attacks through push technology are known. The most important step users can take is to educate themselves about the risks and manage them appropriately.

References

Benson, B. "Re: PostScript FAX Security Hole." *RISKS Digest*, 16:56, November 14, 1994.

Brunnstein, K. "Hostile ActiveX Control Demonstrated." *RISKS Digest*, 18:82, February 14, 1997.

Currie III, D.L. and C.E. Irvine. "Surmounting the Effects of Lossy Compression on Steganography." *Proceedings of the 19th National Information Systems Security Conference*, Baltimore, MD, October 22-26, 1996, pp. 194-201.

Garfinkel, S. "Risks of ActiveX." *RISKS Digest*, 18:62, November 20, 1996.

Haney, C. and G. Brickman. *TechWire Q&A: Browser Bug Hunters Share Their Secrets.* Online. TechWire, March 7, 1997. Available: www.techwire.com.

Internet Mail and News Links. Online. Microsoft Corporation. Available: www.microsoft.com/ie/security.

Johns, P. "Signing and Marking ActiveX Controls." Microsoft Technical Report, October 15, 1996.

Laminack, B. "ActiveX Security? TISK, TISK." *RISKS Digest*, 18:86, March 5, 1997.

Lash, A. "IE Flaw Permits Java Mischief." Online. CNET. August 8, 1997. Available: www.news.com/News/Item/0,4,13226,00.html.

Leichter, J. "Re: Comments and Corrections on Authenticode (Atkinson, *RISKS* 18:35)," *RISKS Digest*, 18:86, March 5, 1997.

McCurley, K. "Re: PostScript FAX Security Hole." *RISKS Digest*, 16:56. November 14, 1994.

McGraw, G. "Is Your Browser a Blabbermouth? Are Your Ports Being Scanned?" Online. *JavaWorld*, Volume 2, Number 3, March 1997. Available: www.javaworld.com/javaworld/jw-03-1997/jw-03-securityholes.html.

McGraw, G. and E. Felten. *Java Security: Hostile Applets, Holes, and Antidotes.* John Wiley & Sons, 1996.

Microsoft Internet Security White Paper. Online. Microsoft Corporation, April 22, 1997. Available: www.microsoft.com/security/.

Microsoft Security Management Architecture White Paper. Online. May 1997. Available: www.microsoft.com/security/.

Office 97 Links. Online. Available: www.microsoft.com/ie/security.

Princeton Secure Internet Programming Team. *Security Tradeoffs: Java vs. ActiveX.* Online. April 28, 1997. Available: www.cs.princeton.edu/sip/java-vs-activex.html.

Princeton Secure Internet Programming Team. *HotJava 1.0 Signature Bug.* Online. April 29, 1997. Available: www.cs.princeton.edu/sip/news/april29.html.

Quarterman, J. *1997 Users and Hosts of the Internet and the Matrix.* Online. Matrix Information and Directory Services, Austin, TX, February 11, 1997. Available: www.mids.org/press/pr9701.html.

The Singapore Privacy Bug. Online. July 25, 1997. Available: www.netscape.com/flash4/assist/security/index.html.

Sirer, E., S. McDirmid, and B. Bershad. *Security Flaws in Java Implementations.* Online. April 23, 1997, Available: kimera.cs.washington.edu/flaws/flaws0423.html.

Sirer, E., S. McDirmid, and B. Bershad. *Security Flaws in Java Implementations.* Online. June 23, 1997, Available: kimera.cs.washington.edu/flaws/vacuum/.

Stein, L. *The WWW Security FAQ.* Question 62. Online. Available: www-genome.wi.mit.edu/WWW/faqs/www-security-faq.html.

Wallach, D., D. Balfanz, D. Dean, and E. Felten. *Extensible Security Architectures for Java.* Technical Report 546-97, Dept. of Computer Science, Princeton University, April 1997.

Weber-Wulff, D. "Electronic Funds Transfer without Stealing PIN/TAN." *RISKS Digest*, 18:80, February 1, 1997.

Yellin, F. *Low Level Security in Java.* Online. Available: www.javasoft.com/sfaq /verifier.html.

Young, S. "Netscape Bug Uncovered." Online. CNN Financial Network, June 12, 1997. Available: cnnfn.com/digitaljam/9706/12/netscape_pkg/.

Referenced Web Sites

ActiveX Exploder Control	www.halcyon.com/ mclain/ActiveX	Fred McLain's site that demonstrates ActiveX can be dangerous.
ByteCatcher	www.save-it.com/ byteftpx.htm	Where to pick up the ByteCatcherX control.
CERT Coordination Center	www.cert.org	The original Computer Emergency Response Team that warehouses security alerts.
Cybersnot Industries	www.cybersnot.com	The site of the WPI students who demonstrate online the ability to start programs on your desktop from remote Web sites via MSIE.
Gamelan	www.gamelan.com	A repository and resource for cool Java applets.

Kimera Group	kimera.cs.washington.edu/flaws	The University of Washington group that found discrepancies between different Java Virtual Machines.
Marimba	www.marimba.com	Bringing automatic software updates to your desktop using push technology.
Matrix and Information Directory Services	www.mids.org	This site publishes Internet usage. You can use its data so long as you reference the site.
Microsoft Internet Explorer Security	www.microsoft.com/ie/security/update.htm	The site to find out the latest officially acknowledged security problem with Microsoft Internet Explorer.
Netscape Security	www.netscape.com/flash4/assist/security/index.html	The site to find out the latest officially acknowledged security problems with Netscape's products.
Open Group Institute/John LoVerso	www.opengroup.org/~loverso/javascript	John LoVerso's Web page that demonstrates privacy breaches via JavaScript.
PointCast Network	www.pointcast.com	Leading developer of push technology.
Princeton Secure Internet Programming Team	www.cs.princeton.edu/sip	The Princeton group that found many of the Java security flaws.
WWW Security FAQ	www-genome.wi.mit.edu/WWW/faqs/www-security-faq.html	The ultimate online Web security FAQ.

Chapter 3

Securing the
Data Transaction

This chapter presents the security issues associated with the most talked about component of electronic commerce—the data transaction. Although a great deal of resources have been spent on developing secure data transaction protocols, the result has been a plethora of confusing and competing mechanisms to transmit information. This chapter organizes the different protocols into meaningful categories and presents their strengths and weaknesses. To securely participate in e-commerce, it is important to realize what security attributes are and are not provided by a given protocol. For example, which protocols encrypt data, which authenticate clients as well as servers, which handle payments, and which offer nonrepudiation? How are these security attributes provided for a given protocol? What is the difference between electronic cash and electronic transfer? This chapter objectively answers the questions asked above to allow information technology professionals and consumers to intelligently choose the right protocol for their needs. Even if the decision has already been made, the security implications for using a given protocol can be understood.

There are two fundamentally different types of data transaction systems touted for e-commerce: *stored account* and *stored value*. Stored-account payment systems are modeled after existing electronic payment systems such as credit and debit card transactions in which a corresponding account of credit (or deposit) is maintained. In contrast, stored-value payment systems use bearer certificates much like hard cash. The bearer certificate resides within the personal computers or smart cards and is transferred between the parties, as when cash changes hands. Both systems offer the ability to facilitate commerce over the Internet and the ability to reduce costs over similar transactions in the traditional form. As a basis for comparison, Figure 3.1 shows the processing costs for paper-based and electronic transactions.

Stored-account payment systems designed for e-commerce simply represent new ways of accessing traditional banking services to shift funds electronically over the Internet. Transferring funds electronically is not new to the banking industry. Banks have been using the Federal Reserve's Fedwire system to transfer funds and settle payments electronically for years. Some stored-account payment systems use the existing infrastructure for credit card transactions and check clearing; others have built their own payment system based on the model for electronic fund transfers between banks. In stored-account payment, the actual monetary value of the transaction never leaves the bank vaults but is instead accounted for at some time in the future through clearing houses and settlement systems. High accountability and *traceability* are hallmarks of stored-account payment systems and also cause for concern among privacy advocates. With full traceability of commercial transactions, a history of purchases can be compiled to establish personal profiles of spending habits for anyone. These profiles, in turn, can be used for targeted advertising or perhaps for more insidious "big brother" activities. Aside from privacy concerns that already exist in credit card transactions, the primary disadvantage of stored-account transactions is that online verification is necessary. Real-time, online verification can significantly increase the cost of the transaction as well as introduce a delay in the approval of

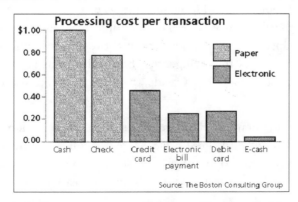

Figure 3.1 Cost of payment transactions by type. Reprinted with permission from the IEEE. M. ter Maat, "The Economics of E-cash." *IEEE Spectrum,* 34:2, February 1997, pg. 69. Copyright 1997 IEEE.

transactions. Three case studies of popular stored-account payment systems are presented later in this chapter with a discussion of both their functional and security attributes:

*   First Virtual's Internet Payment System
*   CyberCash's Secure Internet Payment System
*   Secure Electronic Transaction (SET)

Stored-value systems, in contrast, attempt to replace cash with its electronic equivalent, *e-cash*, by transferring a unit of money between two parties. The transfer of value is instantaneous because it does not require approval from a bank, and banking accounts are neither credited nor debited during the transaction. The security stakes associated with stored-value systems are much higher than with stored-account systems because of the absence of control and auditing and the possibility of undetectable counterfeiting. For example, some stored-value smart cards have secret keys embedded in them that are used to generate e-cash. If the secret key is unmasked, it may be possible to mint e-cash that is indistinguishable from genuine e-cash. In a completely anonymous stored-value system, the counterfeiting of e-cash may go undetected for long periods of time.

The security concerns of using stored-value systems constitute one reason e-cash is typically used for small-value transactions such as purchasing a soft drink from a vending machine. Another more motivating reason is the size of the currently untapped small-value transaction market. A lot of small-value transactions can add up to a whole lot of money. Some estimates place the worth of all small-value transactions each year at over $8 trillion. This is one reason the major credit card companies are attempting to roll out e-cash systems very quickly.

The lack of privacy resulting from complete control and auditing is one of the reasons stored-value systems are being considered today as alternatives to stored-account systems. Paying for goods or services in cash provides a level of anonymity desired by the public—as well as criminal elements. Even now, there are restrictions on the anonymity that occurs in cash transactions. For example, the payer and payee usually have to be within close proximity of each other in order to physically exchange the cash. Stored-value payment transactions can eliminate this problem because a purchaser can pay the recipient anonymously without ever having to meet. The parties can be next door or on different continents—with stored-value transactions, it does not matter—and they may not even know each other's physical location. Also, the value of currency that can be transported is limited by physical factors such as volume and weight. The U.S. government no longer mints bills over $100 denominations to prevent huge sums of money from being transferred in secrecy. It is estimated that the average briefcase can hold roughly $1 million [Gemmel 1997].

E-cash transfers, of course, are not limited by physical characteristics of weight and volume. Consider that the Federal Reserve's Fedwire system transfers over $1 trillion every day. Stored-value systems can transfer and count large sums of money instantaneously, whereas in hard currency systems, transferring and counting large sums of money introduce significant delays. Traceability, or the ability to determine who is exchanging how much in a given transaction, is also built into today's hard currencies. Serial numbers printed on currency can be used to trace depositors of "hot" bills into legitimate banks. Stored-value systems have the ability to bypass some of these controls. In addition to providing privacy for well-intentioned individuals, anonymity in monetary value exchanges can lend itself to untraceable criminal activities. Finally, stored-value systems can be designed so that transactions are not traceable, but in practice, stored-value systems will need to strike a balance between privacy to meet consumer demands and traceability to deter and detect illicit activities on the Net.

Several e-cash protocols are introduced in this chapter, including DigiCash, CyberCoin, Mondex, CAFE, and Visa Cash. DigiCash strikes a unique balance between privacy and traceability by employing a method called *blinding*. Blinding prevents traceability of payment transactions over the Internet, while also providing full control and audit over double spending and redemption of electronic coins. While the balance between end users' privacy and the traceability of payments might be a good idea, backing from major commercial banks is necessary to gain market share. Mondex International is supported by MasterCard; Visa International has already been rolling out Visa Cash in high-visibility field trials such as the 1996 Olympics in Atlanta. This chapter compares and contrasts these protocols and looks at the potential big winners in the small-value transactions market.

To be sure, these systems will evolve, newer systems will be introduced, and at some point in the future, standards may even be established. Even now, there are proposals and prototypes for integrating stored-value and stored-account systems onto smart cards to give consumers the ability to pay via e-cash or to pay from credit lines or accounts of deposit.

Before launching into the e-commerce payment systems, one must recognize existing protocols widely used in securing Web-based transactions. The Secure Sockets Layer (SSL) is the de facto secure protocol for e-commerce transactions today. Although SSL does not provide mechanisms for handling payment, it does offer confidentiality in Web sessions and authentication of Web servers and, optionally, of end users, too. Next, this chapter covers the SSL protocol in some depth to provide a basic understanding of what SSL secures and how it secures Web sessions. The second, less widely used comparable secure protocol introduced here is Secure HTTP (S-HTTP). S-HTTP is a connectionless protocol that wraps messages in a secure digital envelope. Although its relative obscurity may relegate it to a historical case study, the mechanisms it employs to secure Web-based transactions are worth studying for an explanation of how cryptography is used to provide confidentiality, authentication, data integrity, and nonrepudiation in transactions.

Secure Channels

The Internet is inherently an insecure channel for sending messages. When a message is sent from one Internet site to another, the message (or *packet*) is routed through a number of intermediate sites before reaching its destination. And unlike the voice circuits that carry our conversations, a fixed path is not established for all messages passed between the message originator (source) and its recipient (sink). Dynamic routing algorithms can alter the flow of the packet through the Internet depending on the traffic conditions between the many links that route the message to its destination. The intermediaries that transfer packets from link to link are generally unknown to the source and sink in a transmission (though they can be traced). Any surreptitious intermediary can intercept, read, destroy, or modify an Internet packet that is passed through its interface.

Figure 3.2 shows how a packet is routed through the Internet from Bob through an intermediary to Alice. The data contained in the packet is essentially exposed for anyone along the path who cares to read it. This is similar to sending a postcard in the U.S. mail. You may trust that anyone who handles the postcard will not care to read it, but more than likely, you would not write anything that is confidential. Internet sessions should be viewed in the same way. The Internet Protocol (IP) is inherently insecure and provides opportunity for ill-intentioned individuals to read other people's transmissions. Confidential data should not be sent in an Internet session unless a secure channel is established. As Figure 3.2 shows, several protocol layers handle the packet from the time it leaves Bob's mail client until it reaches Alice's mail client. The application layer is made up of Bob's and Alice's mailer programs. The other layers are responsible for carrying the data reliably from its source to its destination. As the figure illustrates, a spy can intercept and read packets that are routed through its Internet interface.

The Internet Protocol, which is responsible for routing a packet to its destination, does not guarantee delivery of packets, correct ordering of packets delivered, data integrity of the packets, or timeliness of delivery—let alone security, privacy, or confidentiality. The Internet Protocol was originally designed to simply interconnect as many sites as possible without imposing undue burdens on the type of hardware and software executing at different sites.

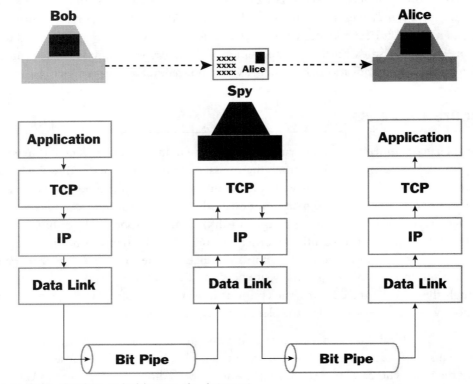

Figure 3.2   Packet switching on the Internet.

That is, the Internet was designed to accommodate *heterogeneous platforms,* so people who are using different computers and operating systems can communicate. The IP is the universal language that different platforms must be able to speak in order to communicate. For this reason, it was designed to be simple yet scalable. To address the shortcomings of the IP and provide more reliable service, protocols were designed and "stacked" on top of the IP. This means that in addition to using the IP to communicate, other protocols can be layered to provide reliability and security. For example, the Transport Control Protocol (TCP) is stacked on top of the IP to provide reliable end-to-end service. The combination is known as TCP/IP and is used by most Internet sites today to provide reliable service. TCP/IP will ensure that data packets received out of order are reordered before being sent to the recipient application. In addition, TCP/IP will request retransmissions for packets that are lost in transit or that are corrupted by noisy channels. Even so, higher-level protocols are necessary to provide secure communications.

Using SSL to Establish Secure Sessions

Netscape's Secure Sockets Layer, or SSL for short, provides a secure channel between Web clients and Web servers that choose to use the protocol for Web sessions. This is an important point because unlike the standard Internet protocols such as TCP/IP, SSL must be selectively employed by the Web client and server in order to use the protocol. Fortunately, this process is easy. Usually by simply clicking on a designated SSL Web page link (or by typing the appropriate URL prefixed with https://), a Web client will invoke the protocol to connect to an SSL–enabled server.

SSL is a layered approach to providing a secure channel. That is, SSL is simply another protocol in the network protocol stack that rides on top of the TCP/IP stack. Figure 3.3 shows the relation between SSL and other network layers used for Internet communication, including secure protocols and payment systems. Recall that the TCP protocol provides reliable, but not secure, transmission of packets. SSL provides secure communications, authentication of the server, and data integrity of the message packet. Notice from Figure 3.3 that the SSL resides underneath the application layer. Since each layer uses the services provided by the layer beneath it, applications that use SSL will have the secure connection provided by SSL, the reliable delivery of packets provided by TCP, and the routing of packets provided by IP. In reality, there are lower layers in the network protocol stack not shown in Figure 3.3 that provide access to the network and the means for sending data over a particular medium.

Because SSL resides on top of the TCP/IP layers, SSL can potentially secure the communications of any number of application-level protocols that communicate over the Net. For example, protocols used to transfer files such as FTP, protocols used to deliver news (NNTP), protocols used to initiate remote login sessions (telnet, rlogin, rsh), and other application-level protocols can, in theory, use the secure services provided by SSL. As of this writing, however, SSL secures only Web sessions. So, even if you are using SSL, do not assume that your mail and file transfer sessions are secure. This is particularly important when one is communicating with a merchant. Most browsers will inform the user when data is being submitted in a form that is being sent insecurely—that is, without encryption. The user must also realize, though, that any mail sent to the same merchant through the browser mailer will also be insecure. For this reason, sensitive information such as credit card numbers should not be sent via e-mail. In the future, SSL may support encryption of other popular network services such as mail, FTP, news, and telnet. In the meantime, buyers must beware of insecure methods of communicating sensitive data.

SSL secures the channel by providing end-to-end encryption of the data that is sent between a Web client and Web server. Refer back to Figure 3.2, which depicts data sent

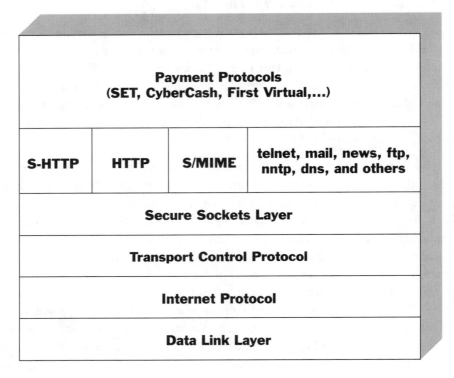

Figure 3.3   Protocol stack for Internet communications.

over the Internet. Adding SSL to the protocol stack will secure messages against prying eyes that may occur anywhere along the route from client to server. Although an intermediary may be able to see the data in transmission, the encryption will effectively scramble the data so that it cannot be intelligently interpreted. However, the technology should also not be oversold. Data that resides on the Web client's machine and on the Web server's machine, before it is encrypted and after it is decrypted, is only as secure as the host machines. For example, if a bank customer sends a request for a statement of account activity over an SSL-protected session, the request will be encrypted and the returned account activity information will be secure; however, once the balance activity is saved to a file on the customer's hard disk, it may be available to read by anyone on the customer's LAN (via shared file systems) and perhaps even the Internet. Likewise, data stored on the bank's server may be vulnerable to eavesdropping. For example, a noted Internet service provider (ISP) stored several of its customers' credit card numbers in a file on the Web server. This was a big mistake because anyone on the Internet was able

How Confidential Data Can Leak from Secure Sessions

In early March of 1997, Daniel Klein, a Pittsburgh-based consultant, reported a vulnerability in the GET method used to retrieve data from Web-based forms. The vulnerability illustrated how confidential data sent to authenticated sites in a secure session can be leaked to other sites for which the data was not intended. Because the vulnerability is made possible by the HTTP network protocol, the problem exists regardless of which Web browser is used.

The confidential data is leaked as follows. When a user engages in a secure session (e.g., SSL) with a Web site, the user may, in the course of the session, fill out a Web form that contains confidential data, such as a credit card number. Now, the credit card number and the rest of the Web session will remain encrypted and intelligible only to the Web site to which the session has been secured. The site can use HTTP's GET or POST method to retrieve the data. With the GET method, the data entered in the form is sent as part of the URL request to the site. With the POST method, the data is encapsulated in a packet that is sent along with the rest of the data in the HTTP request. Regardless of which method is used, the data is always sent encrypted in an SSL-secured session. The key difference, however, is how the transaction is logged in Web site server logs. When the GET method is used in the transaction, the data parameters in the form are logged in the Web server logs; data retrieved via the POST method is not. Since the user trusts the Web site to properly handle the confidential data in the first place, this may not be a problem.

The problem arises when the user jumps to another site (that has no business knowing the user's credit card number) after submitting the form. The next site may be keeping a record of where the user was "referred" from. That is, the server logs of the next site will record the previous site the user jumped from before arriving at its Web page. What makes this a more insidious problem than the typical privacy concern is that if the user entered confidential data in a Web form from the referring site, this confidential data will be recorded in the *next site's* referrer log if the GET method was used to retrieve the data. Obviously, this data was not intended for the next site, and worse, the user does not even know that the confidential data entered in a secure session has been leaked to another site.

The GET method vulnerability illustrates the lack of privacy in Web surfing. Not only do users leave a calling card when they hit a site, but they also let the site know where they came from and potentially any sensitive data they may have submitted to the last site. Finally, it is important to realize that even if the POST method is used and a secure protocol such as SSL is employed, the data inevitably ends up in plain text on the Web server's host machine. The privacy of that data is now only as good as the security of the Web server and the scruples of the people handling the data.

to retrieve this file through the Web! The bottom line is that SSL secures the communication channel but does not secure data that resides on client and server machines. Chapters 4 and 5 examine the server-side security issues at length and review ways of securing host machines so that the data that resides on Web client and Web server machines will remain secure.

The Role of Certification Authorities

In addition to securing the channel via encryption, Netscape's SSL provides authentication of the merchant's server. This means that if the channel has been successfully secured, the Web client is also assured that the server has been endorsed by a certification authority (CA) that the Web client also trusts. The endorsement is not similar to an endorsement from *Consumer Reports*. The CA will endorse only the identity of the Web server. This means that end users can be sure of the *identity* of the Web site that they are connecting to, but there is no assurance of the quality of the Web content. When is Web content an issue for end users? Parents may be concerned about which Web sites their children surf—particularly those that contain adult content. Some Web sites may also contain active content that may violate the security or privacy of the end user as discussed in Chapter 2. Visiting a Web site authenticated by a CA provides assurance only of the Web site's identity—not of its content.

Most Web browsers now come out of the box with built-in trust of certification authorities. The inclusion of CAs in the browser software means that users implicitly trust any of the Web sites certified by these CAs. The sites establish trust by building the public signatures of certification authorities into the browsers.

Figure 3.4 shows the trusted CAs that are built in with Netscape's Navigator 4.x. The signatures are used to verify the identity of Web sites when connections are made. In order to support secure connections and to be authenticated, a Web site must register with a certification authority that is also on the list of trusted CAs in the end user's browser. The process of registering with a CA establishes the identity of the Web site. Once the identity is confirmed, the CA signs the server certificate with its own private key. It is important that this key remain private or else the certification can be impersonated and the trust established with the CA from Web clients would be abused.

When one hits a Web site over an SSL session, the certificate of registration is downloaded to the user's Web browser. The signed certificate is compared with the public signatures of CAs stored in the browser software. If the certificate signed by one CA matches the CA's corresponding public key in the browser, the Web site will be authenticated. The details of the authentication and secure connection protocol are presented

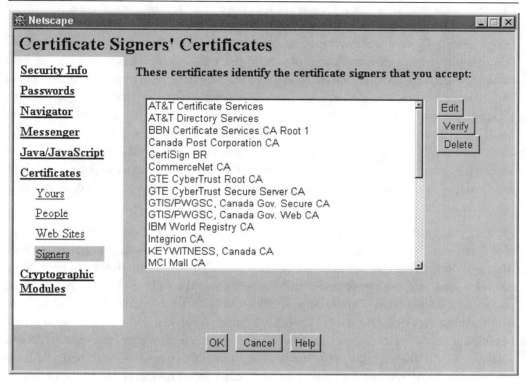

Figure 3.4 Trusted certification authorities.

later in How SSL Works. From a user's perspective, it is important to realize that trust is already established in browsers by default. This means that users implicitly trust any sites approved by these CAs—even if they are unaware that they have placed their trust in these sites. Also realize that certificates can be removed or added at the user's discretion.

Users of the Netscape Navigator 4.x know when a site has been authenticated and a secure channel has been established by the presence of a solid lock icon in the lower left corner of the browser interface. When a secure channel has not been established, the lock is open. Users of Microsoft's Internet Explorer will see an icon of a lock in the lower right corner of the browser when a secure session has been established. When the Web session has not been secured, the icon is absent. Even with the presence of the lock icon, what is not apparent is the party with whom the channel has been secured. It is entirely possible that a Web site has registered itself with a CA under one name and address while advertising itself as another in the content of its Web pages. For example, consider a Web site that registered with a trusted CA under the URL www.citibank.org. A user visiting this site and seeing a banner for Citibank might assume that the Web site was an official Citibank site—especially if a secure session was established with authentication. In fact, the site may be run by a rogue group or a competing bank. One clue that an impersonation might be at work is the suffix of .org in the URL address. Like most commercial entities, Citibank's Web address ends in .com rather than .org. Impersonations of this variety have occurred in practice, particularly among politically charged organizations. During the last presidential election, more than one political party or candidate was spoofed by Web sites established by an opposing party. The danger of this type of impersonation rises when consumers are misled into believing that they are dealing with a legitimate financial corporation. It is hoped that a CA will not allow an egregious error that makes this conjured Citibank example possible. But what assurance does the user have that one will not?

Sometimes just the appearance of a legitimate facade is enough to convince people to give away sensitive information, such as user account IDs, passwords, and personal identification numbers (PINs) for bank accounts. Scams throughout the history of commerce have demonstrated how people are easily duped given the right context. A bogus ATM placed in a Manchester, Connecticut, mall was able to steal thousands of dollars from unsuspecting shoppers [Peterson 1993]. The machine was placed by thieves who either obtained it on the black market or stole it from some other location (this also occurs in practice). While the machine dispensed money until it ran out, the real theft occurred because the ATM recorded account numbers and PINs. The thieves were sophisticated enough to roll out their own ATM cards programmed with the confidential account information. These counterfeit cards, in turn, were used to withdraw thousands of dollars from customer accounts at legitimate New York City ATMs operated by Citibank and Chemical Bank.

This example illustrates how just the context of an ATM in a familiar location is often enough to lure unsuspecting victims. How can Web users know the true identity of the site they are visiting? Unfortunately, the lock icon conveys little information—only that a secure connection has been established and that the site has been authenticated. The secure connection means that the data sent between the Web client and the Web server will be encrypted and not readable by any third party. However, what if the Web server belongs to a criminal organization that is impersonating a legitimate business? The authentication only means that the organization has been registered with a trusted certification authority.

Perhaps the best method to verify the identity of the site you are connecting to is to read the detailed information that accompanies the certification of a site. In Microsoft's Internet Explorer 4.x, you can view the security properties of the Web page by going down the File menu to Properties, then clicking on the Security tab. If the current document has been downloaded via a secure session, the various properties of the secure channel are available to be displayed.

Figure 3.5 shows the certificate properties in the Netscape Navigator 4.x browser that are downloaded after the Wall Street Journal Interactive Edition Web page is authenticated. This certificate is partitioned into two information fields: subject and issuer. Under the subject field, the name of the company that was registered (Dow Jones & Company Inc.), the name of the Web site (The Wall Street Journal Interactive Edition), and its Web address are displayed. Under the issuer, the certification authority (RSA Data Security Inc., Secure Server Certification Authority) and the properties of the secure channel are displayed, including the secure channel protocol and the level of encryption used (RC2, 40-bit international RSA encryption). In Netscape Navigator Version 4.x, you can display the document security information by clicking on the lock icon and then pressing the View Certificate button. To minimize the risk of sending sensitive information to an impostor, inspect the server certificate to confirm the identity of the Web site. The danger is that by not inspecting the certificate, a user may be lured into trusting a Web site that is actually an impostor.

Web Spoofing

Web spoofing was succinctly illustrated by an attack that was recently demonstrated by the Safe Internet Programming team at Princeton University [Felten et al. 1997]. The team's technical report demonstrates how Web users can be conned into a "shadow" world of the Web, where all Web requests and returned Web pages are routed through an attacker organization's site. The attacker organization has the ability to capture, modify, or drop Web requests at whim. Two consequences of this type of attack are that all Web requests from a user's browser may be monitored, and they may be altered. The attack is best described by illustration. Figure 3.6 shows the sequence of events for the Web spoofing attack. During the first step, the end user must be lured into hitting the attacker organization's Web page. The attack organization could place a link to the Web page from a "hot-list" of sites to surf on someone else's page or even include the Web URL and/or Web page in an e-mail message. Again, the appearance of legitimacy or sometimes simply the context in which the page is hit is usually all it takes to con a casual Web surfer. This job is made even easier on the Web, because almost anything goes in today's Web pages. For example, sending a link to a Web page to check out an interesting essay or graphic may in fact be a diversion for luring an unsuspecting surfer into the attacker's Web. Once the user is snared in the attacker's Web, every subsequent Web page access from the attacker's page will be into the shadow world forged by the attacker's server.

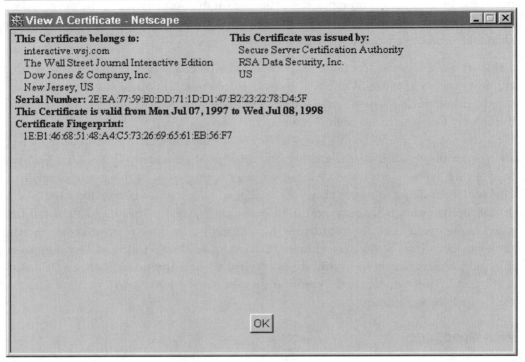

Figure 3.5 Certificate of authentication.

Suppose that the attacker's Web page contained a link to Quicken's Financial Network (www.qfn.com), which allows you to check the latest quote from a stock of your interest. When you click on this link from the attacker's Web page, the attacker's Web server will intercept your request and the subsequent response from QFN. At the minimum, the attacker's organization can log all Web hits throughout the Web session—even if you jump off links from other pages. Even worse, the attacker can rewrite the returned pages to present only the information the attacker organization wishes you to see. The quote of a stock price may be altered, for example, to cause you to buy more of a company's stock or to sell off existing shares. These steps are illustrated in Steps 2, 3, 4, and 5 in Figure 3.6. In Step 2, the requested URL is forwarded to the real Web site that was requested. The returned Web page is routed through the attacker's Web server in Step 3, at which point the attacker may choose to simply log the Web hit or alter the Web page's contents (Step 4). Finally, in Step 5, the spoofed Web page is returned to the user's client browser.

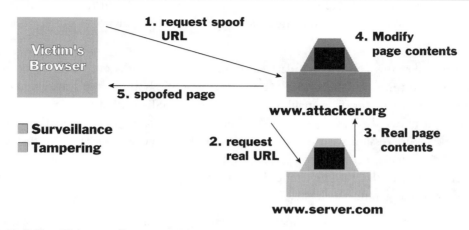

Figure 3.6 Web spoofing.

The attack is implemented fairly simply. Once the Web user is lured to the attacker's Web site, the attacker's server rewrites all URLs to include the attacker's Web address as a proxy to obtaining the requested Web page. For example, when the user attempts to access QFN via a hot link, the Web address would be rewritten as http://www.attacker .org/http://www.qfn.com. All links embedded in QFN's Web page could be rewritten similarly through a script that automates this process.

Prepending addresses with proxies is actually commonplace in many legitimate applications. For example, when users access the Web from behind a firewall, the address of the firewall Web proxy can simply be prepended to the Web site address. The firewall proxy will receive the request and forward it to the desired site. A more interesting example of URL rewriting occurs when users hit the Anonymizer Web site (www.anonymizer.com) to surf anonymously. The idea behind the Anonymizer Web page is to provide privacy in Web surfing. Realize that whenever you surf the Web, you are giving out all kinds of information about yourself, including potentially your name, e-mail address, place of employment (and its location), your machine name and IP address, the machine's operating system, and your Web browser type. If, instead, you used the Anonymizer proxy to surf Web sites, this information will not be offered up to any of the sites you surf— thereby protecting your privacy. To use the Anonymizer proxy, simply prepend any Web addresses with http://www.anonymizer.com:8080/. You can do this manually, set it up in the browser proxy options, or jump to links off the Anonymizer Web page. Of course, the

Anonymizer could be keeping track of all the sites you surf. With the attack described here, it could even alter your returned Web pages, but the Anonymizer site professes not to do this.

What makes this attack particularly insidious is that it works even if the user establishes a secure connection using SSL. Remember that SSL both encrypts the channel and authenticates the server. This attack can occur over an SSL-secured session if *the attacker organization* rather than the genuine Web site is authenticated. This authentication will provide a secure session with the attacker organization that serves as a proxy to the rest of the Web. Since a secure session is denoted by a simple icon in the browser's interface, the user will be misled into believing that a secure session has been initiated and authenticated with the genuine Web site.

Despite the potential to be duped, users can find out when a Web session has been hijacked. A simple method is to examine the URL address displayed in the browser's URL window. Certainly, if the Web address has been prepended with a proxy, this is a telltale sign of surveillance or tampering activity. Bear in mind that legitimate proxies such as the Anonymizer are sometimes used, as are firewall proxies that provide Web access from behind a firewall.

Another method to detect Web spoofing is to examine the display at the bottom of your browser when the cursor is placed over a Web link. The browser display shows the address of the Web page that will be requested when you click on the link. If this address is either prepended with a proxy or different from the Web page you think you will be visiting, then again, the Web session may be hijacked. Both methods should be practiced in casual Web surfing, but an attacker organization can overcome these inspection methods by rewriting the browser interface using JavaScript. For example, after being lured into the attacker's site, the user's browser client may execute a JavaScript program downloaded from that site that cleverly changes the appearance of the browser interface. The JavaScript program can change the display of the URL window so that it shows the URL of the expected site without the prepended attacker's proxy. It can also rewrite the display of the Web address at the bottom of the browser to display only the expected Web address. The user can prevent this attack by simply disabling JavaScript in the browser software.

Perhaps the most surefire method to detect this kind of Web spoofing attack in SSL-secured sessions is to inspect the certificate of the Web site. The certificate will reveal the identity of the Web server to which the secure connection is established. For nonsecure Web sessions, the best advice is simply to disable JavaScript and to pay attention to the URLs when connecting to Web sites.

Although most Web surfing poses risks of privacy infringement, the most disturbing aspect of the Web spoofing attack is the ability of outsiders to tamper with Web pages and subsequently alter the behavior of the parties engaged in a Web session. Consider the Citibank Web request example described earlier. Suppose that a user hit a link for www.citibank.com. Assuming that the attacker was indeed capturing all the Web requests, the attacker organization could rewrite this address to another Web page, such as a bank impostor. If the impostor's Web page presents a familiar Citibank interface to the user, the user may very well not realize that the bait-and-switch occurred; consequently, the user may unknowingly give away sensitive information such as banking account numbers and passwords—the online version of the ATM scam.

The attack can also work in the reverse direction. The attacker organization may alter a confirmation notice of purchase from a merchant, thus instigating a duplicate purchase. The attack exploits the fact that users do not necessarily inspect server certificates, the Web document source code, or even the URL to determine *who* is being authenticated. Finally, it is worth mentioning that the researchers with the Princeton Secure Internet Programming team (www.cs.princeton.edu/sip/) have implemented a demonstration version of this attack.

To summarize, it is useful to review the security features SSL does and does not provide. SSL provides a secure *channel* for communicating between Web clients and Web servers. Because it was developed as a network layer above TCP/IP, it also has the potential for securing other types of network sessions such as remote logins, network news, mail, and file transfers. Currently, SSL 2.0 and SSL 3.0 provide only secure Web sessions. The security of any data that resides on the client's host machine and the server's host machine is not protected in any fashion by SSL. This means that once you send confidential data to a Web server over SSL, you must also trust the recipient to properly handle the data. If the recipient is careless with the data, it may very well end up in the hands of people you would not have authorized. If the recipient's host system is insecure, computer criminals may bypass the security provided by SSL completely by retrieving confidential data right from the server's host through security holes. Chapter 5 addresses this last issue.

As for SSL server authentication, the most important point to remember is that it is imperative to check *which* server has been authenticated. It is entirely possible to communicate securely with an authenticated server (one that has been endorsed by a trusted certification authority) that is impersonating the site you think you are connecting to. Before sending confidential data to an authenticated site, inspect the site's server certificate to confirm the identity of the site. Finally, it is important to note that SSL 3.0 supports strong client authentication. Client authentication is the way that a server can verify the identity of clients who are connecting to their Web sites. When a Web server needs to restrict access to its Web pages, documents, and other files on its Web site, it can use client authentication to permit only authorized users to retrieve access-controlled documents. The role of client authentication in securing the Web server is discussed in detail in Chapter 4.

How SSL Works

Now that we know what SSL can and cannot do, it is useful to understand how SSL works from a bird's eye view. Recall that SSL serves two functions: authenticating the Web server and/or client and encrypting the communication channel. To accomplish these two functions, SSL uses two different encryption technologies: *public key (asymmetric) encryption* and *private key (symmetric) encryption*. Public key encryption is used to authenticate the server and/or client and to exchange a private session key between the Web server and client. It is the exchange of the private session key that makes symmetric encryption possible for secure communications. It is possible to use strictly public key encryption to conduct secure sessions, but it is inefficient, and the performance would be too slow to be practical for Web sessions. Symmetric encryption and decryption, by contrast, can be performed significantly faster than public key encryption. There is a performance penalty in using SSL and any encryption algorithm in general; however, the delay imposed by symmetric encryption is acceptable in most Internet applications.

Using symmetric encryption by itself, though, poses problems, particularly when two parties without a prior relationship are communicating. The problem is that in order to communicate securely using symmetric encryption, both parties have to agree on a shared secret in advance. If the parties do not know each other, agreeing to a secret key in advance of a message or transaction can be difficult. For example, in e-commerce applications, the consumer and the merchant in all likelihood will not know each other before engaging in a business transaction. The shared secret is used to encrypt a message as well as to decrypt it. Figure 3.7 shows how private key encryption is used to secure communications. Bob and Alice want to communicate over the Internet using a private key encryption standard such as the Data Encryption Standard (DES). Fortunately, Bob and Alice met previously and agreed to a shared secret, the secret key. Bob uses the secret key to encrypt an e-mail message. The encrypted e-mail message, now in a form called *ciphertext*, is sent over the Internet to Alice. Alice uses the same key to decrypt the message and read it. Because the same key is used to encrypt and decrypt the message, private key encryption is called symmetric encryption. Unless Bob or Alice has shared their secret with someone else, the message cannot be intelligently interpreted by anyone who may have intercepted it on its route from Bob to Alice—barring brute-force attacks against weak encryption.

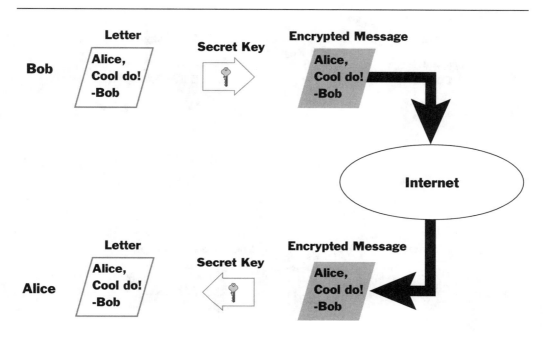

Figure 3.7 Symmetric encryption.

Another problem with symmetric encryption is that it does not scale well to a large community of people who may want communicate with each other using secure channels. The number of private keys necessary grows with the square of the size of the community [Baldwin and Chang 1997]. Clearly, this requirement becomes unmanageable for even a few people who wish to communicate with each other securely. Public key cryptography offers an elegant solution to the problems of symmetric encryption. Public key cryptography is known as asymmetric encryption because a *different* key is used decrypt a message than the one used to encrypt the message. Public key cryptography uses two keys: the public key that can be shared with anyone and a private key that is known to only one person. The two keys work together much like a mechanical lock and key. The private key unlocks the code for the message encrypted with the public key. In this respect public key cryptography can be used to form a secure channel for Bob and Alice, as illustrated in Figure 3.8.

In this example, Bob and Alice keep their private keys secret from each other. However, Bob knows Alice's public key, and Alice knows Bob's public key. In order to send a secure message to Alice, Bob encrypts the message using Alice's public key. Since

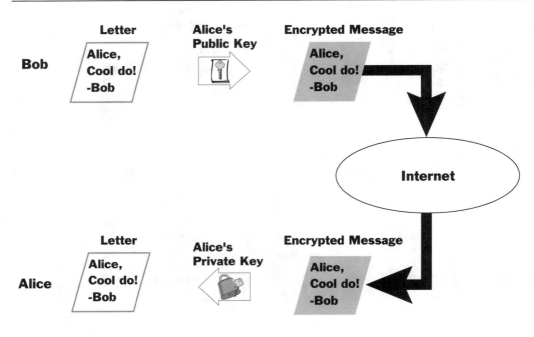

Figure 3.8   Public key encryption.

Alice's private key is the only key that can decrypt the message, only Alice can read it. Interestingly, this also means that Bob cannot decrypt the message he sent to Alice. Likewise, to send a secured message back to Bob, Alice would need to encrypt the message using Bob's public key.

The example of Figure 3.8 does not really illustrate the value of using public key encryption technology in commerce applications. Encrypting messages and communication sessions is best handled by the more efficient symmetric encryption algorithms illustrated in Figure 3.7. Public key cryptography has found its value in Internet-based sessions in authenticating the server and/or client, securely sharing a private key between strangers, and providing unforgeable digital signatures. These methods can be combined to form a secure digital envelope that will not only provide confidentiality of messages, but also authenticate the identity of a sender and provide proof that the message has not been tampered with in transit. Techniques to create secure digital envelopes are presented later in this chapter. The means by which SSL provides these secure properties are discussed next.

Consider the case of a Web shopper who wishes to purchase a book over the Internet from a bookseller. The shopper and the merchant do not know each other. The shopper wants the transaction to remain confidential so that only the merchant will know which book was purchased and what credit card number was used in the transaction. Figure 3.9 shows the steps taken to set up an SSL session. When initiating a secure connection, the shopper's browser sends a "Client Hello" to the server that consists of the suite of secure protocols that the browser supports and a random challenge string generated by the browser. The random challenge string is unique to this session and will be used at the close of the initialization to verify that a secure session has been set up. The suite of secure protocols consists of key exchange algorithms for agreeing to a private session key, private key encryption protocols for transaction confidentiality, and hashing algorithms for data integrity. Before setting up the secure connection, SSL will attempt to authenticate the server. In response to the Client Hello, the server will respond with a "Server Hello" consisting of an X.509 standard server certificate, an acknowledgment that the server can support the protocols requested by the client, and a random connection identifier. As with the random challenge string, the connection identifier will be used at the close of the protocol to determine if a secure session has been set up.

The bookseller's certificate must be endorsed by a certification authority that the client's browser trusts in order for the server to be authenticated. The client's browser will then check the digital signature on the server certificate against the public key of the CA stored in the browser's table of CAs. If the merchant server certificate is endorsed by a certification authority, it will be signed through use of the CA's private key. The endorsement of the certification authority is verified when the browser checks the signature using the public key stored in its table of CA's public keys (see Digital Signatures sidebar).

Once the merchant server has been authenticated by the browser client, the browser will generate a master secret to be shared only between the server and client. This secret serves as a seed to generate a number of keys used for both symmetric encryption and data integrity. The master secret is encrypted with the server's public key and sent to the merchant.

From this point on, public key encryption is no longer necessary for this session. Efficient private key encryption algorithms such as RC2 (40-bit encryption) and RC4 (128-bit) can be used to secure all subsequent messages during this session. From the master secret, both the server and client will generate two sets of symmetric key pairs to secure incoming and outgoing messages. Because the server and client have agreed to a common protocol and they are both using the same master secret, they will generate identical symmetric key pairs. One key pair is used to encrypt outgoing traffic from the

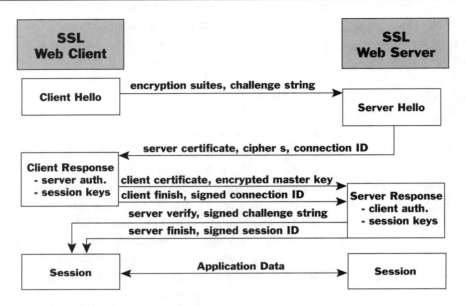

Figure 3.9 Setting up an SSL session.

client and to decrypt incoming traffic to the server. In other words, the client's outgoing write key equals the server's incoming read key. The other symmetric key pair is used to encrypt the server's outgoing messages and to decrypt the client's incoming messages. For security purposes, it is important to note that the client browser generates the master shared secret. This provides assurance from the client's perspective that the server is not reusing the same symmetric encryption key pairs for other sessions. In addition, the master secret is randomly generated for each new session. Even if this key were compromised by chance, it could not be used to decrypt other sessions with other merchants or future sessions with the same merchant.

Two final handshakes are used to verify the secure setup of the session. The "Client Finish" in Figure 3.9 encrypts the server's random connection identifier using the client-write key. If the server started with the same shared secret, the server's read key will decrypt the random connection identifier. The server will know that a secure connection has been established if the decrypted connection identifier is the same as the one the server sent during the Server Hello. The "Server Finish" completes the setup of the secure channel. The server uses the server-write key to encrypt the challenge string sent by the client during the Client Hello. The encrypted challenge key is sent back to the client. The client decrypts the challenge using the client's read key and compares it with the challenge originally sent to the server. If the comparison checks properly, the client will have assurance that a secure connection has been established. Recall that the random challenge was sent to the server during the client hello in plain text form that could possibly have been intercepted by a third party. Although this may have seemed foolish at the time, the final step of encrypting and decrypting the random challenge provides the assurance of security. Because the master secret is known only to the server and client and this secret was subsequently used as a seed in encrypting and decrypting the random challenge, the client can be assured that a secure connection has been established with the server that was challenged during the client hello. Through this series of handshakes involving public and private key cryptography, the Web shopper can be assured of a secure connection to an authenticated merchant server.

Securing Web Sessions Using S-HTTP

The Secure HyperText Transfer Protocol (S-HTTP) is a secure extension of the HTTP that serves up Web pages. S-HTTP was developed by Enterprise Integration Technologies, commercialized by Terisa Systems (www.terisa.com), and distributed to the CommerceNet consortium. By itself, the HTTP does not provide any secure properties for Web sessions. Web servers can implement some secure properties such as basic access control. Access control mechanisms can prevent unauthorized access to a server, but they do not provide confidentiality in data transactions. Without some means for protecting the data transaction, passwords used to access secure portions of a server may be captured in plain text by third parties and subsequently used to grab confidential data. The S-HTTP provides a secure means for clients to communicate with Web servers. Unlike SSL, S-HTTP runs at the application layer parallel with the HTTP and other network services. Figure 3.3 shows the relationship of S-HTTP, HTTP, other network services, SSL, and secure payment systems.

S-HTTP provides a means for communicating securely with a Web server. The protocol was designed to be general enough to provide broad support for a number of different secure technologies, including symmetric encryption for data confidentiality, public key encryption for client/server authentication, and message digests for data integrity. These technologies may be used singly or in combination during a transaction. S-HTTP was also designed to be interoperable with nonsecure HTTP services. This means that S-HTTP can be used to access Web pages that do not implement the S-HTTP protocol for nonsecure communications. The secure technologies may also be specified by one party or the other. In other words, a client may specify that the Web session require confidentiality via symmetric key encryption, while the server may require client authentication through public key cryptography.

Digital Signatures

Digital signatures can be used to endorse an electronic document in a way that can be later validated for authenticity. A valid digital signature does *not* imply that the person or organization named by the signature is also the author of the document. For example, it is a simple matter to digitally sign your co-worker's e-mail and forward it to your boss. The signature should more appropriately be construed as an endorsement of the document. Endorsing documents may be appropriate in many situations. Consider a memo drafted by administrative staff that involves a change in company-wide policy. The individual staff member charged with drafting the memo may not have the authority to implement a companywide policy change. Before sending the memo over the companywide e-mail alias, this employee can have the chief executive endorse it. When the memo is received by the company staff, the chief executive's digital signature will be checked, and if confirmed, it will serve as an executive endorsement.

Digital signatures have an important role in securing e-commerce. They are used by certification authorities to endorse a server's Web site certificate, and they can be used to endorse consumers' certificates, too. The certificate is not an approval of the content, but simply an endorsement of the identity of the Web site. The certification authority verifies the identify of the Web site for a particular Web address.

The process of digitally signing the server certificate is shown in the top half of Figure 3.10. Once the certification authority approves the Web site's server information, a message digest of the information is formed. The message digest is a method of reducing an arbitrarily long message into a fixed-length digest that is unique to that digest. The message digest is encrypted with the private key of the certification authority. The encrypted message digest is attached to the server information in a standard X.509 server certificate.

The bottom half of Figure 3.10 illustrates how the server site can be authenticated by a client browser when it is connecting to a Web site using SSL. The client browser will compute a message digest of the server information stored in the certificate. The client browser will concurrently decrypt the message digest using the public key of the CA. A simple comparison of the message digests will reveal if the server information has been tampered with. If any of the information in the server certificate is changed, when the new digest is computed, it will differ from the previously encrypted digest. If the decryption or the comparison fails, an insecure connection will be established or the connection can be canceled. Otherwise, a secure connection can be established with an authenticated server.

The secure properties for a session are negotiated between client and server during initialization of the connection. When negotiating a secure Web session, the client or server may specify that a specific secure property be Required, Optional, or Refused. If one party specifies that the property be Required, that party will accept a connection with the other party only if the secure property is enforced. For example, the server may require that the client's browser use message digests to provide data integrity of the transaction. This way, an online broker of stock trades can positively verify that the client requested 40 shares of stock rather than 400. The stock broker may also be interested in nonrepudiation as a secure property. Nonrepudiation is a property of the transaction that positively confirms that a particular client did indeed request the transaction in question without having the ability to deny making the request. In current phone-based trades, client-broker conversations are often taped (with the permission of the client) and replayed for both data integrity and nonrepudiation. In an online transaction, there may be some question as to whether the client made the request or someone else pretending to be the client made the request. Nonrepudiation can be established if the client is required to digitally sign the requested transaction using public key cryptography.

The process for signing certificates illustrated in Figure 3.10 can be applied similarly by an individual wishing to endorse an electronic document, such as a request to purchase stock. The recipient broker will be able to verify the client's private signature using the client's public key. S-HTTP provides the ability for a Web server to require client authentication; however, this option requires that the client first obtain a public/private key pair.

Unlike with SSL, the negotiation of secure properties occurs through an exchange of packet headers in S-HTTP. Whereas SSL used special handshakes to establish the parameters of the secure connection, S-HTTP defines a specific security negotiation header for packets sent during the Web session. The security negotiation headers can define the type of secure technologies to use (symmetric encryption, client/server authentication, data integrity), the specific algorithms that the party will support, the direction in which the party desires the property to be enforced (sending or receiving), and the mode in which the property is requested (required, optional, refuse). The required level was discussed in the preceding paragraph. The optional mode specifies that the negotiating party will accept a particular secure property but does not require it for a connection. The refuse mode states that the negotiating party will not or cannot enforce the specified secure property.

Once the secure properties for a session have been negotiated, S-HTTP secures the session by encapsulating the data within a secure envelope. The secure envelope supports

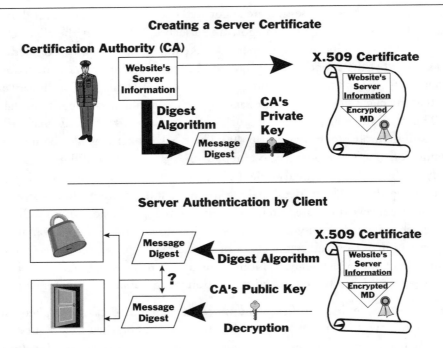

Figure 3.10   Digital signatures.

confidentiality of the Web session contents, message integrity, and authentication of clients and servers. The process of creating a secure digital envelope with these three properties is illustrated in Figure 3.11.

Consider that Alice wants to send Bob a personal letter. If Alice were to use the old-fashioned U.S. Postal Service, she would enclose the letter in an opaque envelope so that its contents could not be seen in transit to Bob. To ensure the document's confidentiality in an Internet session, Alice would generate a secret key randomly and use it to encrypt the letter via symmetric cryptography. Using symmetric cryptography is more important in Internet sessions, where a number of messages may be exchanged and the performance penalty of public key cryptography is too great. Alice will use Bob's public key to encrypt the symmetric key for the first message in the session. Since only Bob can decrypt the symmetric key, the symmetric key will remain private between Alice and Bob. Thereafter, all messages exchanged between Alice and Bob in this session can be encrypted with the symmetric key. The first process in Figure 3.11 illustrates encrypting Alice's letter using the secret key. The second process shows how the secret key is encrypted using Bob's public key.

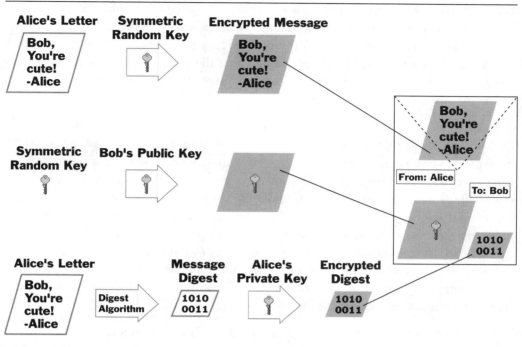

Figure 3.11 Creating a secure digital envelope.

There are two other secure properties that Alice and Bob desire in their Internet session: authentication and data integrity. Bob would like to know positively that it was Alice who sent the message. In the letter analogy, Alice would probably sign it with her signature, which Bob would recognize as uniquely hers. To ensure that the letter is not altered or tampered with during transit, Alice would seal the letter, too. She can assure these two secure properties for her electronic messages as well. A message digest of her letter, which generates a unique signature of the message, can be computed. Alice will then encrypt the message digest using her private key. The encrypted message, the encrypted symmetric key, and the encrypted message digest are all included in the secure envelope sent to Bob as shown in Figure 3.11. When Bob receives Alice's message, he will be able to verify that Alice sent the message, that the message has not been altered in transit, and that it is highly unlikely anyone could have interpreted the encrypted message's contents. Bob first decrypts the encrypted symmetric key using his own private key. He can use the symmetric key to decrypt the contents of the letter Alice sent. First, he will decrypt the message digest using Alice's public key. If Alice's public key properly decrypts the digest,

Bob will know that it was Alice's message, much as he would recognize Alice's signature on a letter. To ensure that the message has not been altered, Bob will recompute the message digest of the letter and compare it with the message digest that Alice signed. If they are identical, Bob will have positive assurance that the message integrity has been preserved. Now that they both know the secret key, they can send future messages without encrypting the secret key.

In the example, Alice would, of course, write the recipient's address on the outside of the envelope so that the courier knows where to deliver it. In similar fashion, S-HTTP uses message headers to specify the address of the recipient. Intermediate routers on the Internet can read the message header, but they will not be able to read the contents of the envelope if it has been encrypted. As mentioned previously, the message headers also identify the secure properties that have been negotiated for the Web session. The secure properties can also be renegotiated at any time during the Web session. The parties have the ability to use only some of the secure properties of a transaction. For example, if Alice did not care if anyone read her message to Bob, she could have sent it on a postcard with her signature and Bob's address. In this case, the Web client would negotiate authentication and perhaps data integrity, without symmetric encryption.

In summary, S-HTTP provides the user with the ability to communicate securely with a Web server by selecting the desired secure properties of the transaction. Both S-HTTP and SSL provide the ability to communicate securely with Web servers. Both can be used to ensure confidentiality, authentication, and data integrity. Their approaches, however, are quite different. Because SSL encrypts the entire Internet session at a lower-level protocol layer, it may ultimately be used to secure other Internet services at the application layer. S-HTTP supports a vast array of options for enforcing the secure properties. The options that are supported make S-HTTP flexible but more difficult to configure for the Web site developer. Although SSL has a number of options for enforcing the secure properties, the options are preconfigured in the browser and servers, making SSL easier to use. Finally, the prevalence of Netscape's servers and browsers in the marketplace today makes SSL the dominant technology for securing Web sessions.

Stored-Account Payment Systems

The secure protocols described in the preceding section provide a means for secure communications between Web server and client. These protocols are somewhat general in that they can be applied to any Web-based session, whether or not it involves commercial transactions. In the case of SSL, the protocol operates at a low enough layer of the network protocol stack that other Internet services may be secured as well. These protocols, however, do not provide a means for transferring payment between merchant and consumer. Payment system protocols go beyond simply securing the channel; they also specify the means by which commercial transactions will be paid. Figure 3.3 showed payment system protocols executing on top of the application layer, well above the network protocols such as TCP/IP and SSL. Recall that in a network protocol stack, higher-level protocols use the services provided by the lower-level protocols. This means that in theory, the payment protocols can use the services provided by S-HTTP or SSL, much as FTP sessions could in theory use the secure services provided by SSL. In reality, SSL currently provides its secure services to only the HTTP protocol, and the payment systems have defined their own secure technologies.

Electronic methods of payment are now commonplace and accepted forms of payment by merchants and consumers alike. As proof, in 1995 four clearing houses in the United States handled roughly 3 billion transactions valued at $13 trillion over their private networks [Sirbu 1997]. It is also noteworthy to consider that fraud exists in the current electronic payment systems. Although fraud constitutes a fraction of the total number of transactions, a small percentage of the total value of all transactions is still a very large amount of money. Banks and credit card issuers realize that fraud will always be a factor in any monetary payment system and have since developed risk management models that accept the expense due to fraud as the cost of doing business. For Internet-based commerce systems, the concern over security is not so much the nickel-and-dime type of fraud, but rather vulnerabilities in the system that may allow clever and scheming criminals to wage large-scale fraud against banks and credit card issuers.

To this end, a number of protocols for supporting credit card types of transactions have been defined and implemented for e-commerce. An overview of three protocols for payment systems that have established themselves in today's burgeoning e-commerce market are presented next. They are First Virtual, CyberCash's Secure Internet Payment System, and Secure Electronic Transaction (SET). Bear in mind that like many technologies entering this rapidly changing market, one or more of these payment systems may dominate the market or may be forced out of the market altogether. Some of the protocols will adapt to meet market demands as e-commerce usage grows. Other entries into the market will undoubtedly surface in the coming years. The success and failure of these protocols and others will be determined by traditional market forces of supply and demand. The protocols that deliver convenience with the required level of security from the perception of consumers will most likely succeed. Any system that is more difficult to use than the current credit card payment systems is unlikely to be adopted in the short term by consumers.

First Virtual

First Virtual (FV) (www.fv.com) implemented and deployed one of the first Internet commercial payment systems, First Virtual Internet Payment System, in October of 1994. Interestingly, FV does not use cryptography or a secure means of communicating. Rather, the system of payment is based on an exchange of e-mail messages and the honesty of customers. First Virtual serves as a broker to credit card transactions between consumers and merchants. A consumer must first establish an account with FV. The account is secured with a Visa or MasterCard credit card. After signing up with FV, a customer is assigned a VirtualPIN. The VirtualPIN serves as a proxy for the credit card number, which FV keeps. An annual fee of $2 is charged to the customer's credit card.

The process for buying a product over the Web using FV is straightforward. Once a consumer is interested in a product offered by a participating FV merchant, the consumer requests the product by e-mail or attempts to download it over the Web. For instance, a consumer interested in purchasing software from a participating FV merchant site can ask to download the software directly from the site via the HTTP protocol or FTP. The merchant will in turn request the consumer's VirtualPIN. If the VirtualPIN is valid, the merchant gives the consumer permission to download the product or sends the product via e-mail. Bear in mind that because no cryptographic protocols are used, it is possible that the VirtualPIN may be intercepted en route to the merchant. In addition, privacy of transactions is not assured because the contents of the Web session or e-mail may be captured and interpreted by network sniffers. The merchant sends FV the details of the transaction. Once the product is downloaded, First Virtual will contact the purchaser to confirm the purchase. The consumer has a few days to review the product before deciding whether or not to keep it. The consumer must acknowledge FV's request for confirmation in one of three ways: YES, NO, or FRAUD.

If the consumer agrees to the purchase, the consumer's credit card will be charged by FV. First Virtual will wait 90 days before paying the merchant. If dissatisfied with the product, the consumer has 90 days to report the dissatisfaction to FV. If no report is made, the payment is made by FV, and no recourse for refunds is available. First Virtual is able to earn dividends on the float during the 90 days. The consumer also has the option to decline the purchase. If the purchase is declined, FV's consumers are expected to remove the product (such as software) from their own systems. This system is based on the honesty of FV's consumers. FV has built in some controls to monitor flagrant abuses of the system, in which a consumer repeatedly downloads software while refusing to pay. In these cases, FV will suspend the VirtualPIN so that subsequent transactions will not be validated. If an FV customer receives an e-mail confirmation note for a purchase that was not requested, the customer can reply with FRAUD. Replying with the fraud warning will result in the immediate cancellation of the VirtualPIN. Although the confirmation procedure prevents most fraudulent behavior, it would not be too difficult for a determined criminal who intercepted a VirtualPIN in the first place to intercept and halt messages intended for the FV customer.

The most attractive feature of this protocol is its simplicity. No special software is required for consumers to purchase products over the Internet. Furthermore, the payment method uses the existing credit card infrastructure for payments. This means that consumers do not need to establish new accounts with new banking institutions in order to shop on the Web. In spite of the lack of secure mechanisms, First Virtual claims over 180,000 buyers, and 2650 merchants were registered to use FV as of September 30, 1996.

CyberCash

Unlike First Virtual's Internet Payment System, CyberCash's Secure Internet Payment System uses cryptography to protect the transaction data during a purchase. CyberCash (www.cybercash.com) provides a secure protocol for credit card purchases over the Internet while using the existing back-end credit card infrastructure for settling payment. Rather than protect the entire Web session, much as SSL does, CyberCash defines a protocol to facilitate and protect credit card payment transactions over the Internet. The key difference between secure Web sessions and secure payment protocols is that secure payment protocols provide a method to assure merchants payment while providing consumers assurance of credit card number confidentiality.

Secure Web protocols, on the other hand, leave the payment details up to the merchant. From a consumer standpoint, secure payment protocols have other advantages over secure Web sessions. Consider using SSL as the secure means for shopping for a product on the Web. After finding the product to purchase on a Web site, you may want to pay for the product using a credit card you use for other everyday purchases. You can send the credit card number securely using SSL to the merchant. From this point on, you have no assurance that credit card number will be safeguarded by the merchant. For instance, the merchant may store the credit card number in a file on the Web server along with every other client's credit card number. At this point, the confidentiality of your credit card number will be only as good as the security of the merchant's computer systems. History has shown how tenuous this confidentiality can be. A well-known Internet service provider in the mid-Atlantic United States did store the credit card numbers of its Internet clients on its Web server. The file was subsequently accessible through the Web to anyone on the Internet, meaning that anyone could have accessed a large cache of credit card numbers and illegally used them.

In CyberCash's system, the payment details of a credit card transaction are specified and implemented in the protocol. From the merchant's perspective, the benefit is that a separate back-office system for batch processing Internet credit card transactions need not be created. Even better, payment is assured for each transaction before the product is sold, much as in point-of-sale (POS) credit card transactions that now occur in (physical) stores. From the consumer's perspective, the important distinguishing feature of CyberCash's protocol is that the credit card number is protected—even from the merchant's eyes. The problem of trusting the merchant with the credit card number is resolved when the number is encrypted with CyberCash's public key so that only CyberCash can read it. In every transaction, only the consumer, CyberCash, and the participating banks are privy to the credit card number. The protocol makes it possible for the payment to be authorized even without the merchant's ever seeing the consumer's credit card number.

The protocol for authorizing and paying for a transaction is not unlike the protocol now followed in standard point-of-sale credit card transactions. As in POS transactions, the details are transparent to the consumer, but they are presented here to illustrate the process by which credit card transactions can be secured on the Internet. In any credit card transaction, several parties are involved: the consumer, the merchant, the merchant's bank, and the credit card issuer. CyberCash has inserted itself as a broker for the transaction (and the technology) between the parties. For its role, CyberCash collects pennies on each dollar of the transaction. Figure 3.12 shows how a transaction is processed and secured over the Internet using CyberCash's Secure Internet Payment system.

As in other Web-based shopping, the consumer surfs the Web until an appealing product, such as a book, is found. After the consumer selects the book, an invoice detailing the purchase price is sent from the merchant to the consumer (Step 1). The consumer approves the purchase by selecting the CyberCash Pay button in the consumer's browser, launching an "electronic wallet" from which the consumer selects one of the credit cards that is registered with CyberCash. The browser sends the payment information encrypted with CyberCash's public key (Step 2). Furthermore, the contents of the transaction are digitally hashed and signed for authentication and integrity.

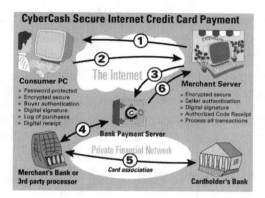

Figure 3.12 CyberCash Secure Internet Payment System. Reprinted with permission from CyberCash Inc. (1997). http://www.cybercash.com/cybercash/shoppers /shopsteps.html.

The merchant strips off the order form and signs and forwards the encrypted payment information and order request to CyberCash (Step 3). Upon receiving the transaction request, CyberCash decrypts the payment information using its own private key. The credit card number will be decrypted and available only to CyberCash. CyberCash verifies the integrity of the order forwarded by the merchant. Recall that the consumer digitally signed the order, which means that a message digest of the order was created and signed using the consumer's private key. CyberCash will verify the digital signature using the consumer's public key and regenerate the message digest of the order. If the message digest computed from the merchant's request checks against the consumer's signed message digest, CyberCash will know that the order's integrity has been preserved. Because the merchant also signed the forwarded request, CyberCash can authenticate the identities of both parties to the transaction. In this respect, CyberCash handles all the authentication requirements rather than leaving it up to the consumer and the merchant to verify each other's identity.

In Steps 4 and 5, CyberCash can broker the transaction for the merchant, the merchant's bank, and the consumer's credit card issuer. The transaction amount is forwarded to the merchant's bank (Step 4), which then seeks authorization from the credit card issuer for payment (Step 5). The request for authorization usually is made through the credit card's association; sometimes it is made directly to the card issuer. The credit card issuer either approves or denies the transaction based on the purchase amount, the available credit line, and any other information, such as whether or not the card has been reported stolen. The approval or denial is sent back to CyberCash, which then sends this information back to the merchant (Step 6). If the purchase request is approved, the merchant's bank is paid by the credit card issuer (generally a bank, too); the merchant also has the chance to refuse the transaction request. Performing this request online in real time (typically 15 to 20 seconds from Step 1 through Step 6, according to CyberCash) allows a merchant to determine the ability of the consumer to pay. It also saves transaction costs that would otherwise be charged to the merchant if the request were to be later denied in a batch processing example.

It is important to note that in Steps 4 and 5, the transaction requests are made over dedicated private networks rather than the Internet. This does not mean that the information is necessarily secure—only that it is not vulnerable to attacks made from the Internet. Traditional POS transactions are routed over private networks, too, which means that the same level of trust placed in traditional credit card transactions can be placed in the requests made in Steps 4 and 5. Additionally, once CyberCash unwraps and decrypts the data of the transaction request, the data may exist in plain text behind CyberCash's firewall. This data will then be only as secure as CyberCash's computer security. So, in truth, the problem of credit card numbers being stored in plain text on servers has not really been solved; it has only moved to CyberCash. Still, having your credit card number stored on a single server (CyberCash's) is more attractive then having it stored on many servers distributed over the Internet.

In order for this payment system to work, a lot of software must be distributed among the involved parties. Consumers must sign up for CyberCash software. The software can be integrated in participating vendors' browser clients or downloaded from CyberCash. CyberCash's consumers must also generate a public/private pair based on RSA's encryption technology that is used to authenticate order information. The merchants must also install CyberCash software called the CyberCash Library on their merchant servers. To stimulate the growth of this business, CyberCash makes this software available free of charge to its participating consumers and merchants. Some analysts believe that requiring special client and server software makes this system less apt to be adopted universally on a large scale. However, with strategic agreements with browser vendors, CyberCash can have its electronic wallet distributed with the browsers to overcome the disadvantage of requiring people to download software.

The credit card authorization to the participating banks is made over traditional processing channels. Although this method may seem slightly outdated, it could, in fact, be a wise strategy for bringing banks into the fold. By using the existing credit card processing infrastructure, CyberCash is able to provide e-commerce business to banks and credit card issuers without requiring high capital expenditures that may otherwise be necessary to enter this market.

In summary, CyberCash's Secure Internet Payment System provides a method for securely handling the payment for goods purchased through e-commerce transactions. This protocol goes beyond securing the Web session; rather, the protocol also provides assurance to merchants and consumers that the payment is authorized by a credit card issuer, that the merchant's bank will be paid, that the order was correctly received by the merchant and the broker, and that the parties to the transaction are authenticated by CyberCash.

CyberCash also supports micropayments for low-valued merchandise such as images and text articles using a stored-value system. CyberCoin, CyberCash's solution for developing a secure payment system and fee structure for small-value items, is introduced later in the discussion on e-cash protocols.

Secure Electronic Transaction

The Secure Electronic Transaction (SET) is an emerging *standard* for secure credit card payments over the Internet. The open standard specifies the mechanisms for securely processing Internet-based credit card orders but does not specify the implementation. SET can be applied in a real-time environment such as a Web session or in a store-and-forward manner such as electronic mail. This flexibility accommodates merchants that prefer either the online POS transactions that are performed in real time and those that prefer a batch method of processing many transactions periodically. The significance of the standard lies more in its origin than in its current implementations. SET is an industry-backed standard that was created by the two most significant credit card associations: MasterCard and Visa. SET was also developed in cooperation with GTE, IBM, Microsoft, Netscape, SAIC, Terisa Systems, and Verisign. The fact that the standard is backed by these highly recognized names bodes well for the future of credit card transactions on the Internet. Consumers tend to place more faith in name brands they have trusted for years than in the obscure cryptographic techniques that underlie the payment protocols. Unfortunately, as for many standards, the specification for SET is too unwieldy in length to prove useful to digest in whole. This section simply summarizes the features that SET provides to securing e-commerce transactions and then describes a typical SET transaction.

SET does *not* specify the shopping or ordering process for Internet goods, the payment method selection, and the platform or security procedures necessary for securing SET client and host machines. This means that a SET transaction can be conducted through the Web or through e-mail. It also means that the process of selecting or negotiating a product between merchant and buyer is not restricted to Web-based access. SET *does* specify that the following security assurances be provided:

Confidentiality. SET does not attempt to secure the order information in a credit card transaction. Rather, SET is concerned only with securing the *payment information*—specifically the credit card number that is subject to fraud. A majority of credit card fraud is a result of merchants mishandling the credit card numbers either by carelessness or by intention. Keeping this information from merchants is one way to reduce credit card fraud. SET specifies RSA Data Security's public key cryptography algorithms to encrypt the credit card number so that only the credit card transaction processing center can interpret it. In some instances, it may be desirable to have the contents of a purchase order remain confidential between the consumer and merchant. Because SET executes at a high layer of the network protocol stack, in theory SET can use the services of a lower-level secure layer such as SSL to encrypt the entire Web session. Current implementations of SET do not support this feature, however.

Data integrity. A risk of any electronic communication is that the data sent from one party to another may be corrupted in transit. In electronic commerce applications, a corruption in information can have unintended financial consequences. Mathematical algorithms that employ message digests and digital signatures can be used to ensure the integrity of data in transit against random corruption and malicious tampering.

Client authentication. As in any credit card transaction, the merchant must be able to confirm that the client is a legitimate cardholder for the specific credit card presented. Digital certificates can be used to verify that a consumer is authorized to use the offered credit card in an Internet-based transaction. A consumer obtains a digital certificate from the financial institution that issues the credit card. The digital certificate contains the identity of the consumer and the consumer's public key. The certificate is digitally signed by the financial institution as an endorsement that the consumer is authorized to make a purchase backed by the credit of the financial institution. The digital certificate is offered by the consumer to the merchant for purposes of identity verification. If the signature on the digital certificate is matched by the public key of the financial institution (or its proxy), the merchant will have assurance that the card holder is legitimate.

Another technology specified by SET is the use of signed digital envelopes for sending orders. Signing a digital envelope combines confidentiality with other secure assurances such as data integrity and nonrepudiation (see Figure 3.11). Consumers sign a digital envelope with their own secret key. The consumer's private key signature is verified by the merchant who compares the signature with the consumer's public key (that is stored in the digital certificate). Once it is signed, the consumer cannot deny having placed the purchase order, unless the consumer was careless with the privacy of the secret key.

Merchant authentication. Consumers, too, require assurance that the merchant is a legitimate participating merchant in the credit card's association and that the merchant's identity is known unequivocally to the consumer. The use of digital certificates as described in Figure 3.10 can be used to verify the identity of the merchant, to authenticate the merchant as a legitimate participant in the credit card transactions, and to initiate secure communications with a merchant.

A typical SET transaction is illustrated in Figure 3.13. SET transactions are performed by a sequence of message exchanges among the consumer, the merchant, and the merchant's bank.

The following are the steps in a typical SET transaction:

Consumer sends request for transaction to merchant. Recall that SET does not specify the method for selecting or negotiating the product or purchase price.

Merchant acknowledges the request. The consumer and merchant exchange their digital certificates in the first two steps of the protocol, if they have not done so previously.

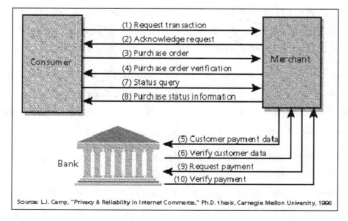

Figure 3.13 Secure electronic transaction. Reprinted with the permission of the IEEE (Copyright 1997). Source: M.A. Sirbu. "Credits and Debits on the Internet." *IEEE Spectrum*, Vol. 34, No. 2, February 1997, pg. 26.

Consumer digitally signs a message digest of the order and encrypts credit card number. The digital signature can be verified by the merchant to provide both authentication and nonrepudiation. The merchant also computes a message digest of the order and compares it with the received message digest to assure data integrity. The consumer's credit card number is encrypted with the public key of the merchant's acquiring bank. The card number is encrypted with the bank's public key in the hope is that credit card fraud will be significantly reduced because the card number will not be intelligible to merchants. In reality, it remains to be seen whether the merchant's bank will share the credit card number with its merchants. If the merchant chooses to process the transaction in real time, the merchant will proceed with Steps 4 and 5 immediately to seek verification that the consumer's bank will pay. The merchant may also decide to process credit card transactions in batch cycles, in which case, the merchant may skip to Step 6 and later perform Steps 4 and 5.

The merchant sends the purchase amount to be approved and the credit card number to the merchant's bank. The merchant's bank uses the traditional back-end settlement system infrastructure to determine if the consumer's line of credit will cover the purchase.

The approval or denial is sent back to the merchant. The approval or denial sent back from the credit card association is propagated back to the merchant via the merchant's bank.

The merchant confirms the purchase with the consumer. The merchant sends the consumer confirmation that the purchase has been approved or denied. At this point, the consumer has the ability to query the merchant as to the status of the product delivery (Steps 7 and 8), and the merchant has the right to ask the bank for payment into the merchant's account (Steps 9 and 10).

The consumer sends a status inquiry to the merchant. This feature allows the consumer to ask about the status of the purchase order. For example, if the consumer has authorized payment for a good, the consumer will want delivery as soon as possible.

The merchant responds to the purchase status inquiry. The flip side of the consumer's request is the merchant's response. The merchant does not want to release the good before payment has been received (Step 10). If the merchant is processing transactions in batch cycles or if the delay for real-time processing is too great, it may not be practical to hold up delivery of the good until payment is received. Some protocols now being implemented allow for the immediate delivery of the good before payment is even approved, with the caveat being that the good is encrypted with a private key known only to the merchant. Once the payment is approved, the private key is sent (perhaps in a secure envelope) to the consumer to decrypt the product.

The merchant requests payment to the bank. This payment can be made immediately as in a typical POS purchase, or it may be made periodically in batch requests.

The bank sends confirmation of payment. The merchant's acquiring bank will obtain funds from the consumer's credit card issuer through the back-end settlement infrastructure that currently exists. When payment has been deposited in the merchant's bank account, a notice of deposit is sent to the merchant.

SET currently supports only *credit card* transactions online. Not supported are debit card payments that are directly subtracted from a consumer's bank account and added to the merchant's bank account. SET also does not address stored-value payment systems, which are addressed in the next section. As consumers demand different types of financial payments such as debit cards and stored-value cards, standards will likely emerge in these areas, similar to the way SET has standardized secure payments using credit cards.

Several implementations of SET are now becoming available. CyberCash supports the SET standard for credit card payments. RSA Data Security has also rolled out its own SET-compliant credit card payment software called S/PAY. In the future, many more implementations that are SET compliant are likely to enter the market because the standard is open for all to implement. What makes this point particularly relevant is that the competitive advantage that companies such as CyberCash have in the way of secure protocols will be diminished because other companies will be able to develop SET-compliant secure payment systems. The most significant development in the release of the SET standard was not the protocol itself or the secure technology, but rather the backing of the two largest credit card associations. This kind of large industry backing makes secure credit card payments a viable option now for many consumers to join the Internet commerce market.

Stored-Value Payment Systems

Electronic cash (e-cash) represents one of the most exciting, innovative, and risky forms of accepting payment. It replaces currency with its digital equivalent, and in stored-account payment systems, the money always resides in a bank account. Transactions simply credit or debit the value of the bank accounts for the parties to a transaction.

Stored-value payment systems, on the other hand, place the value directly on hardware tokens, such as personal computers or smart cards. The goal of stored-value payment systems is to have the advantages of hard-currency systems over an electronic medium. This method frees the customer from seeking approval from a financial institution prior to engaging in a transaction. It could also provide privacy in transactions.

Pros and Cons

Stored-value systems have the potential for preserving the privacy of traditional cash-based transactions while exploiting the advantages of electronic transactions. One limitation of hard-currency systems is that the buyer and seller usually exchange the value face to face, or at least in close proximity. They may want to remain anonymous in some transactions. Even though cash is generally thought of as anonymous, it is possible for authorities in cooperation with banks to trace the flow of hard currency by using the serial numbers recorded on bills. Table 3.1 shows some of the other advantages and disadvantages of traditional hard-currency systems. Stored-value systems would like to exploit the advantages of hard-currency systems while overcoming their disadvantages by using an electronic medium for payment.

Several reasons exist for using stored-value payment systems over both traditional cash-based and stored-account payment systems. First, credit and debit cards require approval of a banking system—which introduces delay, removes anonymity, and is more expensive. In a stored-value system, payments can be instantaneous and potentially anonymous, and the cost per transaction is smaller (see Figure 3.1). Stored-account payments are inherently traceable because banks are required to approve all transactions. Traceability means a loss of privacy for consumers and their spending habits. Stored-value

Table 3.1 Attributes of Traditional Hard Currencies

Advantages	Disadvantages
Not easily traceable	Costly to transport and protect large amounts
Instantaneous payment between parties	Easily lost or stolen
Can be passed from person to person without interference from banks	Can be forged by color copiers
	Requires parties be in close proximity for exchange

systems support low-value transactions unlike most credit card and debit card transactions for which the expense of the transaction cannot be justified for low-value transactions. The proximity of payer and payee is not an issue for electronic payments. Parties can be next door or across the world. Stored-value systems can provide anonymous payments but a traceable receipt of payment. This method provides privacy of purchases while discouraging illicit sales of merchandise or services.

Likewise, there are several high-security risks for going to a stored-value payment system. First, obtaining a secret key from one device may have potential for allowing its use as a master key for many devices. Extracting the secret key also makes counterfeit money indistinguishable from e-cash minted by an authorized issuing bank. In off-line stored-value payment systems, traceability of transactions may be lowered, resulting in a higher potential for undetected fraud. Although anonymous payment systems are important for maintaining individual privacy, they are also the preferred method of payment by criminals for bribery, blackmail, money laundering, and general purchasing. Therefore, stored-value systems must reach a balance between upholding individual privacy and discouraging illicit activities.

How E-Cash Works

Electronic cash (e-cash) is typically stored in an electronic device, called a hardware token, that has a secure processor and nonvolatile memory—meaning that the memory will not be erased if the system is powered off. To load the token with money, consumers connect to a participating bank terminal and execute a withdrawal from their own account, similar to taking cash out of an ATM. In this case, the cash is represented digitally and is loaded into the memory of the token. The consumer's bank account is debited the amount of money that is withdrawn, while the token's value counter is incremented the corresponding value. Alternatively, the value may be loaded into the token's memory as discrete values each of some denomination. The former representation is called register-based cash; the latter representation is called electronic coins.

To make payment using e-cash, either the purchaser can deal directly with a seller's hardware token device in an off-line transaction or the payment can be made directly with the seller's bank account in an online payment. Off-line accounts provide less traceability and therefore more privacy of the transaction. With an online transaction, the bank must be an intermediary, providing the potential for traceability. The only requirement is that the seller accepts the buyer's e-cash and the two devices agree to the same protocol for the payment transactions. Different banks may issue nonstandard forms of e-cash (similar to different forms of international currency) in which case, exchanging the value may be difficult. As the payment protocols become standardized for stored-value payments (similar to SET for stored-account payments), issues of compatibility will fall by the wayside.

In an off-line transaction, the buyer's hardware token interfaces with the seller's device via infrared communications (in close proximity transactions), dial-up modem connections, or the Internet. The two devices then execute a payment protocol for the value that is to be transferred. The seller's device increases its value by the amount of the transaction, while the buyer's device decreases its own value by the equivalent amount. Because these two devices will have the capability to add and subtract value from their counters or electronic purses, safeguards must be instituted that prevent the counters from being incremented arbitrarily or from duplicating electronic coins in the purse. In an online payment, the buyer's device connects to the seller's bank account, and the value in the hardware device and the seller's bank account are adjusted according to the value of the transaction.

Unlike traditional forms of cash, the electronic cash must ultimately be sold back to the issuing bank (or a participating bank that settles with the issuing bank) because in most e-cash payment protocols, the e-cash exchanged in one transaction cannot be reused in another. This practice reduces the potential for fraud through perfect replication of value. To redeem e-cash, the consumer's token device is interfaced with the issuing bank's terminal, and a deposit protocol is executed. The deposit protocol deposits the electronic cash into the consumer's account while deducting the value from the token device.

Securing E-Cash

The security concerns for stored-value e-cash systems are much greater than for stored-account systems. The main reason is that the lack of traceability can mean that fraud can continue for longer periods of time before being detected. The secondary reasons involve the method used for securing transactions.

The main security concern in a stored-value system is the potential to illegally add value to the hardware token that stores the value. The types of attack that must be protected against are physical tampering of the device to add value and a protocol-based attack that mimics a paying device. A physical attack against a device may attempt to alter the nonvolatile memory to increase the stored value or attempt to capture a secret cryptographic key. The device can be physically shielded so that it is tamper resistant. Alternatively, it may be sufficient to make the device merely tamper evident. That is, the device can be constructed so that any attempt to physically manipulate it in a possibly insecure fashion is self-revealing. Therefore, when the value is to be redeemed at the issuing bank, the tampering will be evident, and the appropriate warning flags should go off before any money is deposited in an account. This method assumes, of course, that some bank personnel will be responsible for inspecting a device, which may not be desirable in an online value redemption transaction with a bank.

The second type of attack to be concerned about is a protocol-based attack. In this type of attack, the device that is having its value illegally incremented is receiving instructions from a device pretending to be a legal payer. The receiving device must be securely designed such that it can distinguish between a legitimate paying device and an illegal paying device staged by attackers. To this end, a number of secure authentication protocols have been developed that usually require the use of a secret key. If the receiving device is presented with the secret key, it will know that the paying device is authorized to transfer its value.

One way to provide this assurance is for both devices to share a secret—a symmetric cryptographic key—that is known only to authorized devices. It would be dangerous to have all devices use a single master key because capturing that key once would provide the means to compromise any of the bank issuer's token devices. To combat this problem, the bank can issue a randomly generated master key to all of its hardware devices but use a unique variant of this key in each token. The symmetric key used for the transaction is a function of each device's unique identifier and the master key. The receiving device must be able to regenerate the symmetric key based on the random master key and the connecting device's unique identifier. The purpose of adding this complexity is that if the key is stolen from the device and discovered, the specific device can be traced and effectively blacklisted so that no further transactions will be accepted from that device [Chaum and Brands 1997].

Even so, this method has several problems. First, the key must be resistant to *replay attacks* wherein a wiretap could potentially capture the key and replay the session to add more value illegally. Challenge response systems can be used to protect against replay or sniffing types of attacks. In a challenge response system, the receiving device sends a challenge string (or numeral) to the paying device. The paying device sends back a response that is a function of both the challenge and the secret key. Even if this response is captured, it will not be valid again as long as the same challenge is not resent.

The second problem with the symmetric key approach is that it gives motive for the bearer of the token to recover the secret key. If the secret key can be recovered, the bearer may be able to arbitrarily add value to the token. An alternative to the symmetric key approach is to use public key encryption (PKE). PKE removes the requirement for a single shared secret among all devices issued by the bank. The main advantage of this approach over a shared secret key approach is that knowledge of the public key does not allow reconstruction of the secret key. Unlike with the shared master key approach, if the token device's security is compromised, the capture of the public keys of paying devices will not provide the attacker the ability to compromise the security of all other paying devices supported by the issuing bank. To prevent replay attacks, the paying device computes a response to the challenge, as described before, except the response now is a *digital signature* based on the device's private key and the challenge. The receiving device uses the paying device's public key together with the challenge to authenticate the device before accepting value.

One disadvantage of PKE is the key management problem that is inherent in any asymmetric key encryption technique. That is, it may be unreasonable for any single hardware token to contain the public keys for all of the paying devices it may interface with in the course of commerce. This problem led to the growth of the practice wherein only the public keys of trusted CAs are necessary to vouch for the authenticity of other paying devices. Another disadvantage of this approach is that even though knowledge of the public keys of other paying devices does not provide the attacker any advantage, the receiving device may be a paying device with its own private key. If this private key is captured by a physical attack against the device, it can be used to pay out its value. The use of tamper-evident secure shielding of physical tokens can be used to combat the physical tampering problem.

Finally, an advantage of asymmetric encryption is the ability to prove to the issuing bank that the value the device accumulated was indeed authorized, rather than forged by physical tampering. Recall that every paying device must present a digital signature—which cannot be forged—to the receiving device in order for the payment protocol to be executed. These digital signatures can be presented to the bank by the receiving device as proof that the accumulated value was received through legitimate transactions from a valid paying device.

Representing Electronic Cash

Electronic cash can be represented either as a value stored in a counter of a hardware device or in the form cryptographic tokens called electronic coins. In a counter-based (a.k.a. register-based) cash system, the value stored in the device is recorded as a numeral in a counter. For example, if the basic unit were 1 cent, a counter value of 10,000 would represent $100. Payments from the device are recorded as debits to the counter, as in a stored-account system, except that the account is stored on a hardware token and a bank would not be required to intervene between the buyer and the seller. Likewise, received payments are recorded in the counter by incrementing its value the appropriate amount. The maximum value the counter can hold is restricted by the width of the hardware register and the fundamental unit of currency that is exchanged.

In contrast, cryptographic coin systems maintain a cache of value denominations in purely information form. The cache can be thought of as an electronic purse that contains basic denominations of cents, dollars, fives, tens, twenties, and so forth. Rather than maintaining a single register (or memory location) that holds the total value in the device, each memory location in the purse contains the value of a given denomination that is digitally signed. The collection of all the denominations constitutes the value held in the device, much as the sum of the values of all the bills in your wallet tell you how much money you are carrying.

Both of these systems require some form of security to prevent theft and fraud. In register-based cash systems, physical security through tamper-resistant or tamper-evident devices is essential to prevent unauthorized modifications to the register value. For instance, without adequate physical protection, external attacks can reverse engineer hardware devices to not only determine their design specifications, but also to modify values held in nonvolatile memories. It is also possible to modify program register values without physically tampering with the device case. For example, subjecting the device to ion, x-ray, or ultraviolet radiation can flip bits in memory that may alter the value stored in a cash-based register. The randomness of the results from this type of attack make them unattractive for controlled attacks. That is, the attack may *reduce* the value as well as increase it, though this may be a risk a criminal is willing to take if chances are that repeated trials will increase the value. One technique that provides protection against these types of attacks is to encode the data stored in memory that is used by the devices. Data corrupted by radiation would be detected through periodic tests. Payment protocols can also enforce the amount of value deducted from the cash-based register by encoding the purchase amount in the challenge sent to the paying device. As long as the purchaser agrees to the price, the paying device will use the encoded payment to deduct the amount from the register that is to be transferred to the recipient.

The second way to represent value is to use cryptographic coins. DigiCash's e-cash system is based on cryptographic coins. Cryptographic coins are represented by discrete units of information, each with its own serial number. Unlike physical cash, a cryptographic coin has the potential for being in more than one place at the same time. Because of the nature of the electronic medium, a cryptographic coin can be reproduced perfectly and distributed widely extremely cheaply. This property opens the potential for fraud by spending the value of a coin many times. The physical equivalent is having the ability to perfectly reproduce a government-issued dime to spend multiple times. To prevent multiple spending of electronic coins in practice, a unique serial number is assigned to each coin and digitally signed by the issuing bank. A different signature is used for each currency denomination. The digital signature verifies not only the note's authenticity, but also its value. Before accepting payment, each recipient must check with the issuing bank that the coin being transferred has not already been spent. If approved, the coin is accepted into the recipient's electronic purse, and the coin is noted as spent by the bank. This means that the recipient can no longer spend this electronic coin but can redeem it with the issuing bank for either a new electronic coin (with a different serial number) of equivalent value or credit in the recipient's account. Each time a recipient receives electronic money, a digitally signed deposit slip is sent from the bank that verifies the authenticity of the money.

E-cash

DigiCash's e-cash is a stored-value cryptographic coin system that facilitates Internet-based commerce using software that runs on personal computers. The value of e-cash is represented by cryptographic tokens that can be withdrawn from bank accounts, deposited in bank accounts, or transferred to another person. The implementation of e-cash is both similar and distinct from that for stored-account payment systems. Unlike in stored-account systems, the value of the money is withdrawn from the consumer's account and placed in an electronic purse that exists on a consumer's personal computer. The value can stay there indefinitely, much like change that sits on a desk. Or it can be transferred to a recipient, which could be a private citizen, a merchant, or a financial institution. As with stored-account systems, though, the bank ultimately simply transfers the value from one account to another through a settlement system. In a traditional cash-based system, withdrawing cash from a bank reduces the cash in the bank's vault. Withdrawing e-cash, on the other hand, adds to the e-cash liability for a particular consumer. The bank will not allow the consumer to assume more e-cash liability than funds exist in the consumer's account. Depositing e-cash reduces the e-cash liability in the consumer's account.

Another similarity of e-cash and stored-account payment systems is that ecash requires the online intervention of an issuing bank in any transaction. The reason for intervention (or more appropriately, authentication) is to prevent fraud due to double spending.

Double spending occurs when the value of a cryptographic coin is spent more than once. Unlike physical coins, for example, digital representation of money can be perfectly duplicated. This could mean that a criminal can spend a cryptographic coin to purchase an item from one merchant and use the same cryptographic coin to purchase an item from another merchant. In order to prevent this kind of abuse, a bank must be able to verify that the coin being used in a transaction has not already been spent in another transaction.

An important distinction between DigiCash's e-cash system and stored-account payment systems is that DigiCash preserves the privacy of the *paying party* in any e-cash transaction. DigiCash uses "blinding," a technique invented by DigiCash founder David Chaum, to provide privacy in payments. The e-cash payment protocol and blinding are best explained by illustration. Figure 3.14 shows how Alice withdraws e-cash from her bank.

Alice would like to withdraw $20 in e-cash from her bank account. In an interesting twist, DigiCash's protocol requires Alice—not the bank—to mint her own e-cash. Alice uses DigiCash's client software to randomly generate a serial number for the coin (see Step 1). Prudence suggests that a large number of digits, possibly 100, will reduce the likelihood of this identical number being randomly generated by another consumer. Now, in order for the electronic coin to assume some value, the issuing bank must digitally sign the number with its private key that corresponds to the desired value denomination. If Alice were to send the serial number to the bank to get it assigned $20 and have it digitally signed, the bank could trace how that $20 is spent. That is, the bank can record the

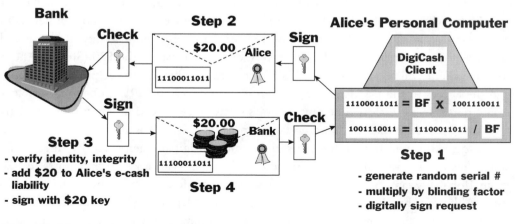

Figure 3.14   DigiCash e-cash withdrawal.

serial number when the coin is issued; then when the coin is later redeemed by the payee, the bank will know precisely to whom Alice gave the money. To prevent this possible invasion of privacy, blinding can be used to obscure the serial number from the bank. Before sending the serial number to the bank, Alice will multiply the serial number by a random number called the blinding factor (Step 1). The blinding factor is a way to arithmetically disguise the serial number from the bank. Because large numbers are hard to factor, it is unlikely that the bank will be successful if it attempts to guess the serial number. Alice will digitally sign the request and send it to the bank (Step 2). The digital signature provides proof that Alice requested $20.

In Step 3, the bank will first verify Alice's signature using her public key. If this step is successful, her e-cash *liability* will be increased $20. The bank then signs the blinded serial number with its private key that is used for signing $20 e-cash denominations. The value of the coin is represented by the bank's digital signature. The signed e-cash is now sent back to Alice's computer (Step 4). After receiving the e-cash, Alice will first check the bank's signature to ensure authenticity. Next, her software client will divide out the blinding factor to restore the original serial number that was generated. Because of the numerical properties of the signature algorithms, the process of dividing the signed e-cash by the blinding factor does not invalidate the digital signature. The e-cash now has a serial number that is unrecognizable to the bank, but it has the bank's digital signature that is used to determine its value and its authenticity. Therefore, when the coin is spent, the recipient will redeem a coin with a serial number for which the bank will have no record—provided that it has not already been spent.

The process of spending the e-cash is illustrated in Figure 3.15. Now that Alice has her e-cash, she will give Bob the $20 she owes him for the concert ticket he bought her. As in every e-cash transaction, a bank is involved in order to ensure authenticity of e-cash and to prevent double spending. Bob will send Alice the request for the $20 (Step 1). Alice's software client will determine if she has $20 in e-cash in her electronic purse. If she does and she agrees to the payment, her software will remove the $20 e-cash from her electronic purse. The e-cash will be sent to Bob's software client this time without her digital signature. Recall that the blinding factor from this e-cash has already been removed. The e-cash Bob will receive has the serial number originally generated by Alice's software. This e-cash was subsequently signed by the bank with a key that denotes its $20 value. Bob's software can check the bank's signature to determine its authenticity and its value. Although this check provides an indication of its legitimacy, Bob must forward the number to his bank to receive credit for the money. This process is performed transparently by Bob's software client. Bob's bank will check Alice's bank's signature on the e-cash by using her bank's public key. From this check, the bank will know the value of the e-cash and its authenticity. The bank will check the serial number (which is different from the blinded serial number originally signed by her bank) against a master list of spent e-cash. If the e-cash passes the verification tests, Bob's bank can credit his account (or reduce his e-cash liability) the $20 that was paid to him by Alice. Once Bob receives a signed deposit slip from his bank, his software client will notify Alice that he received her payment. Notice that since the serial number of the e-cash sent by Alice to Bob is different from the serial number signed by her bank, there is no way for the bank to trace how Alice spent that $20 e-cash coin. If Alice wanted to remain anonymous to Bob (or any other payment recipient) as well, she would need to assume an alias that is used by her DigiCash software client in the transaction.

Rather than having his account credited, Bob may wish to keep the $20 e-cash Alice sent him in his electronic purse. Bob still needs to forward Alice's e-cash to his bank for approval; however, Bob's software client can be configured to handle the authentication by the bank transparently. In effect, Bob will see only that he received the $20 e-cash from Alice. In actuality, Bob is committing a withdrawal type of transaction as illustrated in Figure 3.14 after Alice's e-cash has been credited to Bob's account.

In summary, DigiCash's e-cash provides some of the benefits of a stored-value payment system in a paradigm that is similar to stored-account payment systems for online verification. As in most stored-value systems, the actual value of the e-cash transaction is transferred

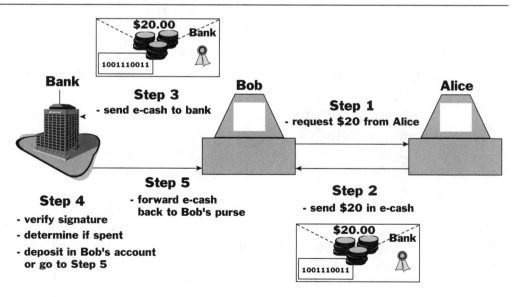

Figure 3.15 Spending e-cash.

between the two parties of a transaction. As in stored-account systems, the bank must intervene in any transaction to authenticate the currency and to ensure that it has not already been spent. Unlike with stored-account payment systems, e-cash provides the payer anonymity that prevents intrusive profiling of personal spending habits. However, because the recipient must obtain authorization from the bank, anonymity of receiving e-cash is not provided. The result is a system that allows anonymous purchasing yet provides accountability for receiving money.

Interestingly, this system makes purchasing illegal goods and services possible over the Internet with impunity, but it provides little incentive for selling illegal goods and services. Because the purchaser knows the serial numbers of the e-cash used to make the purchase and the bank records the serial numbers when the payee authenticates them, the purchaser can indisputably "finger" a seller of illegal goods and merchandise on the Internet. Fingering the party also implicates the purchaser, so there will be little incentive to do this unless the purchaser is cooperating in a police investigation. An interesting side effect is that there will be little value in setting up police "sting" operations on the Internet involving e-cash. Because the identity of the purchaser can be set to an alias and the bank has no way of associating a serial number with its owner, a police sting cannot positively identify the perpetrator of an illegal Internet purchase.

CyberCoin

CyberCoin is CyberCash's payment system for online commerce. It is designed for small-value payment for online commodities such as Web content. Collecting fees for articles, papers, and images downloaded from a company's Web site appeals to individuals and companies producing Web content. The smallest CyberCoin denomination is $0.25. From a consumer perspective, being charged less than $1.00 for an article may be a reasonable value proposition.

Unlike with stored-value systems, wherein the value is stored on some token held by the consumer, the value of the CyberCoins resides with CyberCash. The CyberCash Wallet in the consumer's browser merely enables payment. In this sense, the system fits the stored-account model with the exception that the consumer need not have a bank account. CyberCash actually handles the accounting of purchases between consumers and merchants. By handling the transactions itself, CyberCash can eliminate a large portion of the costs of online transactions via banks, as with CyberCash's Secure Internet Payment System (SIPS). Recall that these costs include online authorization from banks and ACH transactions costs per purchase. By eliminating a large portion of these costs, CyberCash is able to support small-value transactions.

When the consumer purchases CyberCoins from CyberCash, the consumer's funds are held in escrow in an account set aside by CyberCash for the consumer [Stewart 1997]. The consumer's CyberCash Wallet is credited the amount in CyberCoins. When the consumer makes an online purchase with a participating merchant, the purchase value in CyberCoins is transferred from the consumer's CyberCash Wallet to the merchant's CashRegister. CyberCash maintains an account for each participating merchant, too. This account tallies the value of all CyberCoin sales the merchant makes. As with CyberCash's SIPS, the merchant can have the accumulated value of CyberCoins it receives transferred from CyberCash's bank to its own bank account via ACH transactions. However, in the CyberCoin system, the cost of this transaction is borne by the merchant rather than CyberCash. As a result, the merchant is likely to transfer funds only when the value of the transfer is great enough to warrant the cost of the ACH transfer. In the interim, CyberCash earns interest on the funds held in escrow for consumers and merchants.

Because CyberCoins do not rely on bearer certificates (like e-cash), counterfeiting is not possible. Purchases with CyberCoins are possible only for those who first obtain an account with CyberCash; subsequent merchant/consumer transactions are handled by CyberCash via the account ledgers. In this respect, CyberCoin is a stored-account system with minimal costs that enable small-value transactions similar to those in other stored-value e-cash systems. Unlike DigiCash's e-cash system, CyberCoins do not offer anonymity in purchasing, which is a drawback in general for stored-account payment systems.

The market is still undecided about whether CyberCoins will take off. In its favor, CyberCoins leverage an existing infrastructure of personal computers, the Internet, banking accounts, and ACH transactions. Again, strategic alliances with browser vendors can get CyberCash Wallets on people's desktops, which is perhaps the greatest hurdle for CyberCash to overcome. The second hurdle CyberCash will face is convincing consumers to pay for the types of intellectual property on Web pages CyberCash believes will be the market for CyberCoin. The third hurdle is the same one faced by DigiCash: CyberCoin currently runs only on personal computers. The smart card market is growing faster, and having the ability to make online payments via smart cards may allow for a much bigger market.

Smart Cards

In the preceding section, the value that was stored in computers could have been on smart cards. Smart cards represent another form of a hardware token that is used as the interface to an electronic transaction. Smart cards have been around for over two decades under different aliases but are only now being considered instruments of Internet commerce. Smart cards come in several varieties, from simple memory cards, such as prepaid phone cards, to devices with a sophisticated central processing unit (CPU) and a cryptographic coprocessor. The range in prices for these cards varies greatly, too. To purchase a memory card wholesale costs only about $0.25 while a cryptographic smart card can cost as much as $7.00 wholesale [Gorman 1997]. The cost to the end user may be more or less, depending on the channel of distribution through which the card is obtained.

Memory cards have simple hardware requirements to store data in read-only memory (ROM). Most memory cards are secured by a personal identification number (PIN) to control access to the data. Cryptographic cards have the usual hardware chips found in a personal processor: CPU, random access memory, read/write random access memory (RAM), a ROM, and a cryptographic coprocessor for fast cryptographic computations.

Despite the advances in computing on smart cards, simple memory cards dominate the market in terms of production. One estimate is that 600 million out of 800 million smart cards produced worldwide in 1996 were protected memory smart cards [Gorman 1997]. The emergence of cryptographic smart cards, however, should serve to spur Internet-based electronic commerce by providing strong encryption algorithms for authentication and data transport. Many smart cards now employ public key encryption to both encrypt data sent to a payment recipient and digitally sign messages to provide unforgeable proof of identity.

Applications of Smart Cards

In the past, memory cards have been used in single applications such as transit cards, prepaid phone cards, and identification cards for access control to buildings. In order for smart cards to be commercially successful, they will need to perform more than a single function. The recent advances in placing silicon on credit card-sized hardware tokens will mean a greater variety of applications that can be integrated on a single card. Consider all the different types of cards that people currently carry in their wallets that can be integrated onto one or two different smart cards. The following are some of the possible applications that can be integrated in smart cards [Hovenga Fancher 1997]:

- Driver's license
- Social Security card
- Health insurance, blood type, medical allergies, next-of-kin information
- Auto insurance, emergency towing service numbers
- Library card, voter registration card

- School or work ID for access control to buildings
- Access control to Web sites or online databases such as class times and grades
- Digital signatures for e-mail and Web transactions
- Public keys for encrypting data transactions
- Long distance phone card
- Store charge card
- Credit cards
- Debit cards
- Electronic cash

Personal information can be stored in special type of read-only memory called Electrically Erasable Programmable Read Only Memory (EEPROM). This memory can be "burned" with each customer's personal information when it is issued. Unlike other ROMs, EEPROMs are not write-once memory; rather, as new information needs to be added, it can be burned in through programmable devices. Some EEPROMs available for smart cards can now hold up to 8 kilobytes of memory. To put this number in perspective, consider that a U.S. Social Security number requires less than 100 bytes of memory to be stored.

Smart cards are also helping to overcome a critical security issue in public key encryption. When public key encryption is used from personal computers or workstations, a significant concern involves the security of the private key that is usually stored on the machine's hard drive. If the private key can be obtained by someone else, all bets are off. That is, the digital signatures can be forged, nonrepudiation can be disputed, and access controls can be violated. If the personal computer remains locked in someone's own home, the risks are not that great—unless housemates are a risk. In reality, though, many people maintain their private key on shared machines at work in order to use public key encryption. Disk drives are often shared over the network and personal computers are shared among several people, so the security of private keys can be compromised. With smart cards, the private key can be placed not on a shared hard drive, but on a small hardware token that can be carried on one's person. To provide additional security, most smart cards require the user to enter a four- to six-digit PIN to use any of the supported applications. Of course, poorly selected PINs (such as personal birth dates) can compromise the access control to the card.

Some of the leading vendors of Web-based products are now producing software to enable smart card-based interfacing to the Net. Netscape is developing application programming interfaces (APIs) in its Communicator suite of software to support smart card communications on top of its SSL protocol. This means that Web-based applications that run on top of Netscape's software will be able to interface with end users who are connecting through smart cards. Similarly, Microsoft is building support into its Internet architecture to support smart card communication. Near-term key strategic uses of smart cards for Internet commerce will include the ability to securely store and transport public/private keys anywhere. Without a hardware token that can be transported, users currently have to perform their online transactions from their home or work computers. Because the Internet can be reached from almost any computer anywhere, restricting e-commerce to one or two computers has its disadvantages. Smart cards in the future will be used to provide secure Internet commerce sessions from Internet kiosks in universities, malls, airports, amusement parks, and even cafes and coffee shops.

In addition to the owner's private key and other people's public keys, smart cards can be used to store personal digital certificates that are signed by certification authorities. The personal digital certificate is a means for exchanging public keys and providing two parties to a transaction with positive identification verified by a mutual, trusted third party. If consumers want to do business with an online store, they can use the SET protocol, for example, and their smart card to provide the authentication and encryption necessary for the transaction. That is, the consumer and merchant may exchange digital certificates that are signed by a trusted third party. From these certificates, each will know the other's public key in order to communicate securely. The consumer's digital certificate may also be used by the merchant's Web server to provide entry to access-controlled Web pages. Web server authentication can be simplified through use of digital certificates instead of basic password protection. Strong authentication via digital signatures is discussed in more detail in Chapter 4.

Storing Value on Smart Cards

The preceding section presented many of the possible applications that smart cards will be able to support in the future, but one of the most exciting and risky applications of smart cards is storing value for monetary exchange. Unlike credit and debit cards, stored-value cards hold a value unto themselves. Credit and debit cards represent value stored in an account of deposit in some financial institution. Perhaps one of the major innovations in stored-value cards will be ability to perform monetary exchange without online authorization from a financial institution. Stored-value cards have the advantage of being able to perform small value purchases relatively cheaply. Consider that Visa International estimates that the equivalent of $8.1 trillion is spent in cash transactions in the world's top 29 economies [Hovenga Fancher 1997]. Small-value purchases are believed to make up the majority of these purchases. Certainly, having a minute stake in small-value cash transactions can still translate into large revenue. For most credit card transactions, the costs for participating merchants and financial institutions to process small-value purchases do not justify the sales. Smart cards can overcome these costs when the transactions are performed off-line.

Using smart cards for small-value transactions holds many advantages for consumers. First, consumers will not need to carry change. Second, because stored-value cards do not require an account of deposit with a bank, they are suitable to use on travel to foreign destinations where tourists do not typically have a local bank account to draw from. Third, they can be used by children and the destitute who typically do not maintain bank accounts. Finally, as with wireless technologies that are now finding use in countries that do not have a well-developed telecommunications infrastructure, stored-value smart cards may be useful in countries where a well-developed back-end financial infrastructure for processing credit card transactions does not exist.

CAFE

Although DigiCash's e-cash does represent an intrinsic value, online authorization is required from a participating bank in each transaction. Two smart card projects involving off-line stored-value payments that are receiving a lot of publicity are the Conditional Access for Europe (CAFE) project, chaired by DigiCash founder David Chaum, and Mondex cards. CAFE involves several European countries and is supported by the European Commission. The CAFE project uses an extension of the basic blinding paradigm called one-show blinding, also invented by David Chaum. As with the basic blinding paradigm, the idea is to prevent traceability of payment of an electronic coin. The difference lies in the method for detecting double spending. A fundamental weakness in the basic blinding paradigm is that all transactions require online verification, mainly to detect attempts at double spending of a single electronic coin. Because all payments are unconditionally untraceable, the bank could deny approval of payment for the recipient, but it may not ever be able to trace the payment to the payer. The e-cash system, while providing a high degree of privacy for consumers, is unsuitable for *off-line* payment systems such as those used by stored-value smart cards because online verification is not desired.

The one-show blinding paradigm provides off-line payment verification while ensuring that double spending will be positively detected and traceable to the spender. When the consumers is spending an electronic coin the first time, the one-show blinding paradigm ensures that the digital signature used by the paying device cannot be used to provide traceability. If the same coin is spent twice, however, the combination of the two digital signatures positively identifies the party who spent the coin twice [Chaum and

Brands 1997]. The CAFE project has implemented adaptations of the one-show blinding paradigm in electronic wallets and smart cards for off-line payment systems.

Mondex

Mondex (www.mondex.com) is a stored-value system for smart cards that has the backing of MasterCard International. As with DigiCash's e-cash system, Mondex value is a bearer certificate. As with cash, whoever holds it owns its value. Unlike under other payment systems, Mondex value can be transferred from consumer to consumer. In that respect, Mondex value is closest to currency. Furthermore, Mondex does not require online verification. Mondex started as a proprietary network system, but it is now migrating toward the Internet [Stewart 1997].

Mondex was started and spun off by National Westminster Bank PLC, London. A key distinction between DigiCash and Mondex is that Mondex uses a register-based cash system for smart cards. That is, the Mondex value is loaded and stored in a counter in the CPU of the smart card. The value can be passed indefinitely from person to person without requiring the intervention of a bank in the transaction.

Consumers can use Mondex smart cards to pay for merchandise from participating merchants. The transaction begins when the consumer places the smart card in a point-of-sale card reader terminal. The smart card's owner information is transferred to the merchant's card there. A merchant requests payment for merchandise through a signed request that is transferred to the consumer's card. The cards can check the authenticity of the other's digital certificates to ensure proper certification. If the merchant's digital signature is fine, the consumer's smart card sends authorization for payment with an attached digital signature to the merchant's smart card. The consumer's smart card now deducts this amount from its stored-value register. The merchant's card verifies the digital signature again, then sends a signed acknowledgment of receipt. The value of the transaction is added to the merchant's value counter.

Mondex cards support several national currencies. Over 17 banks worldwide participate in a joint venture with Mondex, including Mark Twain bank of St. Louis, Missouri. Mondex value must always reside on a Mondex card—even in the central banks that issue Mondex value. Because the value is stored in a register of the Mondex card, the security of Mondex hinges on the tamper resistance of the Mondex smart card.

Mondex uses cryptographic signatures and tamper resistance to secure the value stored in Mondex cards. Physical shielding is also used to withstand harsh environmental conditions such as cold, heat, moisture, x-rays, and electrical interference. The primary security risk that Mondex faces is a physical attack against the card. Because the card contains cryptographic keys that if recovered can be used to forge Mondex transactions, the card must essentially be tamper proof. Some security experts believe this approach is flawed. Because the bearer of the card has the motivation to recover the key from the card, many believe that the security will ultimately be compromised. The key question is at what price? As long as the cost of extracting the secret key is greater than the derived value, the approach may be successful. If attacks are found that can potentially compromise the keys, it may be possible to transfer forged value to Mondex cards [Campbell 1997].

Mondex has two important characteristics in its favor. First, it has the backing and resources of MasterCard International. This backing by itself is enough to get it off the ground. Mondex plans on rolling out 5 million e-cash cards by the end of 1998. Second, it is the electronic cash payment closest to true currency because of the ability to transfer funds from card to card without intervention by banks. Perhaps its biggest hurdle is that it requires a card reader. Most personal computers are not equipped with card readers. As card readers for PCs become more prevalent and cheaper, these technical hurdles will fall. With Mondex being ported to the Internet, it will probably see more widespread usage. However, it may be used in typical small-value purchases such as vendor machines. Its biggest security drawback is that the card bearer has the incentive to recover its cryptographic keys. If they can be retrieved, attackers may be able to mint their own e-cash. As long as this process is sufficiently difficult, though, this is not a critical threat.

Visa Cash

Visa Cash made its big debut at the 1996 Olympics in Atlanta, Georgia. Like Mondex, Visa Cash is a register-based, stored-value system for smart cards. As such, it has the portability to be used in vending applications outside of the desktop computer. As of mid-1997, Visa Cash had already placed over 6 million cards in distribution.

A distinguishing attribute of Visa Cash is that a sysetm of clearing and settlement is used for payment. This distinction has its advantages and disadvantages. The disadvantage for Visa Cash card holders is that they are restricted to dealing with authorized Visa Cash merchants. That is, Visa Cash cannot be arbitrarily exchanged between any two Visa Cash card holders. Online verification (currently used in credit and debit card transactions) is not necessary for Visa Cash purchase transactions. As a result, the cost of the transaction is small enough to make an economic case for small value transactions. Merchants periodically upload purchase transactions to member banks in batches to obtain credit via a system of clearing and settlement.

The advantages for Visa member banks, however, are quite significant. Visa Cash provides an economic model that makes it viable for participating banking institutions [Stewart 1997]. Visa banks can issue Visa Cash and earn float on the income that resides on the issued cards. In the case of disposable Visa Cash cards, the banks also end up keeping the amount of money that is left on the card when it is disposed. Because Visa Cash transactions are always made with authorized Visa merchants, banks also earn a processing fee for each merchant deposit, similar to the fees Visa banks now collect through POS credit card purchases. The clearing and settlement system also provides high levels of traceability, which is good from a security perspective, albeit less attractive for privacy advocates. However, disposable Visa Cash cards do provide anonymity when purchasing. Mondex has no clear economic model for how banks will profit from issuing Mondex value. Since Mondex transactions can occur indefinitely between Mondex card holders without online intervention, banks cannot collect transaction processing fees. The very features that make Mondex versatile and Visa restrictive for consumers turn out to be economic advantages for Visa member banks.

From a security standpoint, both systems have adopted the model of cryptographic secrets on smart cards. This model gives attackers motivation to crack the cards, but as long as the cost of cracking exceeds the benefit, the threat of security breaches is manageable. Both systems do not offer the anonymity in transaction that DigiCash's electronic cash systems do. But DigiCash is unlikely to be able to compete well against the two most significant players in this market. Ultimately, the winners in electronic cash will be determined by the economic incentives for the marketplace to adopt their usage and the versatility the payment systems offer for consumers.

Summary

Secure communication protocols such as SSL and S-HTTP can be used to secure Web-based sessions including commercial data transactions. Although these protocols can authenticate both parties and provide privacy in the transaction, they do not provide protocols for payment. To fill this void, a number of payment systems have emerged, from CyberCash and SET to DigiCash, Mondex, and Visa Cash. The payment systems can be loosely categorized into stored-account and stored-value payments systems.

The differences between the two systems point to the advantages and disadvantages of both approaches. Stored-account systems provide high accountability, real-time online verification of payment for merchants, and the ability to use the existing back-end financial infrastructure for settling payments between banks. Stored-account systems also provide a high level of security because all transactions are traceable and the value of the transactions never actually leaves the banks. The trade-off for consumers, however, is the lack of privacy provided in stored-account transactions. All transactions are mediated by financial institutions or a third party, so it is entirely possible that complete spending profiles for consumers can be collected and potentially used for purposes that are often equated with "big brother" intrusive oversight.

Stored-value payment systems, on the other hand, offer the potential for anonymity in cash-based transactions rivaled only by that for hard currency. Stored-value systems can exploit the electronic medium in ways that overcome limitations of hard currency. They also hold advantages for consumers who do not ordinarily maintain bank accounts and for countries without well-developed back-end financial settlement systems for stored-account type of transactions. The application of stored-value payment systems to small-value transactions has enabled credit card companies to reach into an estimated $8 trillion market heretofore untapped. Although electronic cash used in stored-value payment systems has numerous advantages, the security risks associated with e-cash have held up widespread adoption. The combination of online verification and the ability to support small-value transactions over the Internet and in specialized applications may end up being the most viable economic model for launching the widespread adoption of smart cards in the United States.

References

Baldwin, R.W. and C.V. Chang. "Locking the E-Safe." *IEEE Spectrum*, Vol. 14, No. 2, February 1997, 40–46.

Campbell, D. "Plastic Treasure ... Not So Smart after All." Online. *The U.K. Guardian*. September 24, 1997. Available: insight.mcmaster.ca/org/efc/pages/media/guardian .24sep97.html.

Chaum, D. and S. Brands. "Minting Electronic Cash." *IEEE Spectrum*, Vol. 14, No. 2, February 1997, 30–34.

Felten, E., D. Balfanz, D. Dean, and D. Wallach. "Web Spoofing: An Internet Con Game." Technical Report 540-96 (revised), Department of Computer Science, Princeton University, February 1997.

Gemmel, P.S. "Traceable E-Cash." *IEEE Spectrum*, Vol. 14, No. 2, February 1997, 35–37.

Gorman, T. "Smart Cards Come to the Web—Are You Ready?" *Netscape World*, Vol. 2, Issue 3, March 1997. Available: http://www.netscapeworld.com.

Hovenga Fancher, C. "In Your Pocket: Smart Cards." *IEEE Spectrum*, Vol. 14, No. 2, February 1997, 47–53.

Peterson, K.M. "Fake ATM Machine Steals PINs." *RISKS Digest*, Vol. 14, Issue 59. May 12, 1993.

Sirbu, M.A. "Credits and Debits on the Internet." *IEEE Spectrum*, Vol. 14, No. 2, February 1997, 23–29.

Stewart, D. "The Future of Digital Cash on the Internet." Online. *Journal of Internet Banking and Commerce*, Volume 2, No. 3, July 1997. Available: www.arraydev.com/commerce/JIBC/articles.htm.

Referenced Web Sites

Anonymizer Web site	www.anonymizer.com	A proxy for surfing the Web privately.
CyberCash	www.cybercash.com	Responsible for online payment systems CyberCash SIPS and CyberCoin.
First Virtual	www.fv.com	Pioneer of an online payment protocol that does not employ cryptography.
Mondex International	www.mondex.com	A stored value system for smart cards backed by Master Card.
Princeton Secure Internet Programming team	www.cs.princeton .edu/sip/	The research group that demonstrated the Web spoofing attack.
Quicken Financial Network	www.qfn.com	Supports Quicken products and provides delayed stock quotes free.
Terisa Systems	www.terisa.com	The primary advocates of the S-HTTP protocol.

Chapter 4

Securing the
Commerce Server

In the last chapter, different methods and protocols for securing e-commerce transactions were discussed. The plethora of protocols that continues to emerge indicates the amount of resources that are being spent in assuring data transaction security. Protocols for e-commerce are also very popular among the computer savvy. Most people are familiar with at least one of the protocols and several of the security properties that are assured: confidentiality, authentication, integrity, and nonrepudiation. In all the commotion over which encryption protocols to use, however, a significant side of e-commerce security has been largely ignored—the security of the commerce server. The commerce server consists of a network server and its software that responds to Internet-based requests. The software typically includes a Web server, mail server, an FTP server, news server, remote login servers, and, of course, the operating system and supporting software. This chapter focuses specifically on the security issues in the Web server software. Chapter 5 addresses vulnerabilities in the operating system and supporting software that run on the network server. The Web server software is integral to most e-commerce applications today. The complexity in both the software and its configuration is a major source of vulnerability in Web sites currently on the Net.

With the presence of secure transaction protocols, it is reasonable to ask: why bother with the server-side security? The answer, once again, is that the security of the system is only as strong as its weakest link. If the server-side security is the weak link, it will certainly be one of the first targets for Internet criminals. Realize that if a malicious Internet user is faced with the prospect of breaking a 56-bit key encryption algorithm that protects the data in transmission or breaking into the server where the data is stored "in the clear," odds are that the intruder will go straight for the server. Because many of the data transaction protocols and payment systems are turnkey commercial systems, the security of the data transaction is purchased with the package. On the other hand, the server-side security must be actively configured, maintained, and assessed periodically.

If the server is not adequately secured, what are the potential losses that can occur if it gets hacked? The most critical information stored on the commerce server probably resides in the back-end databases. This information includes enterprise-critical data that, if compromised, can result in the loss of consumer confidence and potentially litigation. Another large concern is the denial-of-service attack that can occur if a malicious user (internal or external) is able to bring the server to its knees. Denial-of-service attacks cripple the ability of the server to respond to requests, usually by flooding the server with too many requests, too much data, or a combination of both. Anyone can launch a denial-of-service attack against Internet servers with only a little bit of knowledge, without requiring any level of privilege, access, or authorization. For businesses, having an unavailable server is effectively the same as hanging a "Closed" sign on the door. The costs associated with lost business due to unavailability of a server can be staggering, depending on the business of the firm. Some online companies invest heavily in fault-tolerant hardware to continue operation in the face of single computer failures. However, fault-tolerant hardware solutions can be ineffective against flaws in redundant software and protocol-level attacks. Even for companies not involved in real-time commerce applications, loss of Internet service can severely impact the business.

Before Internet service became integral in many businesses, high phone service availability was a requirement. Phone companies early on recognized the importance of high availability for businesses and even mounted advertising campaigns with high availability of phone service as a central theme. Now, with many Internet service providers (ISPs) unable to meet the demands of their rapidly growing consumer base, delivering high availability for Internet service has become one of the leading requirements (and complaints) for most companies and home users connected to the Internet. Until robust protocols for Internet sessions are implemented and deployed, the protocol-level attacks against servers will remain a denial-of-service problem.

Another concern with Web servers is the confidentiality of documents that are placed on the server. If confidential documents are placed in a file accessible by the Web server, unauthorized access to proprietary secrets may be possible. From a system administrator's vantage point, perhaps the scariest scenario is one in which a remote user who has not been granted any system privileges can arbitrarily execute system commands on the server. Given this level of privilege, an attacker can delete or steal files, place Trojan horse programs on the server, run denial-of-service programs, deface Web pages, store cracking tools for other crackers to access, or in the worst case, delete the whole file system.

The Web Server

Figure 4.1 shows the three main components that make up the Internet commerce server: the front-end server software, the back-end databases, and the interface software. Vulnerabilities in any one of these components may allow untrusted users to access confidential documents or even execute system commands. For example, many flawed CGI scripts have allowed malicious users to grab system password files through Web requests. Once they are grabbed, password-cracking programs can usually crack at least one of the account passwords.

The best defense against Web-based attacks is to know where you are vulnerable. Once the vulnerabilities are known, they can be secured. Often, simple errors in configuring the commerce server lead to the most egregious security holes. Testing is the best way to

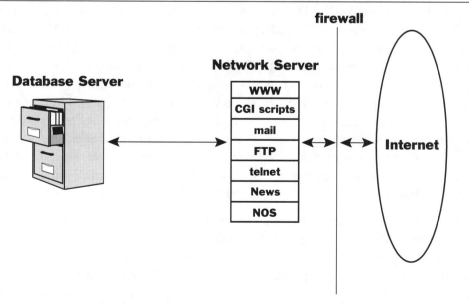

Figure 4.1 Commerce server components.

detect errors in configuration and to determine where vulnerabilities are. This chapter presents common vulnerabilities found in the three components of a Web server.

Interestingly, many computer security experts believe the security of Web servers is so questionable that the server should be placed outside the firewall. The reasoning is that if a malicious perpetrator breaks through the server in an application-level attack, the security of the firewall is breached and the internal machines may be easily compromised. This solution is known as the "sacrificial lamb." In other words, the Web server is considered unsafe and left unprotected for hackers to have their way. For e-commerce applications, this solution is clearly not a viable one. Web servers perform the enterprise-critical functions that must be protected against malicious attacks. This chapter adopts the stance that the server can and must be protected against malicious attack.

The Databases

The back-end software usually consists of relational or object-oriented databases that record transactions, maintain valid accounts, and keep inventory of commercial products. Databases must be access-controlled to prevent unauthorized insiders or outsiders from accessing sensitive data such as client account information or company proprietary data. Consider the recent debacle in the media with the U.S. Social Security Administration's (SSA's) Web site [Garfinkel 1997]. The SSA placed U.S. citizens' Personal Earnings and Benefits Estimate Statements (PEBES) online and made them available to Web requests. These statements provide complete earnings history and detailed financial information for anyone who has ever worked in the United States. To gain access to an individual's record, one only needs the person's name, Social Security number, mother's maiden name, and date and place of birth. Some privacy advocates assert that this information is publicly available and exceedingly easy to find. This means that nosy co-workers, ex-spouses, neighbors, friends, and stalkers can potentially obtain a complete history of anyone's financial earnings through the Web with only basic information about the person. The SSA warns on its Web site that the penalties for abusing the PEBES online database are severe: punishable by up to 10 years in jail and a fine of $10,000 for each offense.

The SSA also claims that it keeps track of who is making requests. Although it is possible to obtain information about the Web user's identity from a Web request, it is also rather easy for the user to remain anonymous. For example, public Internet kiosks in university labs, libraries, and cafes provide free and essentially anonymous Internet access. Because the terminal is shared, it cannot be traced to any one individual, unless the individuals logs on with their true identity. In response to the criticism over potential abuses of privacy, the SSA shut down the server to reevaluate the access control policy. Providing this information online not only is a service to the public, but it also significantly reduces the cost of processing these requests for the SSA. The privacy concerns are real, but so is the need to be able to access this information quickly and cheaply. Securing access to the Web site and maintaining user privacy are the only solution that is acceptable.

The U.S. Internal Revenue Service (IRS) for a number of years has provided an example of how internal access to confidential databases can be abused. The *Washington Post* reported that the IRS fired 23 employees, disciplined 349, and counseled 472 others for illegal browsing of tax records of celebrities, politicians, friends, and relatives [Barr 1997]. A total of 1515 IRS employees were accused of misusing the computers. In 1993 and 1994, a similar government probe reported that more than 1300 IRS employees were suspected of using government computers to illegally browse through tax records. So sensitive were the computer security problems that the government watchdog agency, GAO, feared release of this information could jeopardize the security of the IRS computer systems. Despite the fact that the IRS used sophisticated software to track abnormal browsing of tax records, the abuses were still rampant. The GAO reports that bypassing the software monitor is relatively simple for someone using secondary computer systems. This case illustrates that confidential data must remain protected from outsiders as well as from employees who may have access, but not authorization.

The Server-Side Scripts

The interface software consists of the programs known as Common Gateway Interface (CGI) scripts. These scripts are actually programs that execute on the Web server in response to Web requests. CGI scripts are often used for retrieving information from forms on Web sites and performing online Web site searches, but they are also used to update the back-end databases. CGI scripts make the Web more interactive. Static Web pages that just display content, much like advertising, are now passé. The very nature of computing can make the Web a much more interactive environment in which Web pages can be custom-generated to particular requests. Scripting languages such as Perl are popular for writing CGI scripts because they make program development quick and easy compared with using programming languages such as C. The drawback of using scripting languages is that it is easy to program potentially dangerous functions such as system commands that can be executed in response to Web input. The danger is that the input may be used to execute system commands at the discretion of the user instead of the programmer. These types of flaws have been widely reported and now are favorite targets of crackers who attempt to bypass firewalls by exploiting vulnerabilities in CGI scripts.

Vulnerabilities in any of the three components that make up the commerce server can permit a malicious Web surfer to breach corporate security through seemingly legitimate Web requests. In the following sections, the three components are discussed in detail, with particular emphasis on where potential vulnerabilities may be and how to protect the commerce server from vulnerabilities in these components. In e-commerce applications, where the back-end databases and the digital assets stored on the server and local machines are enterprise critical, providing assurance of security in each of these components plays a vital role in assuring the security of the whole e-commerce system.

Web Server Security

The front-end server software consists of the Web server, also known as the HTTP network daemon, and other network servers such as mail, file transfer protocol (FTP), news, and remote login services. All commerce servers do not require services such as mail, FTP, and news, but many do in fact provide these services, sometimes just because they are started by default. For security purposes, less is better. In the extreme, providing no network services at all will result in a very secure but useless commerce system. On the other hand, providing network services on every available port can open up major holes in the security of the system. Therefore, a balance between security and functional requirements must be reached and articulated in a security policy that meets the business requirements as well as the security requirements. An axiom in software engineering is that the more complex the software grows, the more likely the software will contain flaws. This axiom takes on much greater significance when considered for network daemons.

A network daemon is a program that runs continuously while "listening" to a network port. When a connection to its port is made, the network daemon executes one of a number of functions to handle the request. The functions may be to serve up a Web page, deliver mail, retrieve news, or transfer a file. Again, the more Internet services are offered, the greater the potential for a network intrusion.

The complexity of Web server software has grown as the demand for functions and features in Web applications has increased. The growth in software complexity inevitably results in flaws in the server software—some of which may be leveraged by enterprising individuals into security intrusions. The detection of these flaws requires rigorous analysis techniques and can be quite expensive. The burden of testing software for security should ultimately rest with the developer and vendor of the software, although independent validation and verification labs may assist in the future. Rather than presenting rigorous software analysis techniques that fall under the purview of commercial software developers, this section presents vulnerabilities that are most commonly exploited and can be tested, detected, and corrected at the Web site. The vast majority of security intrusions through firewalls and Web servers result from simple errors in configuring the server. For other good references on Web security see Rubin, Geer, and Ranum [1997], Garfinkel and Spafford [1997], and Stein [1997].

Defense in depth is the best strategy for securing commerce servers. The outermost defense most visible to end users is generally access control or authentication mechanisms. Access control mechanisms in Web servers prevent unauthorized users from accessing confidential files. Beneath the Web server application layer, however, are several other security controls that can be and should be securely configured. Even though different security mechanisms exist at different layers of the server, the mechanisms are not layered in a truly redundant fashion. Rather, breaking through just one of the layers may be sufficient to violate the security of the system. Going back to the chain analogy, the security of the server is only as strong as its weakest link. If the operating system security controls constitute a weak link, the security mechanisms at the application layer, such as the Web server, can be completely bypassed. Equally important to configure securely are the files that make up the Web server. The secure installation of the Web server is addressed next. Readers who are not interested in the technical details of how to install the server securely may skip the next section without losing a basis for further discussion in the rest of the chapter.

Installing the Web Server Securely

Usually, the Web server is installed by the system administrator who has *super user* privileges. The super user, also known as *root* in Unix systems, has the exclusive privilege to read, modify, delete, or create *any* file or directory on the system. When the super user installs the files of the Web server, the super user becomes the *owner* of the files, which indicates the level of privilege required to access the Web server files. The super user can elect to grant access permissions to selected files in the Web server to members of an established group of users or even to anyone with an account on the system. Having the owner of the server files be the system super user has the advantage of showing the high level of privilege necessary to access or modify the server files; however, file access restrictions must be explicitly configured.

The access control permissions will be set according to the super user's default set of permissions for files and can be changed selectively to meet a specific policy. Because the defaults could grant liberal access privileges to other users on the system, the file access permissions for the server files must be evaluated after the server is installed to ensure that the access privileges correspond to the security policy. This evaluation is an important part of the security testing of the server after it has been installed. The following section discusses how to effectively set file access permissions on Web servers.

In order for the Web server to listen to the standard network port, the Web server must be started by the super user. On Unix systems, Web servers can listen to any one of the 65,536 ports normally available for network services, but ports numbered from 0 to 1023 are reserved for "privileged" network services. For example, the Web server may listen to the standard HTTP port 80 or port 443 for SSL connections. Network services that run on privileged ports can be started only by the super user. If network services were to listen on nonstandard ports, the corresponding network clients must know in advance which port to send requests to. For example, to make a Web request to nonstandard port 8080, the Web request would assume the form of: http://www.nonstandard.org:8080.

One advantage of starting Web servers on nonprivileged ports is that the user who starts the Web server need not be the super user. This feature means that potentially any employee in a company or student in a university can start a Web server on a nonstandard port, which may be good from a democratic perspective, but bad from a security perspective. Allowing employees to arbitrarily run network servers opens the possibility of security breaches through these servers. A carefully configured firewall, however, can prevent rogue network services from opening security holes.

Many authors on Web security have espoused the point of view that Web servers should be started on nonstandard ports to reduce the risk of damage in case of a server compromise. Although this view holds merit, it is important to recognize that other security mechanisms exist in many commerce servers to minimize the executing privilege of the Web server. For example, after starting the commerce server from a super user account, the Netscape Commerce server provides an option to switch ownership of the server processes to a nonprivileged account. This option allows the server to be started by the super user on a privileged port but then switch the privilege of the executing server processes to a nonprivileged user. Bear in mind, though, that this option must be configured in order to be active. Apache and NCSA HTTP servers also support an option to have server processes that handle Web requests to be executed by nonprivileged user accounts.

File Access Permissions

File access permissions specify who can read, write, or execute a file from the operating system's perspective. This is one form of access control that can prevent internal users from gaining access to server configuration files, server documentation files, and confidential client files that exist on the commerce server's file system. The files read by the Web server belong in either the *server root* or the *document root*. The server root consists of the files that are installed with the Web server and used for configuration and administration. The document root consists of the Web pages typically written in HyperText Markup Language (HTML) that are served by the Web server in response to client requests. The security concerns for protecting files in the document root are covered in the section Controlling Access to Sensitive Documents. This section discusses the security concerns in configuring the server root.

The files of importance under the server root are the configuration files, the log files, CGI program sources, CGI program executables, and administrative files and programs. Generally, these files are grouped in their own directories with their own access permissions. The server log files record information from Web page accesses that can be used to build a good profile of Web hits. For instance, it can show who is making requests and from what machines and/or IP addresses, the frequency of hits, and from where the requests were referred. Log files also record any errors that occurred during server operation—a feature that is useful for examining security probes. Web servers also typically record transaction information used to generate billing records. The CGI scripts are the interface software programs that execute based on Web server requests. These programs support the commerce functions of the Web server. The configuration of the Web server can reveal a lot about the security of the server. For this reason, the server root files should be neither visible nor accessible to anyone inside or outside the company, except the system administrator who installs and configures the server.

Users outside the Web server's group should not have read or write permissions to any files in the server root. This rule will specifically exclude internal and external users who have direct access to the operating system through internal accounts from modifying the server configuration files. The access control permissions for files in the server root, while barring other users, should allow the Web server to read its files.

Escalating Client Privilege

Probably the most egregious error in configuring the Web server is to set the execution privilege of the Web server processes, which handle Web requests, to the super user privilege level. Misconfiguring the execution privilege of handling Web requests can result in privilege escalation. Privilege escalation occurs when an untrusted and unauthorized user is able to obtain higher privilege in accessing, creating, modifying or deleting files on the server file system than would normally be permitted. Privilege escalation can easily occur in a Web server that is not securely configured. This section explains why.

System administrators may inadvertently facilitate privilege escalation for several reasons. First, the system administrator will typically install the Web server with super user executing privilege. Executing network servers with super user privilege is necessary so that the super user can listen to privileged network ports. Even though the HTTP server listens with super user privilege to the network port, all requests received by the server are handled by another type of process called a child process. A child process is simply a program started by another program (the parent) to service the request received over the network. Child processes can perform simple functions such as serving up a Web page or more complicated functions by invoking CGI scripts to service Web requests, such as updating a database. Although the HTTP server may run with super user privilege to listen to a privileged port, the child processes that actually handle network requests do not necessarily have to run with high privilege. The mistake that is often made in configuring the network server is that the child processes are given the same super user privilege as the network daemon process.

Why is this dangerous? If a network request, such as a malicious Web page request, can exploit a vulnerability in either a child process or a CGI script, the request can potentially execute commands on the server host machine with super user privilege. This means that a relatively anonymous user on the Internet may have the ability to read files anywhere on the server host and its trusted machines and modify or delete files and directory structures, including possibly the sensitive database information. Programs may be placed and executed on the server by the malicious intruder with the purpose of capturing transactions as they occur and account passwords as they are typed—all possibly without knowledge of the system administration staff.

The appropriate safeguard is to configure the server either to switch its executing privilege to a nonprivileged user or to configure the child processes to execute as nonprivileged users. This way, if a malicious request exploits a software flaw in either the child process or a CGI script, at least the damage done by a renegade child process is restricted to the minimum privilege level of the child process. The privilege level of the child processes is set in the configuration file for the HTTP daemon.

Accept These Options at Your Own Risk

Even if the server execution privilege is set conservatively so that privilege escalation is unlikely, other options in the Web server configuration have security ramifications if misconfigured. These are as follows:

Automatic directory listing. Most servers come configured with automatic directory listing turned on. This means that if a Web browser points to a directory where no index.html file exists, the Web server will by default return the listing of the directory. This is especially dangerous for interface software directories, where CGI program sources and executables reside. If the directories can be listed remotely, the program sources may be downloaded for examination. Any flaws in the programs may be discovered through inspection by a malicious user. The bottom line here is that, if possible, automatic directory listings should be turned off, or alternatively, every directory in the document root should have an index.html file.

Server Side Includes (SSIs). SSIs provide the ability to embed commands in an HTML document (Web page). When the HTML document with the embedded command is requested over the Web, the command executes *on the Web host* with the privilege of the Web server. The exec SSI command is particularly dangerous. Using exec, the following command could be embedded in an HTML Web page document:

```
<!-- #exec cmd="/bin/cat /etc/passwd" -->
```

This command would retrieve the system password file (if not shadowed) on a Unix system to anyone who hit the Web page in which it was embedded. SSIs should be disabled in the server configuration in order to prevent this kind of hazard from occurring in practice.

Symbolic link following. This feature provides a means for extending the document tree in a "covert" manner. Symbolic links allow the creation of a file in one directory that points to a file in another directory. Once created, the referred file can be accessed as if it existed in the directory where the link is created. Unless the full file information is displayed in a directory listing, it is easy to misconstrue the file link as the file itself. Symbolic links extend the document tree to other directories outside the file system originally defined for the Web server. The danger is that a symbolic link may point to a directory where the Web administrator has little knowledge or control over the files (such as CGI scripts) that may be called through Web requests. This option should be disabled.

The guidelines above will help to prevent egregious errors in configuration; however, the configuration of the server ultimately must be set and tested according to a well-defined security policy for each site. Setting the configuration of the server according to a sound security policy is simply the first step in ensuring the security of the server host. See Lincoln Stein's WWW FAQ [1997] for more helpful advice on setting up a secure Web site.

Controlling Access to Sensitive Documents

For most companies putting up Web pages, access to files and documents on the Web server must be restricted by necessity. Some companies may use the Web server as an intranet to serve documents to internal employees. Some merchants may establish accounts with clientele that allow privileged access to certain parts of the Web server while prohibiting access elsewhere. More specifically, business practices will dictate strict security requirements that prevent one client from accessing the records of other (and possibly competing) clients. Web servers use access control mechanisms to prevent unauthorized access through the Web to documents and files. These mechanisms must be configured and tested, however, to be effective. Three types of access control mechanisms are generally available for protecting confidential documents through Web access:

- Client hostname and IP address restrictions
- User and password authentication
- Digital certificates

Though the implementation of these access control mechanisms may vary from server to server, the security issues in using these mechanisms encompass all Web servers. In this section, the strengths and weaknesses of these methods are discussed.

Client Hostname and IP Address Restrictions One of the most basic access control mechanisms is to restrict access to Web pages based on the requesting client's IP address or host name. In other words, the Web server can restrict access to certain Web pages or all Web pages on a site to specific client host names or IP address ranges. A Web request to a document on the server includes the host name of the client and its IP address. The server can use this information to determine if the request is from a site that is authorized to view the Web document. Before engaging in this check, however, many Web servers provide the option to double-check the client's advertised host name against the IP address that is sent with the request.

The Web server can use the Domain Name Service (DNS) to check to see if the host name that was sent agrees with the sent IP address. The DNS is a naming service provided to Internet hosts that associates machine names with IP addresses. Without the DNS, we would have to remember the IP address of every machine to which we send mail, make Web requests, and perform other Internet services such as read news and remotely login. (Imagine, for instance, having to remember people's Social Security numbers instead of their names.) Because Internet services require specific IP addresses in order to route packets, any request to a machine name must be "looked up" by a DNS server to determine the named machine's IP address. A reverse DNS look-up involves sending an IP address to a DNS server and receiving the name of the machine in response. This is similar to looking up a phone number in a phone book and finding the name of the person associated with it.

Sometimes Internet crackers will create a pseudo host name to attempt to fool Internet server machines as to the identity of the machine sending the request. This type of attack is one type of "spoofing" wherein crackers attempt to fool the target host about their true identity. A good security practice is to drop all connection attempts from machines advertising a host name and IP address that do not agree with DNS tables.

To check the authenticity of the host names and IP addresses, the Web server can do two look-ups using the local DNS server. First, the server will look up the host name using the IP address from the Web request. Then, the Web server will look up the IP address using the returned host name. If the IP address returned from this second look-up matches the IP address that was sent with the Web request, the check has passed. This check is called a double-reverse look-up. If the IP address returned by the DNS server does not match the IP address sent with the packet, the connection is dropped. This type of checking is perhaps the simplest form and is not particularly strong. That is, this check can be defeated through some well-known DNS name server attacks. However, it is a simple check to perform, provides additional defense in depth, and is a feature that many Internet network services provide as a means of weeding out problematic requests. It is often the case, too, that reverse look-ups can fail not because of maliciousness, but simply because the requesting party failed to correctly configure its name server files.

Assuming that the Web request passes the double-reverse client look-up, the Web server can check to see if the client is authorized to visit the access-controlled Web page, based on the client's host name or IP address. Access control lists (ACLs) can be created for the Web server to identify the hosts that are allowed to access particular Web pages. Conversely, ACLs can be used to specifically deny particular hosts from accessing Web pages. ACLs can be thought of as sets of rules that are evaluated in sequence for every Web page request. In general, it is a good idea to first deny everyone and then allow specific hosts access in the ACL because errors in allowing specific hosts result in inconvenience rather than security errors. This is shown in Figure 4.2.

The opposite tack is to allow everyone and deny specific hosts. In this case, errors in denying specific hosts (such as an incomplete list) can result in security breaches rather than mere inconvenience. Assuming that the ACL will deny everyone and allow specific hosts, the Web server will attempt to match the host name in a Web page request with the list of host names in the ACL for the requested page.

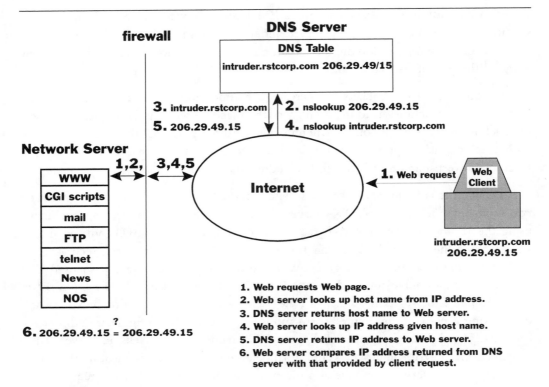

Figure 4.2   Host name and IP address authentication.

Alternatively, the ACL may be set up to check Web requests against IP addresses rather than host names. This method is slightly more secure because it is a little more difficult to spoof an IP address than it is to spoof a host name. If the IP address match is successful, the document is delivered (if no other access control mechanisms are in place); otherwise, a message defined on the server is sent back to the client. This feature can be used to restrict sections of the Web document root to particular sites where access is explicitly permitted. In the case of a general commerce application in which client requests are accepted from anywhere, this feature may not be used. On the other hand, some commerce applications may involve building and maintaining Web pages for a specific client. In this case, it would be wise to restrict access to those pages to the client based on strong authentication using digital certificates.

As mentioned, restricting access based on host names and IP addresses is not considered a strong form of access control. This restriction might keep out the inquisitive surfer, but it will not keep out a determined cracker for very long. The crux of the problem is that the server is implicitly trusting the information sent by the client request in order to make its access decision. Restricting access based on machine host names is not a good idea because host names can be easily spoofed. That is, a remote client can easily send a host name in the Web request that is different from the client's actual host name. Restricting access based on IP addresses rather than host names is a little safer, and it can also increase the reliability of the service, particularly when the DNS look-up fails for host name-based restrictions. However, determined hackers armed with the right tools (available over the Net) can spoof their IP address as well. That is, hackers can make it look as if the request originated from another machine or even domain.

User and Password Authentication User authentication is the process whereby the Web server verifies the identity of a requesting client, usually based on some user identification and password. In order to set up user authentication, the server administrator must first establish a database of legitimate users with their corresponding user IDs and passwords. Users can, of course, be added or deleted from the database. In most Web servers, the database is stored in a simple flat-file format with user IDs and encrypted passwords. The second step to establish user authentication is to determine which resources on the server require protection from unauthorized access. That is, the server administrator must explicitly declare which sections of the file system must be access controlled.

Although Web servers provide the ability to authenticate users before they access sensitive documents, the process of actually setting up the access controls can be difficult and rife with errors. Errors in configuring the access control lists (ACLs) can open security holes to the confidential documents that were intended to be protected. For this reason, the security access mechanisms should always be tested after being configured and before sensitive documents are placed online.

Another aspect of securing an ACL file is the selection of passwords. Many companies that establish Web user accounts with clients will allow the clients to pick a password or pass phrase of their own choice. Inevitably, some clients will pick passwords that are easily guessed, such as their middle name, their pet's name, signs of the zodiac, and English words. If a malicious intruder is able to obtain the password file created by the authentication mechanism, password cracking software can be run on the captured password file to attempt to guess passwords. It takes only a single cracked password to compromise the security of the resource that was protected by the access control.

Even worse, some Web servers do not use an encryption algorithm to scramble the password that is stored on the server. Rather, they use a simple encoding algorithm that is trivially decodable. On appearances, the password is not intelligible, but with standard Unix utilities, the passwords can be decoded without too much difficulty. This form of encoding is not meant to be a strong form of security protection but rather a minimal form of security to discourage relative novices from cracking codes. A stronger form of protection would use an established encryption algorithm such as the Unix crypt algorithm or the Digital Encryption Standard (DES) in its various forms of strength. The first issue with user authentication, then, is the selection and protection of passwords to prevent unauthorized access from easily guessed passwords.

The second security issue in user authentication is to determine if access control should be centralized or distributed. This choice also determines whether the access control lists are statically or dynamically evaluated. Most Web servers provide the option to create a single centralized access control file or a set of access control files that are distributed across the resources to be protected. In a centralized access control scheme, a single configuration file lists all the resources (directories and files) that require access control. This file is statically evaluated once during server initialization. Any changes made to the access control list will require the server to be reinitiated in order for the changes to take effect. In addition to specifying which resources are to be access controlled, the central ACL file must also point to the user password database.

The central ACL file is referred to anytime a client requests a document that has been configured to require authentication. Whenever a password-protected Web page is requested, a user authentication window will pop up in the user's browser client, provided that the client understands the authentication protocol of the Web server. In order to access the requested Web page, the user must enter a valid combination of user ID and password. The user ID is compared with that on the access control list, and the entered password is encoded or encrypted with the same algorithm that was used to create the password in the database file. If the entered user name and password match identically an entry in the specified table, the user is authenticated, and the Web page is delivered to the user's browser. This process is illustrated in Figure 4.3.

One advantage of a centralized password file is that it can be easily maintained by the system administrator. That is, users can be easily added or deleted from the file, and passwords can be checked for strength. The other option is to distribute access control over the resources that are to be protected. Rather than creating a central access control file, the distributed scheme creates an access control file in the directories of the protected

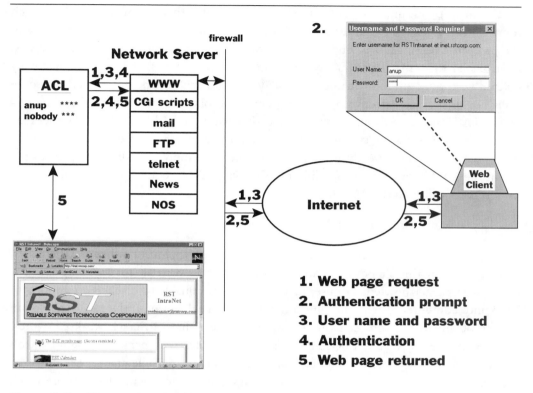

Figure 4.3 User authentication.

resources. The access control file identifies the authorized clients by storing user IDs and their encoded passwords. One advantage of the distributed access control scheme is that it supports access control by local users who do not have the privilege to modify the Web server configuration file. For instance, if users create their own Web pages and wish to restrict access, they can place their own access control file in the directory of the protected resource. Another advantage is that if directories are moved to different file partitions, a central configuration file need not be modified because the access control moves with the protected directory. The most significant advantage of distributed access control, though, is that it is dynamically evaluated. That is, every time access to a protected resource is requested, the corresponding ACL file is reread and reevaluated. This means that changes made on the fly will be implemented immediately rather than require reinitialization of the server.

The main disadvantage of distributed access control is that file maintenance is much more difficult. A system administrator who is responsible for maintaining the security of the protected resources will find it much more difficult to maintain 10 or more access control files than a single file. Also, distributed access control files may be incidentally deleted or moved by local maintainers of Web pages without being noticed for some time. For this reason, effective operating system controls must be established for the distributed ACL files, too. A bug known in an early version of the NCSA HTTP server may even overcome operating system controls. The bug permits a remote client to grab the password database file directly from a Web browser by simply including the path to the file in the URL. For example, sending the following URL request to one of the buggy Web servers will grab the ACL file:

> www.victim.org/confidential/.htaccess

In addition to naming the required users and the access control policy for the confidential directory, this file points to the location of the password file for accessing the protected Web page. Knowledge of user names by itself is valuable to crackers attempting to break into computer systems through authentication mechanisms. If the password file can also be obtained, password-cracking software may be utilized to crack weak passwords. Because the Web server must be able to read the ACL files, the operating system controls cannot prevent this particular bug from providing a knowledgeable cracker access to the ACL file. The best policy for these types of bugs is either to obtain the software patch from the software vendor or obtain the next release version of the software after ensuring that the bug has been removed.

It is important to use the security controls that provide a level of protection commensurate with the value of the assets to be protected. The basic user authentication mechanisms described in this section, even in combination with IP address restrictions, can still leave a corporate site's sensitive documents vulnerable to a determined attack. The basic user authentication mechanisms do not encrypt user IDs and passwords as they are sent over the wire. That is, when clients authenticate themselves to the Web server, the user ID and password are effectively sent in the clear on the Internet. This means that anyone sniffing the line between the end user's LAN and the Web server's LAN can potentially capture the user ID and password. Once they are captured, the spy will be able to access sensitive documents as long as the IP address restrictions, if any, are met.

Combining IP address restriction and user authentication serves as a good deterrent to the casual hacker; however, most hackers that can capture user IDs and passwords over the Internet can also learn how to spoof IP addresses to breach both types of basic access control mechanisms. To make matters worse, many Web servers do not require users to reauthenticate themselves during the same terminal session every time another Web page in the same authentication realm is requested. An authentication realm is the region of the Web server file system that is protected by an ACL. It may consist of a single Web page or the whole Web site. Reauthenticating every time a Web page is requested on a Web site is a major hassle for end users, so many Web servers will provide the user with a "cookie" that in this case can be used as an admission ticket back to the site. Receiving a cookie is similar to getting a stamp on your hand when you leave an amusement park midday. The cookie verifies the user's admission to the authentication realm for a certain time period that can be configured, much as the stamp lets you back into the park throughout the day.

The cookie certainly provides a convenience for the client, but it also makes the job of Internet sniffers much easier. In standard authentication sessions, the cookie is not encrypted. This means that every Web page access during a session to an authentication realm is an opportunity for malicious snoops to capture the cookie. Once it is captured, snoops can use the cookie to access the Web pages for themselves and then possibly change the password. Some Web servers provide the ability to combine the IP address of the client with the cookie to require that the cookie be presented from a specific IP address. The server would then authenticate not only the user ID and password, but also the IP address from where the request is made. This practice might thwart the cookie thief, unless the thief spoofs the IP address as well. If these security issues are a real threat or the assets to be protected warrant defenses against these types of attacks, a secure channel, such as SSL, should be used to protect the Web session.

Clearly, many forms of defenses exist, and corresponding attacks can subvert the defenses. This kind of cat-and-mouse game will continue as long as people continue to use the Net or until some magical solution for securing the Net is found. The key, however, is not that a magic bullet is necessary to eliminate problems in security, but rather that the defense mechanisms employed should effectively manage the risks of putting sensitive documents on the Net. The take-home message is that the level of defense mechanisms employed to protect sensitive documents should be commensurate with the sensitivity of the protected documents. This decision must be made *before* documents are placed on the Web and codified in a security policy that is tested early and tested often.

Strong Authentication Using Digital Certificates The techniques presented up to this point for protecting sensitive documents on Web servers from unauthorized eyes can be considered basic forms of access control. The two techniques restrict access to documents based on the machine host or based on a user name and password. These techniques can also be combined to provide a higher level of secure access than using either mechanism by itself. These methods, while useful in discouraging the casual hacker, can be ineffective against a determined and knowledgeable Internet cracker. Spoofing IP addresses is a well-known technique in the underground Internet community; the basic password authentication method suffers from the weakness that user names and passwords are sent in the clear over the Net. To provide higher levels of secure access, strong forms of authentication exist that use signed digital certificates and symmetric encryption that can verify *both* parties to a Web session as well as provide a secure Web session.

The Secure Sockets Layer (SSL) protocol can be configured to authenticate the Web server or to authenticate both the server and the client. The latter option is now available in SSL version 3.0, but it was not supported in SSL version 2.0 and prior versions. Currently, this feature is not widely implemented, but as more Internet users obtain digital certificates, its use may grow to be more widespread.

Authentication in SSL is performed as part of the handshaking protocol. Authentication of the Web server is described in detail in Chapter 3 and is briefly summarized here. Following this summary, authentication of the Web client using digital certificates is developed. Authentication of end users using digital certificates is a stronger form of authentication than the basic authentication mechanisms that were described earlier. The signed digital certificates verify the identity of Web clients before they are granted access to sensitive documents.

Authenticating Web servers using SSL begins when a request is sent to the server's secure Web protocol port. The server responds by sending back a signed digital certificate. The digital certificate contains the server identity information as well as the Web site's public key. The certificate must be digitally signed by a third party, the certification authority (CA), that both the Web client and the Web server trust. If the client's browser accepts the signed certificate, the client's browser is accepting a third party's nod that the server is truly who the server says it is. It is the responsibility of the server to register with a CA, and it is the role of the CA to verify the identity of the server. The client also must agree to trust the certification authority. This trust is performed implicitly in many client browsers. For example, Netscape's Navigator Web browser embeds several CAs' public keys in its browsers that it distributes. Once the signed certificate is accepted by the Web client, the client generates a session key that is encrypted using the server's public key. The session key is used for a symmetric encryption session between the Web client and the Web server.

If the Web server wishes to authenticate the client, the server can use either basic password authentication or signed digital certificates. The problem with basic password authentication is that user names and passwords are sent over the Net in the clear. This means that the user names and passwords can be captured by intermediaries between the Web browser and the Web server, then subsequently used to gain unauthorized access. In contrast, performing the same type of password authentication over a secure Web session such as that provided by SSL is secure from this type of attack. Even if the user name and password were to be intercepted during transmission, they would be totally unintelligible because SSL encrypts the contents of all data sent in a session.

The procedure for authenticating the Web clients using SSL is similar to the procedure used to authenticate Web servers. In fact, the same protocol for authenticating the Web server and generating the private session key as summarized above and detailed in Chapter 3 is performed first. To confirm that a secure session has been negotiated, the Web server returns an initial client challenge phrase encrypted with the private session key negotiated by both parties to the Web session. If the client decrypts the encrypted challenge phrase and finds that it is the original challenge phase that the client sent, the client will know that the session has been secured. The procedure for client authentication begins when the server requests that the client present a signed digital certificate. The server will send its own challenge phrase encrypted with the private session key to begin the client authentication. This challenge phrase will be used subsequently to confirm that client authentication has been successfully performed.

For the user to participate in strong client authentication, the user will have had to have obtained a priori a digital certificate signed by a trusted certification authority. If the client does not have its own digital certificate, the client will respond to the server's challenge with an error message. If the client can respond, the client software will first prompt the user for a secret pass phrase. If it is correct, the client will respond to the server. First, the server challenge phrase and the server's digital certificate are digitally hashed. This digital hash is signed through the client's private key. The client software will then send the signed digital hash together with the client's digital certificate to the server, using the channel secured by the private session key.

The server will now be able to positively verify the identity of the client from the response message. First, the server will check the client's digital certificate by checking the signature of the certification authority against its list of trusted CAs. If this check works, the server can accept the public key of the client into its database of public keys. This check by itself, however, does not prove that the owner named in the digital certificate actually sent the digital certificate. To verify the identity of the Web client sending the certificate, the server first checks the signed digital hash sent by the Web client using the public key for the Web client that was received and verified in the preceding step. If the digital signature on the digital hash agrees with the public key of the Web client, the Web server will have positive identification that the person named on the digital certificate also signed the digital hash. The server will also create its own hash of the digital certificate and the challenge phrase using the same hashing algorithm as the client. The digital hashes will be compared to verify that the challenge phrase and digital certificate sent by the Web server are properly received.

The final step of the client authentication is completed when the Web server sends a unique session identifier to the client encrypted using the private session key. Use of the session identifier is similar to the way the cookies were used for basic authentication. This session identifier can be used to grant access to any of the Web pages within the authentication realm of the authenticated session. This step will eliminate the necessity for the client authentication process for every subsequent Web page access within the authentication realm during the current Web session. Unlike cookies used in basic authentication, the unique session identifier is encrypted using the private session key and thus immune to sniffing attacks.

In summary, strong client authentication provides the ability to combine signed digital certificates and symmetric encryption in a secure channel to positively identify end users accessing a Web site. This strong form of authentication can be used to transparently grant access to confidential pages by using the digital certificate presented by the end user's software client. Strong client authentication does not suffer from the weaknesses of IP spoofing in host-based authentication or from captured passwords or password files that may compromise basic password authentication. When employed in an SSL session, the mutual authentication of client and Web server provides positive identification of each party via a trusted third party to each other party to a transaction.

One of the problems with this approach is the requirement that individual end users obtain digital certificates from a certification authority. In some cases, these certificates may be free for a low level of identity-verification by a CA. In other cases, an annual fee is associated with the certificates. The larger hurdle is just getting consumers to go through the process of obtaining a digital certificate. As more and more people use the secure mail and secure Web access features of Netscape Communicator 4.0 and Microsoft Internet Explorer 4.0, personal digital certificates will become more commonplace, overcoming this barrier.

Dangerous CGI Scripts

CGI scripts provide the interactive nature of Web pages and give rise to commercial functions. The dangers that CGI scripts introduce are particularly relevant to e-commerce. CGI scripts provide an essential role for facilitating the business of commerce. In fact, as the Web assumes a greater role in the daily business functions of companies, more and more programs that execute on the commerce server will be developed and commercialized. As the needs of businesses grow, the complexity of these programs will grow accordingly.

One of the most pressing concerns in securing the commerce server is the potential for CGI scripts to act maliciously on behalf of remote Web client requests. The fact that CGI scripts execute on the server based on input from untrusted Web clients is enough to make most security experts queasy at the notion of allowing CGI scripts to exist on a server. The problem is made worse when enterprise-critical applications reside on the server. The enterprise-critical applications usually include transaction software, mail, bulletin boards or news, and the database of commercial transactions and users. The risks that CGI scripts pose to the server include the ability for remote Web clients to execute system commands that may do the following:

- Read, replace, modify, or remove files
- Mail files back over the Internet
- Execute programs downloaded on the server such as a password sniffer or a network daemon that will provide unauthorized telnet access to the server
- Launch a denial-of-service attack by overloading the server CPU with a computation-intensive task such as exhaustive file system searches

The growth of both Internet and intranet Web applications means that it is no longer feasible to bar CGI scripts and other programs from executing on the Web server. Many security professionals in the field have felt that the dangers of using CGI scripts should preclude their use in enterprise-critical applications. This option, of course, is not feasible for e-commerce.

Mitigating the Dangers of CGI Scripts

Several steps can be taken to reduce the dangers inherent in executing Web applications on the server. The steps range from properly configuring the server to performing rigorous analysis. Deciding which steps to take will depend on both the security requirements of the merchant and a cost/benefit trade-off analysis that must weigh the cost of ensuring security against the potential loss of assets due to security violations. In banking and finance, the potential for monetary losses can be staggering, and the level of security required for online applications will be very high.

This section describes ways to reduce the hazards of executing CGI scripts on the server. Taking these simple precautions can eliminate a large portion of the configuration problems that often provide access to intruders. Even with a commerce server properly configured, programming errors in CGI scripts can introduce vulnerabilities in the security of the whole system. The best policy to eradicating these vulnerabilities is to develop CGI programs with prudent security practices in the first place. This approach is taken up later in this chapter in the Designing More Secure Software section. Regardless of whether CGI scripts and other Web applications were developed with security in mind, these programs should be analyzed to determine if they contain errors that may result in security intrusions. Another good reference for analyzing and writing secure CGI scripts is Rubin, Geer, and Ranum [1997].

As with vulnerabilities described previously in this chapter, the most common vulnerabilities that exist on the server as well as the simplest to fix are related to the configuration of the server files. Simple errors in configuration can result in handing over excessive privileges to an untrusted user. First and foremost, the executing privilege of the server must be minimized to a nonprivileged user. The executing privilege of the server is of paramount importance to CGI security because CGI scripts are executed by the Web server with all the privileges of the Web server. If the Web server executes under super user privilege, a vulnerable CGI script can inflict severe damage on the corporate systems of the online merchant. The execution privilege of the server is set as a configuration parameter in the configuration files installed with the Web server.

Another step that can be taken to minimize the dangers of CGI scripts is to configure the directories from which CGI programs can execute. Some servers will execute any program ending with .cgi or .pl from anywhere under the server root. This is dangerous because stray or malicious CGI scripts can be placed anywhere under the myriad directories that exist under the server root. CGI scripts that have not been analyzed for security should be considered potentially dangerous to the security of the server. If the server is configured to execute CGI scripts from anywhere on the local system, employees can maliciously place dangerous CGI scripts in locations where the system administrator may not consider looking. Take the case in which local users are allowed to create their own Web pages in their own working directories. With the server configured to support individual Web pages in users' own directories, the commerce server is effectively extended outside the scope defined in the global configuration file. Care must be taken to prevent CGI programs from executing from within the extended server/document roots. Probably the simplest, most effective way to prevent this kind of danger is to restrict the directories from which CGI scripts can execute. Preferably, a single directory under the server root should be established from which only approved CGI scripts can execute. This directory is typically called the cgi-bin and is used to store the CGI binary executables. It will also typically store *shell scripts* such as Perl scripts, which are often used in developing CGI scripts. The server can be configured so that when any script or program in this directory is requested in a Web request, the program will execute rather than have the source downloaded.

Another directory to be aware of is the cgi-src, which may hold the software source code for many of the CGI scripts. The cgi-src directory should be guarded from unauthorized access to prevent vulnerabilities in CGI script sources from being exposed to internal users and untrusted Web clients. Back-up files of CGI scripts and sources created by text editors should also be removed from the cgi-bin and the cgi-src directories. The back-up file names usually follow a known convention such as adding a tilde character (~) to the end of a file name. Back-up files should be removed because, first, they are no longer necessary once development and testing of the CGI script is finished, and second, the file access permissions of back-up files are not usually monitored as the program's primary source. Carelessness in setting the file access modes may result in the back-up file sources being accessible to internal employees or to untrusted Web clients. With the back-up source code in hand, analyzing the vulnerabilities of the primary program may not be a far stretch.

Once the cgi-bin and source directories are established and securely configured with appropriate access control mechanisms, the origin, purpose, and any modifications of every single CGI script must be accounted for. If the CGI script does not serve a purpose for the business needs of the commerce server, it should be removed. A cause of frequent security intrusions is carelessness in leaving CGI scripts that came out of the box with the server distribution and that serve no other purpose except to demonstrate CGI utilities. These programs exist on many servers because they are installed with the server. Flaws in several of these programs that are widely distributed have resulted in security intrusions through the Web server. These programs often serve no useful business purpose for the Web site, so they should be removed to protect against vulnerabilities that are widely distributed.

After a stable set of CGI programs has been established for the CGI bin and source directories, a digital hash, such as MD5, should be made of the directories. This hash will serve as a reference for a stable version of the server. Periodically, the CGI directories (in addition to other executable program directories) should be rehashed to determine if the contents have been modified. In a comparison of the periodic hashes with the initial stable hash, any changes such as modifications, additions, or deletions of CGI executables will be detected. Publicly available programs such as Tripwire (ftp://coast.cs.purdue.edu/pub/COAST/Tripwire) support digital hashes for this purpose.

Malicious intent aside, even casual carelessness can result in the execution of CGI scripts that were not intended to be placed on the server. For example, older versions of an installed httpd server that have not been removed from the server host machine may have cgi-bin directories that contain a number of outdated CGI scripts. Failure to either remove the old cgi-bin directory or update the CGI programs may result in old vulnerabilities resurfacing. This error has actually been the source of a number of security problems in Web servers in sites throughout the Web. In the now infamous case of a serious Web server vulnerability, an error in a C function distributed with the NCSA/Apache server (Version 1.4 and prior) opened up a gaping security hole in the Web servers of many sites that use this server. The C function, escape_shell_command ( ), was designed to remove potentially malicious nonalphanumeric characters from the inputs sent Web servers from untrusted clients. This function was used not only by the Web server itself, but also by a CGI program called phf, which was compiled and distributed with the Web server in the cgi-bin directory. Unfortunately, the escape_shell_command ( ) function failed to remove one of the special characters that, if used in combination with system commands by the phf program, can potentially result in an untrusted client executing arbitrary system commands on the server.

News of this vulnerability spread quickly through the underground hacker community before reaching the system administrators of the NCSA/Apache Web servers. A number of incident response alerts and a software *patch* were released to fix this vulnerability in the installed versions of the vulnerable server. In addition, the next release version of the server fixed this vulnerability. However, as is often the case in system administration, software patches are not applied and software is not upgraded if it appears to be working fine as it is. This "don't fix it if it ain't broke" philosophy is pervasive throughout the system administration community. It has made securing systems particularly difficult because even when vulnerabilities are discovered and patches are disseminated, they are often not implemented in the installed software, leaving these systems vulnerable to attack. Crackers know this and take advantage of this situation to attempt simple probes on systems to see whether well-known vulnerabilities have been fixed. Unless regular audits of the system are conducted, it may be difficult for a system administrator to know whether the system is being violated through a vulnerability like that described here.

To make matters worse, some of the sites that did patch the vulnerability in the C function or upgrade to version 1.5 failed to remove or update the compiled version of the old phf program. This meant that even though the software source code had been patched, remote Web clients could still take advantage of the vulnerability of the old version by accessing the phf program—even if this was not being used for the business of the Web site. This example illustrates how careless errors can leave the gate open to malicious Web users who exploit CGI vulnerabilities. This problem has become so well known that warnings have been posted to numerous news groups and mailings to check system logs for attempted accesses to this program. Drop-in replacements for the phf program exist that notify a site's administrator when this program is being accessed via Web clients.

A potentially dangerous error is to include shell interpreters in the cgi–bin directory. Shell interpreters are programs that execute instructions from a shell script on the host machine. A shell script is simply a file (or program) with instructions written in the language that the shell interpreter understands. One primary difference between a shell interpreter and a language compiler is that interpreters allow interactive execution of instructions. Instructions entered from either a shell prompt or a shell script are executed immediately as they are read by the interpreter. In contrast, a language compiler, such as C, reads a program file in its entirety and compiles the program into a lower-level representation called a binary executable. Once the binary executable is created, it can be directly executed by the processor. Shell interpreters are often used in the development of CGI scripts because they allow rapid program development in a high-level scripting language such as Perl, Tcl, or Python. As an instruction is written, it can be executed immediately to provide constant feedback and debugging.

In contrast, programming languages like C require entire functions or modules to be written and compiled before any testing can begin. Many of the shell scripting languages also make programming tasks such as searching on regular expressions, executing system commands, accessing input/output functions, and creating graphical interfaces easier than programming in a compiled language.

Two trade-offs, however, are inherent in programming in an interpreted language. First, the performance of executing an interpreted program is much worse than that of executing a compiled program. For large-scale applications, this performance hit will preclude using interpreted languages for development. Second, a security trade-off exists. The very same features that make programming in an interpreted language easier make interpreted programs, or shell scripts, much less secure. For example, Perl makes it exceedingly simple to use an untrusted Web request as an argument to system call. In C, on the other hand, functions are written to parse the Web request, to build the argument, and then to execute the system call. It is this level of difficulty in building potentially dangerous system calls in C and the ease with which it can be performed in Perl that makes shell scripting in interpreted languages dangerous from a security perspective.

CGI scripts prove to be dangerous when a system call can be executed from a Web request or if the Web request can result in the creation of a Unix shell. In order to exploit these types of vulnerabilities, the wily hacker must first know about the existence of system calls from within the shell script and then must figure out how to exploit flaws in the instructions that make the calls. If flaws in the instructions do exist, it may be possible to leverage the flaws to execute commands of the cracker's choice on the server. This process is of course simplified when CGI script sources are distributed with the server software, as with the phf problem previously described.

Early documentation in Netscape and other servers recommended placing the interpreters—including the Perl shell interpreter—in the cgi-bin directory to ensure that the CGI scripts that require the shell interpreters can find them. If the shell interpreters were installed in an obscure directory on the file system, the CGI scripts may not be able to find the interpreter when called, which would result in a failure to execute the CGI script. However, rather than suggesting that the script be changed to reflect a different location, the documentation proposed that a simpler solution would be to move the interpreters to the cgi-bin directory where they would be easily found by the scripts.

Unfortunately, placing the shell interpreters in the cgi-bin is an incredibly dangerous practice. Executing a system command is as easy as executing the shell interpreter from the Web request with any system command that is desired. When shell interpreters are included in the cgi-bin, the challenge for crackers to execute arbitrary commands on the server becomes a "no-brainer." The interpreter can be accessed directly from the Web, and arbitrary commands can be executed on the server in response to untrusted Web client requests. Interpreters take commands and execute them immediately, so no compilation is required on the part of the untrusted Web client, making the job that much easier. What can a cracker do with a shell interpreter? Basically, anything the server can do. So, if the server is executing with super user privilege, the cracker will become the super user. Even executing as a nonprivileged user, a cracker can frequently grab the system password file, which can usually be cracked easily. Once a cracker does the damage, the cracker can alter the log files using commands through the shell interpreter to cover the cracker's tracks.

Database Vulnerabilities

The third broad component of the commerce server is the back-end database. Databases are essential for most Web commerce-related applications and are often used for authenticating users before granting access permissions to Web pages. Databases are also used to store commercial transactions or even to query the server for the status of a transaction. In financial applications, databases maintain account information that must be updated when transactions occur, and they also must provide information securely to account queries. The most sensitive data for commercial Web sites will usually reside in databases that exist behind the corporate firewall. Clearly, the database hold the jewels in the Web site's vault. For this reason, access to the database must be carefully controlled.

Fortunately, the people who design Web servers and the people who design databases are getting together to provide secure mechanisms for accessing databases through Web requests. The simplest databases provided with Web servers store user names and associated passwords for client authentication in a flat-file format. Creating a flat-file database format simply involves creating a file with entries corresponding to the desired database fields. Most Web servers provide a program that allows users to be added to the database. The passwords are usually encrypted with a simple encryption algorithm; some even use simple encoding algorithms. Although simple to create and use, flat-file databases don't scale up well to a large number of users. The performance in accessing the database decreases markedly as the number of users grows.

To partially combat this problem, many Web servers now offer a fast flat-file format called DBM for storing and retrieving entries from a client authentication database. The DBM format can search arbitrarily large databases with one file system read. The entries in the database are hashed for maximum look-up efficiency. This hash will make the entries unintelligible to the casual glance, but don't be fooled into believing that the entries are encrypted. If unauthorized access to the file is obtained, the entries can be easily decoded without a secret key. Password entries are usually encrypted before being encoded in the DBM format. Even though the fast flat-file format overcomes some of the performance problems, flat-file formats are not suitable for many commercial database application requirements. Flat-file database formats serve the function of basic user authentication well, but they lack the power to perform advanced query, storage, and processing operations on the database.

To address this need, many of the larger sophisticated database vendors have developed database software specifically for Web applications. These databases can be classified as relational, object oriented, or a hybrid mix of the two. The power provided by relational and object-oriented databases is the ability to write database programs to perform sophisticated processing functions on the data stored within the database. Commercial applications in the financial industries use databases to keep a record of transactions and account activity. In wholesale and retail manufacturing, distribution, and sales, online databases maintain inventory and are now being used to provide just-in-time (JIT) service to store outlets. These commercial applications require large-scale databases capable of performing real-time transactions as well as batch processing according to the business needs of the application.

The database vendors have recognized the importance of integrating their database packages in an online Web-based environment. As a result, many of the commercial Web server vendors have developed interfaces for directly accessing the databases through Web requests. Leveraging the power of databases has made Web-based enterprises such as corporate intranets an efficient means for back-office automation. Although the benefits of placing corporate databases online are persuasive, the security issues are cause for prudence.

To provide security assurance for online commercial databases, some of the leading database package vendors have provided secure mechanisms for storing and retrieving data from the databases. Security-assurance techniques that can be employed range from simple access controls for a database to encryption channels from the Web server to the database as well as encrypted storage of data in the database. If properly employed, these mechanisms can provide a strong level of security assurance. On the other hand, rarely will the security mechanisms be configured out of the box ready to provide high levels of security. Most software packages are configured by default for maximum functionality and minimal security. The so-called "deadly defaults" are deliberately configured in this manner so that the system administrator can get the software up and running as quickly as possible without having to worry about nonfunctional requirements such as security during installation.

One of the fundamental security controls that must be configured is access control, which prevents unauthorized access to the database. Without access control mechanisms in place, anyone on the inside and potentially outside may be able to access, modify, or delete the sensitive data stored in the database. For this reason, most commercial databases offer access control lists and passwords to access different portions of the database. In fact, different access control policies may be enforced for modification or creation of data than for retrieval of data. For example, the database administrator (DBA) may be given access to read or write entries to a database while all other authorized users are given permission to query only the database. Different portions of the database, called table spaces, may also have different access control policies. For example, an accounting group may have a table space created separately from an engineering group's table space. The security policy for the company may dictate access controls on the accounting table space such that members of the engineering group cannot read or write to the table space. On the other hand, the accounting group may be permitted to query but not write to an engineering table space consisting of hours billed to specific contracts.

Depending on the origin of an attempt to access the database, different access control mechanisms may be employed. Access control mechanisms may differ if access is attempted via the Web server than if it is attempted via database programs. Usually the former type of access is received from unknown and untrusted Web clients; the latter type is attempted by internal users who have been granted password-protected access. Defense-in-depth strategies can be employed to control access to the database. Even if an intruder is able to bypass the external access controls and gain access to the internal machines, the database access controls should thwart attempts to gain access to the database.

Consider the case of directly accessing the database from an internal machine. If someone attempts access by directly querying the database using the database software or database application programs, access controls for the table spaces should prevent unauthorized access. To implement the access controls, an authentication file or another table space within the database may be created with user names and encrypted passwords. Users can also be grouped and granted access privilege by group permissions. The important point to remember about password access is that weak passwords may compromise the security of the database. If the user authentication database can be obtained by an unauthorized user (anyone outside the DBA), password-cracking software can be run against the database to attempt to guess weak passwords. For this reason, it is important to ensure that access to the password database file is properly restricted. One can restrict access to the user authentication database by employing appropriate access controls at the operating system layer. This type of layered approach is another example of defense in depth.

Next, consider access to the database attempted through a Web interface. Before being granted access to the database, Web users must authenticate themselves. This process is very similar to access control to Web pages. The Web server can provide authentication of clients before sending a database query to the interface software. The same issues of client authentication by IP address, by user names and passwords, or by digital certificates are pertinent here as visited earlier in the discussion on the Web server. The advantage of using digital certificates is that authorized end users can seamlessly gain access to protected databases with strong authentication and nonrepudiation properties being enforced. Once client requests have been authenticated, the Web server will forward the database query to an interface program, typically a CGI script. Most database software packages will either define the interface to the databases or provide scripts for querying the database. In order to gain access to the queried portion of the database, however, the interface program must have knowledge of the user ID and password.

The alternative is to not provide access control to the database from local processes. This alternative would not be prudent, however. The defense in depth provided by access controls at the database can both prevent unauthorized internal users from accessing sensitive data in the database and thwart an intruder who has gained internal access. Although providing access control to the database from external Web requests as well as internal queries is good, knowledge of a valid user ID and password must also be embedded in the interface programs that handle the external Web requests.

The interface programs will contain the important internal access information, so the programs themselves must be closely guarded. The steps described earlier for CGI scripts will be extremely important to implement in order to protect this information. The danger is that if a script source can be captured by either local or remote Web requests, the user ID and password information to access the database may be discerned. For this reason, it is important that appropriate operating system access controls be implemented for the CGI sources to prevent anyone outside the system, Web, or database administration from accessing the CGI script sources. Furthermore, the Web server should be configured such that CGI scripts can only be executed rather than downloaded. Finally, access to execute the CGI scripts should require the authentication procedure enforced by the Web server.

The last point regarding database vulnerabilities is that even when data is encrypted and sent over a secure link to a database, the data is eventually processed by an application program or a CGI program. If the data is encrypted, the application program must decrypt it to perform the required operations. Programs will often create temporary files when manipulating files that contain sensitive data. If possible, sensitive data should never be stored in temporary files. However, if temporary files are created on the host machine, these files should be wiped as soon as the file has served its purpose. Temporary files created by application programs have been a source of security vulnerabilities in the past. They are especially dangerous because most /tmp directories have extremely liberal access permissions that make it possible for any user (such as a nonprivileged Web server) to access the temporary directories and inspect their contents.

Designing More Secure Software

The previous three sections on the Web server, CGI scripts, and databases have shown how simple errors in configuration can make security intrusions possible. Configuring the commerce server according to a sound security policy can go a long way toward improving the security of the whole system. However, even the most carefully configured site can be vulnerable to the dangers of server-side execution of Web applications. The reason server-side execution is so dangerous is that CGI scripts have the ability to perform any action on the host machine or trusted host network that is granted to the Web server. Unlike Java, which imposes a security "sandbox" around what a Java applet can do on a client machine, most of the programming languages in which server-side programs are written do not prevent server-side programs from executing dangerous actions. So, if a server-side program is programmed to remove all the files on the disk, it will. If it is programmed to mail confidential documents back to a remote client on the Internet, it will. For this reason, configuration of the server is generally not enough to ensure secure behavior on the part of server-side programs such as CGI scripts.

Two types of techniques can be used to prevent the dangers of server-side programs from breaching the security and confidentiality requirements for a Web site. First, server-side programs should be designed and implemented with techniques for minimizing the types of problems that can attributed to security breaches. Second, analytical methods can be applied to detect the existence of either dangerous structures or dangerous behavior in a program. This section presents some of the flaws in software coding that are found in many Internet applications and that are often exploited in breaking into sites or in initiating denial of service attacks. Wherever possible, heuristics for designing secure programs should be used by developers to prevent security problems from ever surfacing in security-critical applications. It is a lot easier to prevent a security problem than it is to detect one. Both the Rubin, Geer, and Ranum [1997] and the Garfinkel and Spafford [1997] books offer tips for writing more secure server-side programs.

Several barriers currently exist to secure program design. First, most developers do not consider the security implications of the programs they are writing. In their defense, commercial software developers are typically under tremendous amount of pressure to develop software under incredibly tight schedules. Whereas commercial software release cycles were 18 months or longer at large software companies in the early to mid 1990s, they are now being squeezed to 6 months or less. This kind of rapid deployment cycle, although undoubtedly good for the quarterly earnings report, can have adverse effects on the quality of the software. The burden of software testing is increasingly being placed on the consumer. Many software companies are putting off software testing to users of the *beta versions* of the software. These preproduction versions are typically loaned to individuals and organizations who agree to provide bug reports in return for free use of the software. This form of testing is better than no testing at all, but it is insufficient for producing quality software. Perhaps because the public at large has become so accustomed to software bugs, it has become acceptable to release buggy software to consumers. This practice will undoubtedly change as software development matures and as consumers stop tolerating software failures. Consumers should not endure crashing application programs any more than they put up with a TV that shuts down periodically. As TVs and other electronic appliances execute more and more software embedded in the electronics, the preceding statement will weigh heavily on the developers of the embedded software.

Aside from tight software development cycles, software is not developed with security in mind because many people (software developers included) believe security is a problem solely for security analysts and system administrators. This attitude could not be further from the truth. Security analysts and system administrators are usually at the tail end of the problem trying to diagnose where security problems lurk and how they can be fixed. In reality, security problems originate from flaws in software design and configuration management. These flaws are leveraged by users of the software by malicious intention or by accident into providing a level of access and privilege that would not otherwise be granted by the program. Defining what is a flaw and what is a feature can be tricky for software. It is often the case that nifty features deliberately put in the software are exploited in ways that the software developer did not anticipate.

Even if software developers realize the security implications of the software, rarely are software developers trained either on the job or in university programs in how to write code that is secure as well as functional. The idea of designing programs to be secure against malicious attack is only recently gaining awareness, particularly among vendors of operating systems and their related utilities. Some design heuristics are quite intuitive. For example, programs should execute with the absolute minimum privilege necessary to accomplish the task. Under no circumstances should a program run with super user privileges unless absolutely necessary. Programs that execute with root privilege do so by setting the user ID (abbreviated by SUID) of the program to root. The SUID root programs are frequently the target of hacks because of the potential for severe server damage if the programs are compromised.

Programmers must be especially vigilant in handling input data. Most attacks against software are launched through malicious commands embedded in the input that the program is reading. Inputs to programs are read through a variety of methods, including forms on a Web page and data appended to the http request sent to a Web site. Inputs are often sent implicitly to a program through *environment variables* set by shells, browsers, and other programs. Inputs can be read as arguments to commands, from keyboard input, from files, from outputs of other programs, and through graphical interfaces. No matter what the entry point for an input to a program is, it must be handled carefully. Many security violations occur when the input sent by the perpetrator was unanticipated by the program developer.

Inputs must be carefully checked for special characters, sometimes called meta characters, which allow execution of system commands by some interpreters. Inputs should be checked to ensure that they are well formed. For example, if the birth date of a field in a Web form should not exceed six characters, the program interpreting the birth data should ensure that it does not exceed six characters. It is not enough to simply limit the size of the field on the form because this data can either be entered directly in the URL field of the browser or posted to the server by a custom-written program that does not abide by form field limits. Similarly, if the number of arguments read should be exactly 10, make sure that exactly 10 arguments are received. If each of the arguments read can be bounded within some range, the interpreting program should make sure that the argument falls within the acceptable bounds. The length of the input as well as the range should always be checked and limited before it is read into a program *buffer*. A buffer is simply a contiguous portion of memory that stores data used by a program. A buffer is overflowed when more data is read into it than space is allocated for the buffer in memory.

Buffer Overflows

Buffer overflows are favorite targets of hackers. When input is read into a buffer and the length of the input is not limited to the length of the buffer allocated in memory, it is possible to overflow the buffer. Overflowing the buffer results in overwriting memory that is not assigned to the buffer. The consequences of overflowing a buffer can range from no discernible effect to an abortion of the program execution to execution of instructions contained in the input. If no adverse effects result from an overflowed input buffer, it can be said that the program is tolerant or robust to this type of attack. It may be difficult to verify this through standard testing, though, because programs will behave differently for different input streams. If the program is designed to protect buffers from unconstrained inputs, formal analysis methods may be able to prove the tolerance of the program to all unconstrained inputs. Even for programs that are tolerant to unconstrained input attacks, these types of attacks should be logged and monitored, particularly for network daemons such as a Web server. This practice provides a means for monitoring and repelling potential attacks against an online commerce site.

In the second case of overflowing buffers, it may be possible to crash a program during execution. As an example, consider the Ping O' Death denial-of-service attack (www.sophist.demon.co.uk/ping/index.html). This attack exploits the ping network client that is commonly used to determine if a remote host is "alive." The ping client uses two instances of the Internet Control Message Protocol (ICMP), ECHO_REQUEST and ECHO_RESPONSE, to determine if hosts on the Internet are reachable. ICMP is a protocol used during standard TCP/IP sessions for sending error and control messages encapsulated in IP datagrams. An IP datagram can hold up to 65,535 bytes of information that includes 20 bytes of header information. The ICMP ECHO_REQUEST uses an additional 8 bytes of header information in the IP packet. Subtracting the header information, a ping request has 65,507 bytes of space in an IP packet with which it can fill other data. However, because the ECHO_REQUEST is embedded in the 28 bytes of header information, no additional data is necessary to find out if a network server is alive.

Fortunately or not, the underlying layers of the Internet can handle information packets with more than 65,535 bytes of information. Large data sets are fragmented into the maximum IP packet sizes, then reassembled at the server. Using the ping program, it is possible to send more than the maximum IP packet size (65,535 bytes) and be assured that they will be reassembled at the server. Because 65,507 bytes of data are available in a ping IP packet, sending more than this amount of data will cause packet fragmenting and reassembling at the server. On Windows machines, this can be performed by the command:

```
ping -l 65510 machine.ip.address
```

The problem that occurs in some operating systems is that when the bytes are reassembled at the network server, they can overflow internal 16-bit variables in the operating system kernel. Executing the command above will cause some operating systems to choke on the data and crash. Do not perform this test on other people's machines because it is considered a denial-of-service attack [CERT-96:26, 1996].

Having the ability to abort or crash a program during execution by sending an unconstrained input can cause serious availability problems for the program. This problem can be unacceptable in the enterprise-critical application of e-commerce in which failure to provide service results in direct loss of business and potentially negative publicity in the media.

The third case of overflowing buffers can result in the most serious security problems for a site. Overflowing program buffers with unconstrained input is a technique widely employed by crackers to attempt to execute commands embedded in the input. Depending on where in memory the buffer is allocated, it is possible that overflowing a buffer will result in writing over a special section of memory called the program *stack frame*. The stack frame is the section of memory that is used to restore the state of the executing program after returning from a function. During the execution of a program, when a call is made to a function, the current state of the program, which includes program variables and internal registers, is saved on the stack. In addition to the program state, the address of the next instruction to be executed after returning from the called function is "pushed" on the stack. This address is known as the *instruction pointer*. So, when the program is finished executing the called function, the next instruction to be executed is "popped off" the stack and loaded in the program counter to execute the next program instruction.

Now, by overwriting the stack with data that overflowed an input buffer, it is possible to change the instruction pointer to another address. In the case of many program crashes caused by buffer overruns, this is exactly what happens. That is, the instruction pointer is overwritten with random or garbage data that does not correspond to a legitimate instruction address for this program. Upon return from the called function, the processor will attempt to execute an instruction from a section of memory outside the program's address space, and a serious error called a *segmentation fault* will result. If a segmentation fault occurs during the execution of a program, the program will normally abort and create a file on the disk called a core file. Most users of Unix systems have experienced the frustration of having a core file dumped on their file system. In some cases, core files have been known to contain passwords that were stored by an authenticating program (such as a Web browser) before crashing. This is a good reason to prevent core files from being created on the file system altogether.

If the input stream that overflows a buffer is carefully crafted, it is possible that the instruction pointer can be overwritten in a principled manner. That is, a specific address can be written into the instruction pointer so that upon return to the calling function, the next instruction to be executed is located at an address of the malicious user's choice. This technique is known in the underground hacker community as "smashing the stack" [Aleph One 1996]. It is also possible to construct the input stream such that the address that is written in the instruction pointer points back onto the stack frame instead of to some other portion of the program memory. With the address pointing back onto the stack, it is possible to execute any instructions embedded in the input stream that have overwritten the stack.

Smashing the stack is illustrated in Figure 4.4. In the program's "main" function, an array variable "large" is defined to have length 2000. This array is filled with 2000 "X" characters. Next, the function "overflow" is called with a pointer to large passed as an argument. In overflow, a new array, "small," is defined with length 100. The stack in the right side of the Figure 4.4 shows how the memory is allocated for the overflow function. The variable small is allocated 100 characters. After small, memory is reserved for the stack frame pointer (SFP), the return instruction pointer (IP), and the pointer that was pushed on the stack when overflow is called. The overflow function simply copies the contents of the large variable array to the small variable array. Unfortunately, the function strcpy does not check the length of the variable it is copying before copying it to small. As a result, the 2000 characters are written over the 100-character-long array, buffer. This means that after the first 100 Xs are copied, the rest of the 2000-character-length array will overwrite the SFP, the return IP, and even the pointer.

After the overflow function finishes executing, it will pop off the return IP address and execute the instruction located at that address. In this example, the address pointed to by X is probably not an instruction, and as a result, this program will probably crash. However, the large array could have been intelligently loaded with input that places a meaningful instruction address at the return IP memory location. After the return IP address is overwritten, the next instruction that will execute could be an instruction of the attacker's choice, most likely one included in the rest of the buffer that was over-written.

This technique is as effective as is being able to access and modify the program source code, recompile it, and execute it on the server without ever having access to the source code. Smashing the stack is one of the primary attacks launched against SUID root programs. In the case of commerce applications, the problem can be especially dangerous if a network server program such as a Web server, mail or news server, login, or ftp server is susceptible to this type of attack—because many network daemons run SUID root. The implications are that an attack launched over the Internet by an unprivileged remote

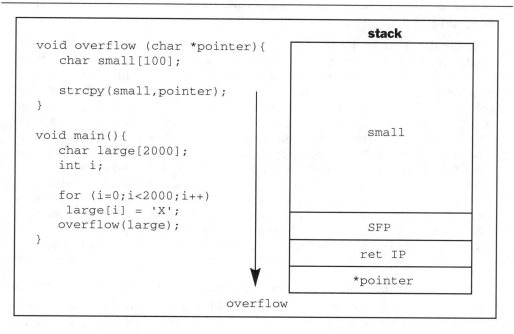

Figure 4.4 Smashing the stack.

user can potentially execute arbitrary commands on the server with super user privileges if the network daemon is susceptible to this type of attack. The problem was a programming error that allowed a larger buffer to overwrite a smaller buffer. The strcpy function call is a dangerous one because it does not check the length of the buffer being written before performing the copy. Instead, using the safer strncpy function that checks the length of the buffer would prevent this buffer overflow.

One of the most notorious cases of a exploiting a buffer overflow flaw occurred in 1988 via a program known as the Internet Worm. The Internet Worm was a program written by Robert T. Morris Jr. to exploit a flaw in the finger server, which runs on many networked machines and provides information to remote clients about the local users. Normally, the finger server is queried through a command of the following format:

```
finger userID@machine.ip.address
```

Program Stacks

To understand the program stack, it is more useful to know why stacks are necessary. High-level programming languages were created in part to make the task of solving a complex problem more simple by using the tried-and-true divide-and-conquer approach. That is, a larger problem is more easily solved if it is broken into its component parts. From an engineering perspective, a system is more easily developed if its components are constructed first and then integrated. In programming languages such as C, programs are modularized by being broken into smaller components called functions. When a function is called from within another function, the flow of execution is changed from the calling instruction to the first instruction in the called function. When the execution of the called function is complete, control is returned to the next instruction in the calling function. So that it "remembers" where to return to in the calling instruction, the instruction address is saved in a portion of memory called the *stack*.

The information returned by the finger server may include the identity of users who are logged on to the queried machine, the length of time a user has been idle at the terminal, the last time a user read mail, the status of mail received, and sometimes additional information that users will provide about themselves such as phone numbers, office hours, public encryption keys, and philosophical statements about life. The finger server can also provide information about which users are currently logged on to a host machine. Although this information may reveal more than is necessary, the Internet Worm did not exploit any of this information in its attack. Rather, the Internet Worm exploited a flaw in the finger server that allowed it to overflow an internal buffer.

The finger server allocated an array in memory (the buffer) of 512 bytes to store the argument of the finger client command. The argument to the finger client command is normally just a user ID and machine name or simply the machine name itself. The function the finger server used to read the argument did not check the length of the buffer it was reading it into, nor did it limit the length of the argument to the limit of the buffer. As a result, if the argument of the finger client sent was greater than 512 bytes, the buffer allocated in memory would be overwritten. This flaw is exactly what the Internet Worm exploited to overflow the buffer and overwrite the stack on many machines it attacked. By overwriting the stack, the Worm was able to execute its own code that it sent in the argument to the finger command. The code written by the Worm created a shell from which arbitrary commands could be executed. Because many finger servers run with root privilege, the Worm was able to execute its commands as the super user. The worm made its point, not by damaging the systems it violated, but by launching the same attack on other machines from each successive machine it conquered through this program flaw. This case has been studied and well documented in the literature [Spafford 1989]. Despite its prominence in the annals of computer security, a very large number of security attacks today exploit buffer overflow flaws in programs. The lesson learned from this attack is that input should always be checked for proper length and format before being further processed in a program.

Analyzing the Security of Software

Perhaps the single greatest cause of security-related flaws is the unexpected events the software experiences. Most software developers program to a specification of what the software is supposed to do rather than what the software *should not* be doing. The same can be said for testing. That is, when software developers test their code, they are testing to ensure that the software delivers the required functionality rather than testing to see what the code can be manipulated to do. It turns out that the latter form of testing does occur, just not by the "good guys." The cracker community is constantly engaged in software testing to determine if software can be manipulated into performing actions that are not in the specifications. That is, they are testing the software to see if they can gain unauthorized privileged access to the host systems on which the software executes. This is exactly the type of testing that should occur in the software development labs *before* software is released.

Software must be tested with at least two purposes in mind. First, the software should meet its required functionality. Second, the software should be tested to make sure it does not behave anomalously to unexpected inputs. The former type of testing uses the tests from the expected profile of inputs. The latter type of testing uses inputs from the unexpected space of inputs. This type of input will frequently "break" programs or cause programs to crash. Testing to break a program is known as *stress testing*. In some cases, the unexpected inputs will cause a program to act outside its jurisdiction of what constitutes acceptable behavior. That is, some programs can be manipulated to perform actions at the behest of the user—in violation of the program's specified behavior. Flaws in CGI programs that can be manipulated to act on behalf of an untrusted client are particularly dangerous. Unless server-side programs are analyzed for these types of flaws, the vulnerability of the commerce server to attacks will be unknown.

Several approaches to analyzing programs for these types of flaws exist. Only recently have these methods been considered in the security-critical area of Web applications. This section gives a high-level overview of the types of analytical methods that can be employed. Most software analysis methods can be classified as static or dynamic. Static methods examine software source code to determine if flaws exist or if dangerous structures are present. Static methods range from manually inspecting source code to automating searches for specific dangerous constructs. Source code is generally inspected during design reviews and "walk-throughs" of the code by people other than the designer of the program. It is often difficult for software developers to identify design errors in their own programs. This is a case in which another set of eyes is needed to see deficiencies or flaws that would otherwise go unnoticed. Certainly any flaw in a Web application has the potential to have security ramifications. Performing design reviews is an important process in developing reliable and secure software. Most good software engineering processes will have design reviews throughout the development of the software. The drawback of this approach is that it is manual and can consume many labor hours. Another drawback of the approach is the difficulty in judging how well the process works. The quality of this process will depend on the rigor by which it is conducted and the skill of the reviewers. These drawbacks have most software engineers seeking more automated solutions to this problem.

Static analysis can be automated to some extent if it automatically searches the source code for constructs that are known to be unsafe. Most text editors have the ability to search on regular expressions to make the search process easier. The difficult part is determining which constructs are unsafe. These constructs are determined through experience and can be gleaned from design heuristics for developing secure software. Using virtually any system command within a CGI program such as Perl system ( ), open ( ), popen ( ), eval ( ), or backticks (`) commands can be unsafe unless they are correctly coded. The danger of security breaches increases when input from Web clients is used in the arguments to these system commands. For example, it is often unsafe to use input received over the Web as part of a system command without first removing meta-characters from the input. Meta-characters are nonalphanumeric ASCII characters that have special meaning to many shell interpreters. All input received from Web clients must be considered untrusted and potentially malicious.

When designing CGI programs, the developer should not assume that user data will adhere to form fields or that the data will adhere to an expected format. Programmers should always anticipate the unexpected. From a design perspective, all input that is processed by the CGI program should be carefully preprocessed to remove (or "escape") all meta-characters. From a static analysis point of view, all sections of the code that receive and process input should be examined to ensure that all meta-characters are removed from the input. An even better solution would be to accept only the range of characters that is legitimate or expected rather than removing simply the meta-characters. Depending on the input, this may be more or less feasible. For example, if the program is reading a birth date, the only range of characters that is acceptable may be [0,9]. The length of this variable should also be restricted to the appropriate number of digits used by the program, such as eight characters for birth date. Based on these design heuristics, a static analysis can search for structures that implement strict control of inputs. If controls are not found, the program may be vulnerable to malicious input. Only a dynamic analysis of the program will be able to determine the true vulnerability of the program.

Many of the common scripting languages used to write CGI programs support functions that make it particularly easy to perform unsafe actions, so it is worthwhile to search for potentially dangerous ways to use these functions. In Perl and the Bourne shell, for example, the eval ( ) command can be used to execute system commands that are included in the argument to eval ( ). Again, if the argument to this function is built from inputs, this can be a potentially dangerous construct. A simple first step for detecting this potential problem is to search on eval ( ). Using backticks (`) in Perl and other scripting languages will cause a Unix shell to be spawned with the text delimited by the backticks to be executed as commands to the operating system. The use of backticks can be statically checked and inspected to make sure that no dangerous commands built from user input can be used as a shell command. Programmers must be extremely careful in using this function, and a static analysis should search for their use. CGI programs written in C have to work a little harder to execute possibly unsafe commands. However, this is no guarantee of safety. Two functions to be aware of in C are the open ( ) and popen ( ) commands. These functions provide the ability to make system calls with arguments that may be constructed from user input. In a static analysis, the CGI program source code should be searched for these structures. If they are found, the construction of these commands should be carefully inspected and then tested (via dynamic analysis) to ensure that they are not vulnerable to attack.

Even more sophisticated static analysis techniques exist for the detection of potentially dangerous constructions in code. Researchers at the University of California, Davis, have developed a static analysis tool for detecting a class of vulnerabilities called Time Of Check To Time Of Use (TOCTOU) flaws [Bishop and Dilger 1996]. These flaws occur when access to a resource is first checked and then later granted. If an attack is launched such that some malicious action is taken between the time access to the resource is checked and the time that access is granted, it may be possible to violate the security of the system. For example, consider a Web server that restricts access to a Web page by using basic authentication. When a user is attempting to access the Web page, an authentication window is launched wherein the user must first enter a valid user name and password. If the page is substituted with another unauthorized document between the time that the authentication occurs successfully and the time that the page is delivered, it may be possible to gain unauthorized access to a confidential document. This attack works by exploiting a race condition that is created when the process of checking and the process of granting access are two distinct steps rather than a single action, known as an atomic action.

The attack may work as follows. The attacker creates a script that attempts to race the server (it could also be a CGI program) to replace the file for which access has been granted before the server delivers the document. The script may create a symbolic link that points from the file that is supposed to be accessed to another file, such as the system password. If the script manages to replace this file with the symbolic link after access has been granted and before the authorized document is delivered, it has won the race, and the confidential document may be delivered. A static analyzer program was written by the U.C. Davis researchers to search for TOCTOU flaws. If they exist, warnings are noted.

Dynamic analysis involves executing the program to detect flaws. Dynamic analysis studies the *behavior* of the application rather than its structure. In practice, programs will often behave differently from the way the designers may have anticipated. Static analysis, by itself, may reveal the potential for vulnerabilities to exist; however, dynamic analysis can confirm the existence of program flaws. Traditionally, dynamic analysis has involved testing a program for functional correctness. That is, a suite of test inputs is generated to test the functions the program is supposed to provide, and the resulting outputs from the program are compared with the expected program outputs. In practice, it may be very difficult to know or to generate the correct output for every input without having a program oracle. An oracle defines exactly what the correct output for every input should be. The existence of oracles for programs is rare for most nontrivial applications. Another problem that stymies testing for correctness is that the number of possible inputs for most nontrivial programs is far too great to exhaustively test a program. This problem by itself precludes proving the correctness of most programs via dynamic analysis.

Showing functional correctness appears to be an intractable problem for most nontrivial programs, so an alternative technique to identifying program vulnerabilities would be attractive. One technique that shows promise is to analyze the behavior of the program, not for correctness, but rather for secure behavior. From a perspective of computer security, we may not be as concerned if a program does not perform exactly as specified, as long as it does not breach the security of the system. Rather than checking that all outputs are correct according to the functional specification, a more tractable problem would be to just ensure that the program does not perform maliciously. Of course, this requires that we can specify what constitutes malicious behavior for a program and that we can determine if this behavior is violated. This approach assumes that it is easier to specify what constitutes a security violation for an application than to define the correct behavior for every input. This assumption generally holds for most nontrivial applications.

Recent research in computer security has developed dynamic analysis techniques to detect the presence of security-critical flaws in software during the development stages of software [Voas et al. 1996]. White-box analysis techniques use knowledge of the program's internal structure to detect the existence of security-critical flaws. Security-critical flaws are those errors in the program source code that can potentially compromise the security of the system in which the software is installed. Unlike static white-box analysis techniques described earlier, dynamic white-box analysis techniques study the *behavior* of the software to quantify characteristics such as security and safety. White-box analysis can take advantage of two types of source-code-level *instrumentation* techniques: *assertions* and *fault injection*.

Instrumentation is the process of inserting yet more program code into a program in order to study its behavior. Assertions are statements that check the state of the program after the execution of an instruction. Assertions can be used to check if certain insecure states have been reached during execution of the program. Once a security policy for an application has been specified, it can be coded in the program through the use of assertions. The security policy is simply a statement of which behaviors violate the security of the application and system in which the software is installed. For example, if a program is not to access the system password file /etc/passwd, this assertion can be coded and checked during the dynamic analysis of the program. The violation of an assertion signifies that the security policy of the application or system has been breached. This information can be collected for statistical analysis about the frequency with which the security policy of a program is breached through standard testing or through fault injection.

Fault injection can be used to simulate anomalous program behavior. For example, if a fault is injected into the evaluation of a branch condition, the program will take a different branch for an input than it would have without the injected fault. Fault injection can also be used to simulate the incorrect computation of program functions. For example, the value returned from a called function can be corrupted and subsequently used throughout the rest of the program execution. Combined with the use of assertions, the security of the program in the face of anomalous behavior can be studied. The purpose of employing fault injection is to determine the effect of potential flaws in a program on the security of the application. The results from fault injection can be used to determine the security-critical sections of a program and also to build in fault-tolerant mechanisms to prevent security violations from occurring during the future execution of the program.

Summary

This chapter takes a critical look at an often overlooked aspect of e-commerce: server-side security. Flaws in any one of the three basic components of the commerce server—the Web server, the interface software, and the database—can be sufficient to allow an intruder access to sensitive company and client data. The chapter presents salient vulnerabilities in each of these components and methods for securing them. In addition, the importance for designing security into software design and the necessity to analyze software for security are underscored. Two take-home messages should emanate from this chapter: First, the commerce server must be secured as much as the other parts of the e-commerce system, and second, regardless of which commerce server is used, no matter how secure a given commerce server is purported to be, the server must be tested in order to provide assurance of security.

References

Aleph One. "Smashing the Stack for Fun and Profit." Online. Phrack Online. Volume 7, Issue 49, File 14 of 16. November 9, 1996. Available: www.fc.net/phrack/.

Barr, S. "IRS Audit Reveals More Tax Browsing." *The Washington Post*, April 9, 1997, A01.

Bishop, M. and M. Dilger. "Checking for Race Conditions in File Accesses." The USENIX Association, *Computing Systems*, Spring 1996, 131–152.

CERT Advisory 96:26, "Denial of Service Attack via ping." Online. CERT Coordination Center. December 18, 1996. Available: ftp://info.cert.org/pub/cert_advisories.

Garfinkel, S. "Social Insecurity." *RISKS Digest*, 19:5, April 7, 1997.

Garfinkel, S. and G. Spafford, *Practical Unix and Internet Security*, Second Edition. O'Reilly & Associates, 1996.

Garfinkel, S. and G. Spafford. *Web Security and Commerce*. O'Reilly & Associates, 1997.

Rubin, R., D. Geer, and M. Ranum. *Web Security Sourcebook*. John Wiley & Sons. 1997.

Spafford, E. "The Internet Worm Program: An Analysis." *Computer Communications Review*, 19:1, January 1989, 17–57.

Stein, L. *The World Wide Web Security FAQ*. Online. September 2, 1997. Available: www-genome.wi.mit.edu/WWW/faqs/www-security-faq.html#contents.

Voas, J., A. Ghosh, G. McGraw, F. Charron, and K. Miller. "Defining an Adaptive Software Security Metric from a Dynamic Software Failure Tolerance Measure." *Proceedings of the 11th Annual Conference on Computer Assurance* June 1996, 250–266.

Chapter 5

Cracks in the
Foundation

Securing the Operating System

As recently as 1990, most desktop computers were considered to be stand-alone machines. Networking of computers on a global scale not only has changed the perception of computers as stand-alone machines, but has harnessed the power of group collaboration, communication, and large-scale, cheap dissemination of information. The paradigm of programming is changing, and today's software developers are programming to the network platform. Most commercial software is now designed to share application documents across networks. Future software technologies will distribute software in tiny parts over many networks that work together as a whole. This type of technology is already being used to solve difficult problems such as brute-force breaking of ciphers. The year 2000 (Y2K) problem is expected to force many companies to scrap legacy systems and start development of software systems that use the network as the platform. Recent programming languages such as Java have the potential to eliminate the dependence of developing programs on a particular machine architecture such as Windows, Macintosh, and Unix systems. This means that software developers can write a program on their favorite platform once, and the program can be run anywhere on any other platform.

The grandest network of all, the Internet, is also an insecure network for connecting the computers that hold the intellectual property of today's corporations. The Internet was not designed to be a reliable—let alone secure—means of communicating. More recently, cryptographic protocols were designed to layer on top of the TCP/IP protocols in order to provide secure communications between network peers. Secure protocols such as SSL have brought privacy and authentication to Web sessions, but they do not secure the computers that are connected to the Internet. This is an important distinction for companies that are now placing their computers (and by implication, their corporate assets) on the Internet.

Corporations that have connected to the Internet are also facing problems with managing the growth of their information systems. Long gone are the days when MIS technical managers could spend a number of years researching, acquiring, and installing information systems to meet the technical support needs of the corporations. The pressure on software vendors to be first to the market has reduced software release life cycles to several weeks down from years. The result is a deluge of new software products in the market for which MIS departments have neither the time nor the resources to effectively evaluate. The current model of free software evaluation copies has made many of these software products free for evaluation by anyone with Internet access. The result is that all employees in an organization can now be their own MIS manager. An employee can now download, install, and evaluate software from the Internet on corporate machines. Frequently, there is little or no control over which software is downloaded and installed. To make this problem worse, there is no assurance that the software is free from viruses or Trojan horses that may damage or steal corporate assets.

Minding the Operating System

Imagine that you are a chief information officer (CIO) responsible for making information technology infrastructure decisions for your corporation. By now, you've had an earful about the dangers of sending sensitive e-mail in plaintext, visiting unknown Web sites, executing active content, installing push technology, and setting up your corporate Web servers securely. So you know that there are some basic decisions you can make to improve the security of your corporate information infrastructure. You buy the latest and greatest firewall to protect your internal machines. You have all versions of Internet Explorer or Netscape Navigator updated to the latest version. You decree a systemwide policy about surfing Web sites and downloading active content. Even better, you are enforcing it using either a system administrator's browser toolkit or a packet filtering solution at the router(s). You obtain a server certificate for your commerce server to support SSL, SET, or one of the other secure Web/commerce protocols. Now you think you've secured your system. Well, you have to a large extent, and kudos to you for being diligent to security. What you have really done is securely set up the applications running on the desktop. What you forgot, though, is the operating system software.

The operating system (OS) is the foundation for any software that runs on a machine. Software interacts with the machine's processor through fundamental calls to a portion of the operating system known as the kernel. But the OS includes myriad software generally called system programs that are installed out of the box with each different platform. Examples include device drivers, a file system, networking software, shells with command-line interpreters, login programs, language compilers, interpreters, and editors. Collectively, this software forms the OS. Building security into software at the application level is necessary for security, but it is not sufficient. Vulnerabilities in the OS and all of its system software can undermine the security implemented at the application level. Despite the best of intentions, flaws in the OS software can produce holes in the security of a machine.

Take Sun's popular Network Information System (NIS), for example. NIS, also popularly known as Yellow Pages, is a method for sharing password files and other critical system configuration files between Unix workstations using a centralized server. This eliminates the need to replicate password and configuration files on each Unix machine in a large network—which would be a formidable maintenance task by any administrator's standard. NIS has been a source of Unix system security vulnerabilities, primarily because it is built on top of RPC, the Remote Procedure Call system. Although invaluable for distributed processes and networked software, RPC has been known for quite some time to be an insecure means of executing processes remotely. When making remote invocations, RPC is generally not configured to authenticate network clients before performing the requested action. RPC can use a weak form of authentication that relies on user and group ID information. Spoofing this information is trivial work for an interested party. A secure form of RPC that uses DES encryption exists, but it is not popularly supported by vendors. NIS normally would not need authentication because NIS clients internal to the network are designed to query world readable files. The security problem arises when an untrusted outside client can connect to the NIS central server's RPC portmapper. If this is possible, the rogue NIS client need only guess the NIS domain name (which is usually set to the site's Internet domain name), and the client can easily grab the system password file—which normally has world readable permissions. This process is automated through a freely available exploit called ypx. From the password file, cracking at least one user account is usually a given.

Clearly, operating system software and configuration is important. This does not mean that end users or system administrators need to inspect the source code for each and every piece of running software on the local machines. The good news is that a properly configured firewall (cheap or expensive) can shield a vast majority of the flawed software running on internal machines from untrusted clients outside the firewall. Although firewalls are commonly used to protect the corporation's resources from the Internet-at-large, they are also effective for protecting internal organizations from one another. The bad news is that a vast majority of firewalls are improperly configured. Until firewalls become easier to install and configure, they will continue to be ineffective against many kinds of attacks. Furthermore, firewalls need to be maintained and monitored by system administrators on a regular basis.

Unfortunately, even a properly configured firewall cannot stop some attacks from breaking into corporate systems because, by design, a firewall lets some network services through. If the firewall were configured to let no services through, the effect would be the same as unplugging the network connection from the back of the machine, but it is infeasible to perform any computer-related work today without access to the Internet. The services normally let through the firewall are the Web protocol, mail, news, and sometimes other network services such as FTP, telnet, finger, and RPC services, among others. These network services connect network clients outside the firewall to network servers inside the firewall. Security problems arise when a network client is able to manipulate the network servers to grant a higher level of access privilege than should be allowed to an untrusted client. These types of attacks are called *data-driven* attacks.

Name Your Poison: Unix or Windows NT

The rest of this chapter focuses on the vulnerabilities in the OS software that can be exploited through legitimate network services (those services offered through the firewall by intention). To bring this discussion closer to home, the vulnerabilities are framed around the two most predominant platforms used for network servers today: Windows NT and Unix. Since the very early days of the Internet, the platform of choice in universities and corporate science and engineering departments has been Unix. Like ice cream, Unix comes in a great many flavors, including SunOS, Solaris, SCO, HP-UX, Ultrix, AIX, Linux, and Irix, to name the popular ones. Each flavor (with the exception of Linux, which is a worldwide collaborative effort) represents a different vendor's interpretation of the original Unix created by AT&T's Bell Labs in 1969. In spite of the long history of Unix, security remains elusive.

With the horsepower of today's Intel processors, a stable, true multitasking 32-bit operating system, and a large base of supporting software applications and software development tools, Windows NT has made a huge impact on the desktop/workstation market. Expensive Unix workstations are now being supplanted by their cheaper and more effective NT counterparts in engineering labs everywhere. Muddying the waters is the claim that Windows NT offers a more secure platform for corporate computing. The heightened presence of NT workstations on desktops has placed the NT OS under a fair amount of scrutiny since 1996. The security claims made by Microsoft have also triggered a backlash reaction by hackers who consider it their mission to dispel the rumors that Windows NT is more secure than its distant Unix cousins. As a result, Microsoft officials have begun to meet with hackers at hacker conferences to facilitate an open dialog on security issues [Lange 1997].

Anyone who monitors the security announcement news groups or mailing lists knows that new flaws in Unix software come out at a rate of almost one per day. The sheer volume of security announcements may lead one to believe that Unix is an insecure platform. Remember, however, that Unix has been around since the early 1970s, and the installed base of Unix users is both very large and full of very technically competent people, whose aim is to improve rather than detract from the security of the OS. With so many flavors of Unix, there are many targets. The flaws tend to be esoteric in nature and typically require some advanced software development skills in order to exploit. Furthermore, the announcements usually convey too little information for would-be hackers. Does the volume of security announcements mean Unix is unsafe to work with in practice? No. Rather, the sheer size and complexity of OS software are what make security vulnerabilities possible.

When Microsoft first released Windows NT 4.0, the marketing department pushed its security features as a competitive edge for businesses. NT 4.0 certainly gave consideration to security, especially when it was compared with Windows 95. For example, the Security Accounts Manager (SAM), which manages user accounts, was added in the NT OS. Without any history of security violations, it is easy to declare a new product secure. After the release of NT, the ensuing barrage of security flaws found by users and skeptics marked another well-known attribute of new operating systems—early releases are almost always buggy. The posts became so frequent that several newsgroups and mailing lists dedicated to NT security flaws were created, and they remain ever active today. The most respected of these is Russ Cooper's NT Bugtraq list (ntbugtraq.rc.on.ca).

Firewalls can protect machines on internal networks from machines on untrusted networks. However, ensuring and maintaining individual host security are as important as installing and configuring a firewall. Organizations that erect firewalls at the expense of individual host security are known in the security community as *crunchy on the outside and soft and chewy on the inside*. Attacks that penetrate the firewall will have an easy time hopping from machine to machine, stealing information and pillaging hard drives if individual host security is not maintained. A great number of books on the market today discuss how to lock down individual host security.[1] Rather than providing a complete guide to securing your desktop machine, this chapter turns its attention back to the network server. Whereas Chapter 4 discusses the Web server software, this chapter focuses on the underlying operating system software of the server host machine. The premise of this chapter is that even if the Web server software is locked down securely, cracks in the underlying OS foundation can permit unscrupulous outsiders access to the server machine, and from there, they can reach the rest of the internal network. The attacks are data-driven attacks made through legitimate services in the firewall. The objective is not to cover all potential vulnerabilities in server machines but to focus on those that exist even behind a well-configured firewall. The first part of this chapter discusses how firewalls operate, what services they provide, and where they fall short. The second half investigates the vulnerabilities of Windows NT and Unix systems to data-driven attacks to network server machines.

Vulnerabilities are classified by category and compared by OS (Windows NT and vanilla Unix). Some vulnerabilities apply across platforms; others are specific to Windows NT or Unix. The objective is not to provide a comprehensive guide to all vulnerabilities in different OSs—this list is too long to cover here and too dynamic to be meaningful. Any listing of OS vulnerabilities is only a snapshot in time that will change on a daily basis. The objective is to identify categories of vulnerabilities that are expected to persist for a useful lifetime of the OS. Therefore, as these vulnerabilities are patched (and many already are) and new vulnerabilities are found, the CIO will have both the wisdom of the types of vulnerabilities found in practice and the yardstick by which to compare the severity of future vulnerabilities.

Firewall Insecurity

Erecting a firewall between digital corporate assets and untrusted networks is essential to preventing security break-ins through vulnerabilities in the OS. Firewalls are the first line of defense against malicious users, placed between the computer network to be protected and the network that is considered to be a security threat. Figure 5.1 shows a sample system architecture, imposing a firewall between an organization's internal LAN and the Internet.

---

[1] A complete reference for system administrators is *Practical Unix & Internet Security*, Second Edition, by S. Garfinkel and E. Spafford. O'Reilly & Associates, Inc. 1996.

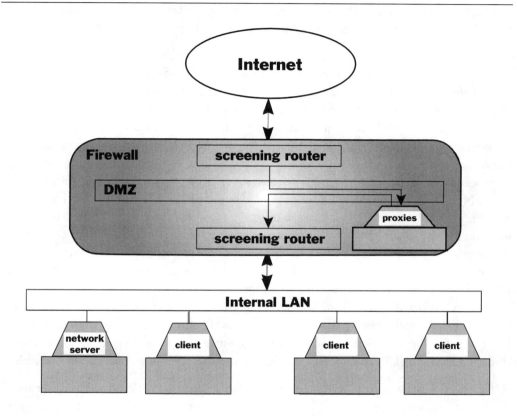

Figure 5.1 A firewall placed between an organization's internal LAN and the Internet.

Though firewalls are typically used to isolate a company's local area networks (LANs) from the Internet, firewalls are also used to partition, isolate, and control access between internal corporate networks. If configured properly, firewalls can prevent most of the scattershot attacks/probes through well-known network scanning tools such as SATAN. In fact, many firewalls are now certified to be resistant against these kinds of attacks. But like encryption, firewalls are not a silver-bullet solution to security problems. This section highlights reasons that firewalls can be ineffective to concerted data-driven attacks.

To provide protection against malicious elements on untrusted networks, firewalls can be erected between trusted and untrusted computer networks. Firewalls are also used to partition and protect data between internal corporate networks called intranets. As the Internet is being increasingly used within companies to interconnect groups that may be geographically distributed, the distinction between the Internet and intranets has blurred to give rise to the latest buzzword—extranets. Extranets are corporate intranets or LANs connected via the Internet.

Although the term firewall evokes the image of a bastion fort, in truth, a firewall is usually some combination of packet filtering routers and a computer that executes a set of proxies. Proxies are simple programs that store and forward network requests based on an evaluation of a set of rules. The rules define which connections are allowed and which are not. One of the most important functions that a firewall serves is to restrict the number of network services that are available to outside connections. Consider that on many Unix platforms there may be a network service running on any one of 65,536 network ports. Network port scanners allow remote computers to determine what services are running on the network ports. Once a service is detected, it can be attacked by packets sent to attempt to subvert the service into providing an unauthorized level of access to the computer. Successful attacks are made possible by bugs in the network services, errors in configuration, or the lack of access-control mechanisms. Firewalls combat these types of attacks by preventing connections to all services except those explicitly permitted by the firewall. What is less well understood is that many attacks are launched through the services that *are* permitted by the firewall. Bugs and features in the supported services can be exploited for malicious gain through legitimate requests to the services offered through the firewall. These types of attacks are the data-driven attacks alluded to earlier.

Firewalls provide control over which network services are offered to the Internet or the untrusted network in general. An easy way to secure a network from external threats is simply to disconnect all access to and from the Internet. Some Internet services such as mail, Web access, and FTP are typically desired in corporations, so disconnecting from the Internet is generally not a popular (or viable) option. On the other hand, simply connecting all internal machines to the Internet without forethought to the computer security can place corporate assets at risk. Firewalls represent a compromise solution between these two extreme positions of security and insecurity. Even though rigorous access controls can be imposed on the types of network services offered, there is the potential for attacks to be waged against a corporate network through errors in configuration of the firewall, around the firewall through backdoors, or even through legitimate requests over network services offered through the firewall.

The firewall serves as a choke point between the Internet and internal machines. That is, all access to and from the network must be routed through the firewall. The firewall proxies can control access to both the Internet and to the internal network by evaluating a set of rules for each connection attempt to a network service. The rules specify which type of network traffic is permitted on either side of the firewall, where connections are allowed from, and to which machines connections are permitted. The rules can also be defined to deny requests from selected sites or domains that have proved to be pesky in the past. When connection requests that do not meet well-defined rules are dropped, many malicious attacks can be thwarted before they ever reach the network server(s). Before the vulnerabilities of the network server machines inside the firewall are addressed, the firewall itself must first be secured.

Locking Down the Firewall

Security starts with simplicity. The general-purpose computer that serves as the firewall must be stripped down to the absolute bare essential services. In this case, stripping the computer down does not mean removing hardware devices (though this may be necessary in the case of modems). Rather, the software programs that are installed and that execute upon start-up must be carefully evaluated. Most computers now come out of the box with networking software and other system services that support a wide variety of functions to accommodate the general-purpose uses of computers. Because the firewall should not be used for general-purpose computing, all of the unnecessary network services and user accounts should be removed. As an example, the network services that support remote login capability should be removed. The firewall should always be configured directly from its console by the designated system administrator. When the remote login capability is removed, the security issues for breaking into the firewall machine may be reduced to physical security. This will not be true, however, if other insecure network services such as a Web server or FTP server are run on the machine. Flaws in the software for these services have been exploited in the past by unauthorized users to gain shell access with high privilege levels on the server host. Removing other user accounts on the firewall host is necessary to prevent users from tampering with the security of the firewall. It is often the case that a firewall machine will come out of the box with a number of default accounts set up, with weak or no password protection at all. These default accounts are usually the first avenue of attack from probing Internet machines. Finally, most firewall software is distributed with port-scanning utilities to determine which network services are running so that any unnecessary services can be detected and removed.

The routers that are part and parcel to the firewall must also be securely configured. Routers can stop many attacks before they even reach general-purpose machines. For example, routers can drop any packets sent to machines that should not be visible to the outside world. Routers can drop packets sent to network services that should not be offered to the outside, as well; an example would be remote login services. Routers are programmed through a table of rules. The rules specify the behavior of the router in transmitting or dropping packets from one interface of the router (e.g., the untrusted network interface) to another (e.g., the trusted network interface). Errors in coding these rules (the rules can be quite complex and nonintuitive to program) can permit malicious attacks to penetrate the trusted network.

Another important, often overlooked, method is to disable remote login services to the router. Many routers are configured by default to allow remote logins to update and configure the router rules. If the remote login service is left running on the router, it may be possible for a malicious user to compromise the router. A malicious attack could rewrite the rules to permit attacks from a user's machine to be passed to the internal network, or the attack could disable the router altogether to implement a devastating denial of service attack. Finally, services such as SNMP running on routers and other perimeter machines can introduce vulnerabilities in the network. SNMP is used for performance monitoring of networks for system administrators to determine network usage. Unless SNMP is secured, a hacker using an SNMP client can probe local SNMP devices to find out a great deal of information about a target organization, such as the network topology. Information on SNMP vulnerabilities and exploits has been publicly released [Danckaert 1997].

Assuming that the firewall machine itself has been secured, what level of security does a firewall provide to the protected network domain? One unfortunate side effect of installing a firewall machine is that the host security of individual machines on the protected domain tends to be relaxed. The notion is that if the front door is locked and bolted, why bother locking the doors to all the rooms in the house? This attitude, however, makes the firewall a single point of failure from which the security of the whole system may be compromised if the firewall is breached. Unfortunately, the house typically has back doors and side doors that are not securely locked or monitored. An example that often burns system administrators is a modem attached to a computer that is also attached to a corporate LAN. Modems are often attached to corporate machines to provide dial-up access for employees at home or on the road. Sometimes, employees will also bring in their own laptops and dial out to their personal Internet service provider to check e-mail through personal accounts. The problem arises if these computers are also connected to the corporate network while the modem passively listens to network requests. A malicious user may be able to completely bypass the firewall by making a direct connection to an internal computer through the modem. Again, if the individual host machine security is relaxed, the user may be able to exploit the web of trust that is woven between internal machines to hop from machine to machine and obtain varying degrees of privilege.

Data-Driven Attacks

Now assume that the network perimeter has been secured so that there are no open front doors, back doors, and side doors. Even with the latest, greatest (and most expensive) firewall in place, corporate assets may still be vulnerable to external attacks. Although firewalls are useful for thwarting attacks launched through nonessential network services, there is little that firewalls can do to prevent data-driven attacks through legitimate requests made to offered services. These types of attacks use the legitimate grammar of the protocol and creative license to trick software inside the firewall to act on behalf of a remote user—in violation of the security policy of the site. Some examples of these types of attacks are presented in the next section.

In practice, most attacks are made possible by errors in configuring the firewall and network servers. Firewalls, unfortunately, do not come out of the box configured for a particular organization. Rather, a secure policy must first be developed and documented unambiguously, and often logic tables must be created for specifying what is permitted and what is not. Because these policies will vary with each organization, the firewall must be customized to adhere to the security policy for the site that it is protecting. Firewalls are typically ineffective for two reasons: first, the security policy is rarely specified unambiguously, and second, errors are made in configuring the firewall to adhere to the security policy (assuming that one exists). The configuration problems extend to the network server programs themselves. Again, even if the firewall is securely configured, errors in configuring a network service, such as the Web protocol (HTTP), can result in violations of corporate security.

Data-driven attacks exploit software services offered through firewalls. For example, sendmail is one of the most commonly used mail servers on Unix machines. Throughout its long history (sendmail is now on version 8, approaching version 9), sendmail has been rife with errors that have resulted in security vulnerabilities. For example, in the past when sendmail was compiled in "debug" mode, it allowed untrusted outside users unrestricted access to the system [Garfinkel and Spafford 1996]. Even now, security-related bugs in sendmail are usually discovered with each subsequent release version. The problem is not that sendmail is poorly written but rather that the size and complexity of the sendmail program make a bug-free implementation a near impossibility. Firewalls can do little to prevent program errors in a network server from being exploited through legitimate requests to the server. They can, however, limit the extent of the damage.

A firewall proxy can impose a restricted file system around an executing application server. With this "jail cell" around a server, if the server program is compromised by an outside request, the extent of damage that can be caused by the intrusion is limited to the scope of the jail cell. In the case of sendmail, a data-driven attack that is able to obtain shell access on the server through a bug in sendmail will be able to access only those files and/or programs in the file system defined by the firewall proxy—provided that the jail cell is invoked when sendmail is called.[2] Of course, any mail that is within the scope of the jail cell may be vulnerable to eavesdropping by a subverted sendmail program.

Another example of the class of attacks on program vulnerabilities relates to Web applications. Web servers known as HTTP daemons may themselves be vulnerable to attack, and the CGI scripts that the server interacts with may also be vulnerable. CGI scripts are released with the HTTP daemon software distribution and are often written by Web site administrators to make a Web site interactive. CGI scripts execute in response to a request received over the network to a Web server. The CGI script will process the remote client's input data and usually perform some action such as to update a database. If the CGI script is written without regard to the security issues with processing user input, it may be possible for a remote client to execute arbitrary commands on the Web server machine. One such vulnerability existed in a CGI script released with the NCSA HTTPd Version 1.4 and earlier [CERT-96:06 1996]. A failure to correctly remove special characters from user input being fed to a shell command can result in the potential to arbitrarily execute commands embedded in a Web request on the server host machine. Even today, the vast majority of attacks against Web servers attempt to exploit this flaw. Using the chroot option for executing programs such as mail servers, Web servers, and CGI scripts can help minimize the collateral damage, however.

It should be clear by now that firewalls cannot ensure network security for those who want some connectivity to untrusted networks, such as the Internet. The second part of this chapter presents vulnerabilities in Windows NT and Unix network server machines that can be exploited through data-driven attacks. In addition, techniques for securing the network server against attacks through these vulnerabilities are presented.

The Network Server Vulnerabilities

Attacks against network servers protected behind firewalls stand a good chance of succeeding if vulnerable operating system software is exposed through the firewall. This section describes vulnerabilities in software running on network servers in both Windows NT and Unix platforms. The vulnerabilities are classified into seven categories by their distinguishing characteristics. The categories are not canonical but rather descriptive. Table 5.1 summarizes the vulnerabilities described for each category by platform. Some vulnerabilities apply generally across Unix and NT platforms; others are platform specific.

---

[2] This feature is made possible by the Unix chroot command that restricts the file system visible to the program that is the argument to the chroot command.

Table 5.1 Network Server Vulnerabilities by Category

Category	Cross Platform	Windows NT	Unix
Deadly defaults	WebServer configuration CGI scripts Guest accounts	Guest account Administrator account Everyone group NetBIOS shares	NA
Web server flaws	HTTP GET method Flawed CGI scripts	Truncate .bat/.cmd flaw Dot–dot flaw ASP flaw GET ../.. flaw 8K URL bug TCP/IP port 1031 flaw	Early NCSA HTTPd versions
CGI script flaws	Mishandling malicious input Interpreters in scripts directory Server-side includes	FrontPage server extensions	Flawed CGI distribution
Networking software vulnerabilities	DNS cache pollution	NetBIOS remote share mounting SMB challenge-response implementation	RPC authentication NIS/YP domain name NFS
Denial-of-service attacks	SYN-flooding Ping O' Death	Out-of-band attack	NA
Weak authentication	Bad passwords Accessible password hashes	SMB password No password salting	NA
OS software holes	Buffer overruns	System registry	SUID root programs Shell escapes

The first category, deadly defaults, consists of those settings of software or system configuration that are insecure and leave the system open to penetration. In this category there are interestingly several that apply cross platform, as well as some specific to Windows NT. As for flaws in the Web servers, some are cross platform, such as those described in Chapter 4, but several are NT specific or Unix specific.

Related to the Web server software are the CGI script flaws. Recall from Chapter 4 that CGI scripts are the server-side programs that execute in response to Web requests. The Flaws in CGI Scripts section contrasts weaknesses in CGI scripts that are cross platform with those that are specific to particular platforms.

Naturally, networking software vulnerabilities also represent an important category of data-driven attacks. The example of Sun's NIS software falls into this category. These flaws tend to be very platform specific, although some vulnerabilities that apply to the Internet protocol are cross platform. Denial-of-service vulnerabilities, described by some security experts as indefensible, form the class of attacks that can bring a server to its knees. Some, like the powerful SYN flood attack, are frighteningly easy to launch. Most denial-of-service attacks are independent of platform, though several have been found to be specific to Windows NT.

A category of vulnerability that seems to be the Achilles' heel of most security systems is weak authentication. Authentication problems have haunted the Windows NT server since its release. Vulnerabilities in supporting software found in most OSs are commonplace across platforms, and several are specific to both Windows NT and Unix.

Flaws in the OS system software may make up the only category that may not be accessible through the firewall. Security flaws in this type of software are found almost on a daily basis. Many do not expose the system to external penetration attacks, but they can facilitate escalation of privilege for internal account holders. Ensuring that this type of flaw is patched can go a long way to preventing successful external penetrations from gaining further privileges and preventing insider attacks from gaining unauthorized privileges.

Caveat Emptor

The most important caveat is that the flaws discussed here represent a snapshot in time. Many of the flaws already have patches, service packs, or release versions available that correct them. The objective of presenting this snapshot is not simply to patch these flaws, but to realize that these categories of flaws will continue to arise in network servers, regardless of the firewall, platform, and vendor. Remember that firewalls are not the panacea to providing network host security. Rather, a combination of firewalls, application-level security, secure protocols, Internet-safe clients, and secured operating system software can provide the optimal solution. This requires an active security maintenance plan on the part of the system administration that includes monitoring security newsgroups, patching software released vendors, auditing system logs, and perhaps even employing real-time intrusion-detection software. No single security plan will provide 100 percent security. Rather, the risks for a particular system must be identified and the appropriate mitigating secure technologies applied.

Burying the Deadly Defaults

The "deadly defaults" refer to the default configuration settings for software installed out of the box. Most software is optimized to fulfill its primary functional objectives with minimal hassle for the user rather than configured for optimal security. Security is often made possible at the expense of convenience and vice versa. When it comes to making a trade-off of convenience for security, most software manufacturers will err on the side of convenience. A good example that illustrates the point is discussed in the sidebar on the Communicator 4.0 Certificate Deadly Default.

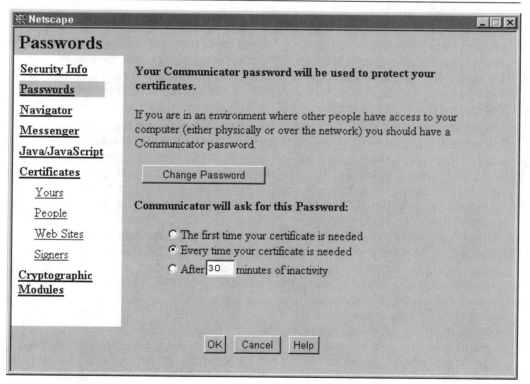

Figure 5.2 Certificate password options in the Security window in Communicator 4.0.

Deadly defaults are also common in software because rarely is there a one–size–fits–all policy for security. Rather, security features are configured for the lowest common denominator in security requirements. If you or your organization are not in the set of the lowest common denominator, you will end up getting the short end of the security stick.

Communicator 4.0 Certificate Deadly Default

An example of a deadly default is the configuration of the Netscape Communicator 4.01a for Windows 95 for secure mail (using S/MIME encryption) and Web client authentication. A deadly default is simply a pre-set configuration that is by default insecure.

In order to use the S/MIME e-mail and present a certificate to a Web site, the user must first generate a public/private key pair and then obtain a certificate from a trusted certification authority. The Communicator automates this process with a few clicks of the mouse. The private key is stored on the user's drive and protected by a password or PIN. If the private key is compromised, the user's digital signature can be forged in Web and e-mail transactions, and encrypted mail can be decrypted by the perpetrator. It turns out that brute-force attacks against the password may not be necessary to compromise the private key if the Communicator 4.0 is used as is, out of the box.

The Communicator 4.0 has one of those deadly defaults that makes forging e-mail and decrypting encrypted e-mail intended for someone else a simple exercise. The Communicator is set by default to cache the password and retain it for as long as the Communicator application is kept open. This means that the user needs to enter a password to access the private key only once. What is deadly about caching the password by default? If the user, for instance, gets up from the terminal at some point in the day, leaving it unattended with the Netscape application open, anyone can sit down at the terminal and send out e-mail signed with the user's personal digital signature. In fact, there is even an option in the browser to automatically sign all outgoing e-mail without user intervention. If the recipient of the e-mail has the user's certificate ahead of time, the recipient of the e-mail will be able to verify the digital signature with certainty. This means that the recipient will have the proof positive (the user's digital signature) that the rightful user sent the mail, when in fact someone else did. The default configuration of caching the password defeats one of the main purposes of employing digital signatures, which is to prevent forgeries. Caching the password can undermine the weight that a digital signature carries. Anytime a terminal is left unattended, anyone can send mail from it, mimicking the user's identity. The point of employing digital signatures

In this section, deadly defaults that apply to Unix, Windows NT, or both platforms are described. Although the deadly defaults will vary with each platform and each flavor of Unix, the most common ones that seem to apply across all platforms are the guest/demo default accounts installed out of the box, dangerous or unnecessary CGI scripts distributed with Web server software, and insecurely configured Web servers. The guest or demo

is to provide a level of assurance to the recipient that the message was truly signed by the person whose identity is vouched for by the signature. If digital signatures are to be used as legally binding power of attorney, default configurations that cache the password can undermine the weight of the digital signature.

As an example, suppose you had an online trading account with a stock broker. To provide higher levels of accountability, the stock broker requires all orders to be digitally signed by clients who possess a certificate signed by a trusted CA. One of your conniving colleagues who knows that you have an online trading account decides to play a "joke." When you get up for lunch, he sits down at your terminal, fires off an e-mail to your online broker (or fills out the online form with the necessary certificate already enabled by the password) to purchase 100 shares of Netscape stock. The order goes through, and you don't know you've just purchased the shares until you see the charge on your credit card bill at the end of the month. Irate, you call up your broker demanding an explanation. The broker presents your unforgeable digital signature as evidence that you placed the order. Clearly, you are in a bind. You alone are responsible for the protection of your private key. Little did you realize, though, when you typed in your password, your private signature could be forged by anyone with physical access to your terminal.

Fortunately, this problem can be fixed before a compromising situation like the example given above occurs. The Communicator 4.0 provides the option to present the password every time it is necessary to sign an e-mail, present a certificate to a site, or decrypt e-mail. This option can be set in the Communicator 4.0 through the Security Window with the Passwords option (see Figure 5.2). The option to request the password every time the certificate is necessary should be enabled, and the default configuration asking for the password only once should be disabled. The other option is to request the password after a period of inactivity. This latter option is less safe than asking for it every time, but safer than the option to ask for it only once. The fact that these options are available to users to configure (if users find them) indicates that Netscape is well aware of the security risks associated with cached passwords. Unfortunately, Netscape came down on the side of convenience, rather than security, in making the default configuration to ask for the password only once.

accounts are set up in the default configuration of the machine when it is installed out of the box. In many cases, guest accounts either do not have password protection or have passwords that may be as guessable as "guest." Many Unix systems have guest or demo accounts set up by default without any password protection. (Problems with guest accounts unique to NT machines are elaborated on shortly.) One of the first tasks of the system administrator should be to eliminate all accounts for which there is no valid associated user. This practice makes sense not only during install, but also during periodic inspections of the password file. If crackers do manage to break into your system, they will often leave back doors open to provide an easy means of reentry in the future. Adding a new user account is an easy way to get authenticated privileged access to the machine.

Default CGI Scripts Another deadly default found across platforms is the inclusion of CGI scripts with Web server software distributions. When Web server software is installed, several CGI scripts are installed in source and binary directories. The purpose of these CGI scripts is generally to provide some sample CGI scripts to demonstrate how CGI scripts can be used and how they are written. The problem with these scripts is twofold. First, they were written for demonstration and educational purposes, not for commercial use. Therefore, they may contain flaws (and several do) that can be exploited by untrusted users to gain unauthorized privilege. Second, because these are installed by default on Web servers everywhere, finding a flaw in one of these scripts may be enough to compromise most of the installed base of a particular vendor's Web server.

Historically, there have been several vulnerable CGI scripts shipped with many of the widely used HTTP servers. These scripts are often overlooked by the installer and left enabled. These vulnerable scripts provide an attacker a very easily discovered means of compromising the system. One such vulnerable CGI script called phf was distributed with early versions of NCSA and Apache Web servers (1.5A and 1.0.3 and earlier, respectively) on Unix systems. This sample script provides an online form for a type of network "white-pages" phone-book look-up. This program was flawed in a way that could give untrusted Web surfers the ability to run arbitrary commands on the Web server host machine. Given the right combination of characters in a request, remote users are able to execute arbitrary commands on the server. Allowing an untrusted user to execute commands that potentially reveal sensitive information or damage files on the system is certainly a serious security hole. This particular vulnerability was caused by a C-language routine called escape_shell_cmd() that stripped out potentially dangerous characters from user input before it was passed to a shell [CERT-96:06 1996]. The routine neglected to strip out a key special character from user input. This special character provides the user the ability to run arbitrary commands appended to the request. This example illustrates that even the smallest of overlooked details can introduce the most gaping of security holes.

A CGI script called test-cgi, which has been distributed with versions of Apache, NCSA, and Netscape Commerce servers, has been found to be vulnerable [CERT-97:07 1997]. Utilizing the character "*" in a query to the test-cgi script will allow the remote user to obtain a filename listing of the contents of the server's cgi-bin directory. The "*" is interpreted by the Unix shell as a wild card, which matches the filename of each file in the directory where the test-cgi script resides. Such a listing can be extremely valuable to a malicious user because it provides the names of other CGI scripts that may be vulnerable to attack.

These examples illustrate that default CGI scripts can be very dangerous to keep on the server. It is very important for the default CGI scripts to be removed from the CGI directories unless they are absolutely necessary. It is important that each and every CGI script in the CGI directories serve a necessary function for the Web server and be accounted for during inspection. This means that the author of each script should be known and the purpose of each script be made explicit. These techniques are the simplest auditing checks that can be performed. Chapter 4 also describes how to properly configure CGI directories and set up appropriate privilege constraints. Later, in the Flaws in CGI Scripts section, flaws in CGI scripts that can pose vulnerabilities to the system are discussed.

Deadly Web Server Configurations Most Web server configuration problems apply across platforms. There are basic configuration problems in Web servers that can leave a Web site vulnerable to security intrusions regardless of which vendor's Web server is installed. Naturally, some vendors' configurations will be less secure than others. The following is a list of the most egregious types of Web server configuration vulnerabilities regardless of the Web server or platform:

> **Execution privilege.** The Web server should execute with the minimum privilege necessary to serve document retrieval requests and execute CGI scripts. The best policy is to create a new user account with minimal privileges under which the Web server can run. On Unix-flavored systems, this account does not need access to a shell. Under no condition should the Web server execute as root on Unix systems. On Windows NT systems, the user should not be the administrator account, which has the equivalent super user privileges.

Automatic directory listing. Most servers come configured with automatic directory listing turned on. This means that if a Web browser points to a directory in which no index.html file exists, the Web server will by default return the listing of the directory. This is especially dangerous for server-side program directories, where CGI program sources and executables reside. If the directories can be listed remotely, the program sources may be downloaded for examination. Any flaws in the programs may be discovered through inspection by a malicious user.

Server-side includes (SSIs). SSIs provide the ability to embed commands in an HTML document (Web page). When the HTML document with the embedded command is requested over the Web, the command executes *on the Web host* with the privilege of the Web server.

CGI directories. Unless otherwise specified, many Web servers will execute a program file suffixed with .cgi regardless of who owns it or where it is located. This can be problematic for unauthorized CGI programs placed in user directories. Because CGI programs can pose security hazards, they must be strictly controlled. Restricting directories from which CGI programs can execute is a necessary first step.

Access control. The directories from which documents and files can be retrieved by anyone via Web requests is specified in the Web server configuration files. Web servers also offer access control mechanisms to portions of the document root. Basic authentication mechanisms restrict access based on user or group names and passwords. Strong authentication uses digital certificates to provide access. These mechanisms are disabled by default. If sensitive or proprietary files are kept within this partition of the file system (called the document root), they may be easily compromised.

Cookie distribution. Some Web servers have the capability to utilize cookies for authentication purposes. Cookies are extensions to the HTTP protocol that allow the server to maintain *state* information about where a user has been and what the user has done. Cookies are sent between the user's Web browser and the originating Web site. A security/privacy problem can arise when cookies intended for one Web server are sent to another. This can occur if the cookies are misconfigured by the Web server. The authentication information and other privacy-related information may then be shared with unauthorized sites. A malicious server can capture a misdirected cookie and gain unauthorized access to the originating server by echoing the captured authentication cookie.

Document/CGI file permissions. Both Unix file systems and the Windows NT file server allow for the establishment of file ownership and read/write/execute permissions. The HTTP server relies on these permissions, coupled with the ACLs, to restrict unauthorized access. Errors in configuring either the OS-level access controls or the Web server access controls can result in the compromise of sensitive files on the server machines. For example, liberal read permissions on CGI directories under Microsoft IIS will allow clients to download the source code to the files within them [Microsoft 1997].

Windows NT Deadly Defaults Windows NT systems have specific default settings for the guest account, the everyone group, the administrator account, the SAM file, and the NetBIOS shares that can prove to be vulnerable to the server-side security.

Every copy of Windows NT has a guest account installed on it by default. This account cannot be deleted, only disabled. In NT Server 4.0 the guest account is disabled by default, and unless the administrator enables the account, users of NT Server 4.0 should not have to worry about this problem. Users of NT 4.0 Workstation and earlier versions of Windows NT do have to worry about this problem. If the guest account is enabled, a serious security risk is involved. When the guest user logs on to the system, the user does not have to input a password. This means that there is no control over who can log in as the guest. If the guest account did not have any permissions, this would not be a problem; however, the guest account is a member of the everyone group, which poses other problems discussed next. The best short-term fix is to disable the guest account on all NT Workstations.

The presence of the everyone group is a fairly serious problem for keeping Windows NT secure because this group has overly liberal access permissions. By default, the everyone group has read/write permission to the /<windows>/system32 directory. This represents a problem because a Trojan horse program, when placed in the /<windows>/system32 directory, will have the potential to grab all of the user passwords. The best solution is to disable the guest account and change the access permissions on the /<windows>/system32 directory such that the everyone group does not have write permissions by default.

Another security concern with Windows NT is the administrator account. The administrator account is susceptible to brute-force cracking. By default, the administrator's login name is administrator, though it need not be. The strength of the password selected for this account is another problem (dealt with in the Weak Authentication section). The most commonly used password for the administrator account seems to be admin or administrator. The second exacerbating problem is that, unlike other accounts, the administrator account does not lock out logins after a certain number of failed attempts. This situation is ideal for a brute-force attempt to break into an account through the front door. Given knowledge of the account user ID and no lockouts enforced on failed attempts, a program can repeatedly attempt to login by guessing the password based on commonly used passwords or permutations of site-specific information. One mitigating factor is that a time delay is introduced after failed login attempts. A quick fix is to change the name of the administrator account to something more obscure. If the account name is changed, crackers may not realize which account is the administrator account, making their job much more difficult. To make the account even more obscure, create a new user name called administrator, with no read/write privileges. This account could fool crackers into spending their time and resources breaking into a nonprivileged account. Of course, any login attempts to this account would also be suspicious and should flag intruder activity.

The Security Accounts Manager (SAM) password file is the cause of yet another security problem with Windows NT. If an emergency repair disk is made (a normal procedure during installation), a /<windows>/system32/ERD directory will be created with a copy of the SAM file that is accessible to the everyone group. A copy of the SAM file combined with a program such as Jeremy Allison's PWDump (see www.masteringcomputers.com/util/nt/pwdump.htm.) can crack the user's passwords. Again, one need only consider the guest account with everyone group privileges to see how simple it can be for an untrusted outsider to gain super user privileges. The fix is to either delete the /<windows>/system32/ERD/ directory or to change the permissions of the /<windows>/system32/ERD directory so that the SAM file contained within can not be accessed by anybody except the administrator.

Finally, the default permission settings for a NetBIOS share constitute another source of deadly defaults with NT. A NetBIOS share is a file share that is created for access to shared resources in a local network. When a new share is created, the default settings allow anyone full access to the share. This means that anybody can add, delete, or modify any file contained within the share. If critical files are contained within such a share, they may be easily compromised. A method to handle this situation is to make sure that each share has the appropriate permissions set to it.

Flaws in the Web Server

The Web server is the front-end software that responds to requests via the HTTP Web protocol. Although firewalls can prevent many kinds of Internet-based attacks, they must let through requests to legitimate services that the host site wishes to provide, such as Web service and mail. It is important to bear in mind that any network service can have flaws that make it vulnerable to attack. For example, the sendmail Unix mail server has a long and storied history of being flawed [Garfinkel and Spafford 1996]. Also, certain versions of FTP servers have been known to have flaws that have been exploited for malicious gain [CERT-95:16 1995] [CERT-93:06 1993]. The requests to these services generally come from unknown or untrusted services, so some of these requests may be malicious in nature.

An important consideration in connecting to the Internet is deciding which services to offer. Once determined, the services must be securely configured and updated to the latest version level or patch level. One way to determine if the version of your server software is vulnerable is to check security announcements from the CERT Coordination Center (www.cert.org). Another way is to check with your vendor for the latest version of the software that has probably fixed all the bugs found up to that release version. In this section, only flaws in the Web server are considered for purposes of illuminating flaws in the basic server of e-commerce transactions.

Flaws in the Web server software, configuration, and CGI scripts can permit malicious requests and unauthorized access to confidential information. Most vulnerabilities found in Web server software are platform specific. The vulnerabilities that apply to Web servers independent of platform have primarily been in flawed CGI scripts and the use of the GET method for retrieving data. (Flaws in CGI scripts are discussed later in this chapter.) Using the GET method to retrieve sensitive information can potentially expose clients' sensitive data (e.g., credit card numbers) to other untrusted sites, even when a secure connection is used. This problem, which was discussed in Chapter 4, is a flaw in the HTTP protocol rather than any one server implementation.

One of the first Web servers to be released and popularly adopted on Unix systems was the NCSA[3] HTTPd server, subsequently commercialized as Apache. Early versions of this server were known to have security-related flaws. The NCSA HTTPd is distributed in source code form, meaning that it can be examined for security flaws. The early examination and testing by users everywhere have not only found flaws, but also led to a more robust server against malicious Web requests. Currently, the Apache and Netscape's suite of servers are the most popular Web servers in the Unix market. Because Netscape's servers are proprietary, the source code is not generally available for inspection and peer review. As of this writing, no security-related flaws specific to Unix Web server software

---

[3] National Center for Supercomputer Applications, University of Illinois

are widely known. This is not to say, though, that flaws in Unix Web servers may not be uncovered in the future.

Flaws in the NT IIS Web Server A number of security-related flaws have been found in the most predominant server for the Windows NT platform, the NT/IIS Web server. Some of these flaws are summarized below. These flaws have been reported on several NT security Web sites, including NT Bugtraq (http://ntbugtraq.rc.on.ca), NT Security (www.ntsecurity.net), ISS's NT Vulnerabilities list (www.iss.net/vd/nt_vulnerabilities .html), and HackNT (www.ilinks.net/~486578/hack_NT/hacknt.html), but they have not been independently confirmed by the author. All of the vulnerabilities listed below have been patched in the most recent release versions of Microsoft's IIS Web server. The best policy to minimize your risk is to make sure your current version of IIS is the most recent release and to ensure that your operating system software is up to the latest Service Pack level. See Microsoft's Web pages (www.microsoft.com/security) for current security news and patches to Microsoft's products.

> **Truncate flaw.** This flaw takes advantage of the fact that IIS does not properly parse input fields to a batch script running on the server. A URL such as www.domain.com/scripts/exploit.bat>PATH\foo.bat will create a file foo.bat. If this file already exists, the file will be truncated, and potentially all of the data may be lost. A server is vulnerable if a batch executable file exists in the scripts directory such as the autoexec.bat file.
>
> **BAT/CMD flaw.** This flaw potentially allows any untrusted user to execute any arbitrary command on the NT server at the behest of the remote user. A URL command sent to the server, such as www.domain.com/scripts/exploit .bat?&commandA+?&commandB, will execute DOS commands on the server. Pressing the STOP button on the browser will interrupt the server from making a log of the command that is sent so that there will be no record of the attack. Adding a +?&time' or '+?&date to the end of the command will cause the server to pause for input.
>
> **Dot dot /..\.. flaw.** A flaw in the IIS server 1.0 potentially allows users to read and/or execute files on the NT server. A URL command such as www.domain.com/scripts..\..\scriptname allows any untrusted user to remotely execute a script or program on the server if the user knows the program name and relative path to the scripts directory. A command line such as www.domain.com/..\.. allows a user to browse and download files outside the

Web server root directory. These attacks allow a malicious user to gain information about the server in the first case; in the second case, the user can execute a potentially malicious script on the server.

Get ../.. flaw. A user can telnet to port 80, enter GET ../.., and cause the IIS server to crash. To fix this flaw, telnet can be disabled.

ASP flaw. Users can download unprocessed Active Server Pages files by entering the standard URL followed by a period. For example, sending the URL www.domain.com/something.asp. to an IIS server will download the unprocessed ASP file to the user. Any security parameters stored in these files can be easily browsed. Through this attack a malicious user can gain information about how to exploit a script. This attacks works on all versions of NT 4.0 that are running IIS 1.0 or 2.0.

8K URL bug. This attack will result in the IIS crashing when it is sent with a large-length URL. The length of the URL can vary, but it seems to be around 8K. The range is reported as 4K to 12K.

Telnet to Port 1031. Another attack that can be used on IIS is a telnet-based attack. This attack works on versions NT 3.51 and 4.0 that are running IIS server. The attacker initiates a telnet connection to port 1031 (the inetinfo.exe port) and types a single character, which causes the connection to close and IIS to crash.

The vulnerabilities described for NT are meant to illustrate some of the vulnerabilities specific to NT's IIS Web server. Although these flaws have been patched, it is important to remember that the server software, OS software, and Service Packs need to be upgraded to the latest versions. The number of vulnerabilities already found indicate that NT is not immune to the security flaws that have plagued many other OSs, including Unix. The fact that NT is relatively new gives even greater reason to believe that flaws will continue to be found at a frequent rate until NT's development stabilizes.

Flaws in CGI Scripts

The Common Gateway Interface (CGI) provides the means for running server-side programs in response to Web requests. CGI scripts are supported in most widely available HTTP servers. CGI standardizes the way in which applications on the server host are passed input from an HTTP request. Because these applications execute on the server machine and receive input of any kind (expected or malicious), they can pose serious security risks to the server if they are not carefully implemented. CGI vulnerabilities apply equally across Unix and NT platforms. The cross-platform problems with CGI are parsed HTML, also known as Server Side Includes (SSIs), shell interpreters left in the scripts directory, and malicious input handling. The problem with SSIs was discussed in Burying the Deadly Defaults. Leaving shell interpreters such as Perl in the scripts/ directory on NT systems or the cgi-bin/ directories on Unix systems poses a security threat. These interpreters will accept any command (malicious or not) from untrusted users and execute them on the server machine. It is a trivial matter to grab confidential documents and password files through this error. Unfortunately, early versions of Netscape documents recommended placing the Perl interpreter in the scripts/ and cgi-bin/ directories to overcome PATH problems for CGI scripts.

Stripping the Input to CGI Most CGI-related security issues stem from failing to remove meta-characters and commands from user input sent to the CGI scripts. These character sequences have special meaning to command interpreters called by these scripts. The result is that an untrusted user may be able to execute arbitrary commands on the server machine if they are embedded in an HTTP request. The phf script distributed with the NCSA HTTPd version 1.4.2 and earlier provides a good example of a CGI script that failed to remove meta-characters with a corresponding large impact on the security of the system. This problem was described in the Default CGI Scripts section.

CGI Security Problems on Windows NT Many CGI scripts have been exploited on Unix platforms, but NT platforms are not free from security problems. For example, a vulnerability in the Microsoft FrontPage Server Extensions has been discovered [Microsoft FrontPage 1997]. This product is intended to allow users to publish Web pages to an Internet service provider. The vulnerable Server Extensions operate under a variety of platforms, including Windows NT, Linux, Solaris, AIX, IRIX, SunOS, and HP-UX. They operate through the use of three CGI executables, which perform the publishing and supporting functionality. Apparently, the application does not filter out raw HTML from entry fields, which when properly exploited, allows users to append content to Web pages for which they should not have authority. A second, possibly more serious, concern is that the Server Extensions also allow users to upload custom-grown CGI scripts onto the server to be executed at anyone's whim. Allowing other people to upload CGI scripts is a bad idea in general.

Measures for Guarding against CGI Exploits The severity of the vulnerable CGI problem increases dramatically if the HTTP server invokes the CGI script while executing under a privileged User ID. The User ID of a process determines the amount of access granted to it. In the case of Unix, if this User ID happens to be 0, signifying the super user, the process may access or delete any file on the system. If a CGI application executing with these privileges is exploited, the results can be disastrous. This problem is circumvented when the HTTP server executes as a user with no special privileges.

To guard against CGI script exploits, all input to a CGI script must be stripped of all characters that have special meaning before being passed to a command interpreter. The use of any routines that may use user input to form the argument to a system command, such as the C library calls popen() and system() or the Perl eval() and backtick (`) functions, should be avoided or used with utmost caution.

An option called "tainting" can be activated for CGI scripts written in Perl. "Tainted" data is data that comes from outside the program and includes any user input, environment variables, or file input. In taint mode, the Perl interpreter will refuse to allow any tainted data to be used in commands that modify files, processes, or any command that invokes a sub-shell [Wall, Chriastiansen, and Schwartz 1996].

The best policy is to audit and control the CGI scripts placed on the server and audit the contents of CGI executable directories. Also, disable or delete any CGI scripts that have no reason for being there, and be aware of what is installed and enabled by default in a server installation. Do not assume that the default configuration of any server is secure by any means. Finally, the CGI exploitation issue is just as relevant (and dangerous) under Windows NT as it under Unix.

More advanced techniques for analyzing CGI scripts may be appropriate for organizations that cannot assume much risk from CGI exploits. For example, it is a good idea to use a package such as Tripwire (see www.cs.purdue.edu/coast/coast-tools.html) to create checksums or hashes of the executable images of each CGI program. The checksums should be regenerated and checked periodically to ensure that the CGI scripts have not been altered or corrupted in any way (or that new CGI programs have been added to the CGI binary directory). Some machines have check-summing functions built into the OS. These machines call the portion of the file system that is checked and rechecked periodically the trusted computing base (TCB). System executables and CGI scripts are appropriate files to include as part of the TCB. The TCB checking functions need to be scheduled periodically to ensure detection of altered files.

Another advanced technique is to inspect the CGI script sources for dangerous programming constructs. For example, opening a system pipe and executing commands with arguments built from user input is a bad idea. Although that may sound esoteric, it is a practice found in many CGI scripts that allows an untrusted user to execute system commands by manipulating the input. Finally, it is a good idea to dynamically test CGI scripts with particular emphasis on using unexpected, garbage, and malicious input before putting CGI scripts up on the Web server.

Networking Software Insecurity

Networking software supports shared file systems, remote logins, interprocess communications, and all manner of Internet services. Network services are so closely integrated with the operating systems of the machines they interconnect that they are often called network operating systems (NOSs). In securing the network server machines, people often overlook an aspect of server-side security: the web of trust that is woven between locally networked machines. Even if the Web server host is locked down tight, a security intrusion in a trusted machine may compromise the security of the Web server or even the critical database server machines.

Cross-Platform Vulnerabilities Many network services have security problems that span all platforms. Authentication in the telnet and FTP protocols involves sending a password in plaintext across the network. The passwords can be intercepted by anyone utilizing a packet sniffer on a local or intermediate network between users' consoles and the remote machine that they are logging into. Basic authentication for Web servers suffers from the same problem. User IDs and passwords are sent in plaintext over the Internet.

The Domain Name Service (DNS) is network service provided for Internet machine name resolution that has proved to be vulnerable across several different platforms. DNS was developed in response to the growing number of machines connected to the Internet. It provides a means for acquiring a host's network IP address based on a more intuitive text host name. Both Windows NT and Unix platforms utilize this protocol. Many of the security problems associated with DNS relate to its provision for caching entries, which speeds up the name resolution. There exist attacks for polluting a server's DNS cache with incorrect addresses. These attacks allow malicious users to redirect Internet traffic to a site of their choosing—effectively allowing them to masquerade as another site. Microsoft's DNS implementation for Windows NT 4.0 is especially vulnerable to such attacks because it uses a predictable means of choosing query IDs for making DNS requests [Microsoft DNS 1997]. Microsoft has addressed this problem. See the vendor's Web site for a hotfix, patch, Service Pack, or upgrade. A good practice in configuring network servers is to require reverse DNS lookups. This tactic will not solve all DNS attacks, but it will thwart a good majority of hackers who use domain names that do not match their IP addresses.

Unix-Specific Network Software Vulnerabilities The example of the vulnerability of Sun's NIS was given early in this chapter (Minding the OS) for how vulnerabilities in OS-related software can compromise system security. Most of the vulnerabilities in Unix networking software relate to software designed to facilitate interprocess or remote communication between machines. RPC is the best example of vulnerable networking software on Unix machines.

The Remote Procedure Call (RPC) protocol was developed by Sun Microsystems in the 1980s to aid in making a group of Unix workstations behave as a single system. RPC has proved over time to be an insecure protocol for interprocess communications. Two file-sharing protocols widely used on Unix systems, NIS/YP and NFS, are based on the insecure RPC. Security problems related to RPC stem from its weak authentication mechanisms. RPC is usually configured to use either no authentication at all or "Unix" (AUTH_UNIX) authentication, which relies on user and group ID information. The problem is that this information is trusted by the server to be correct. This information can be easily spoofed by illegitimate parties to fool the authentication of RPC. A "secure" RPC implementation exists that utilizes DES encryption to address these problems. However, it is not widely used because all network clients must be recompiled to support it.

NIS is vulnerable because it relies on RPC. Recall that the security problem with NIS is that an untrusted host need only connect to a NIS server's RPC portmapper and be able to guess the NIS domain name (typically set to the organization's domain name) in order to acquire copies of the system password file. A freely available exploit utility called ypx will automatically attempt to guess a remote site's NIS domain and fetch its password files (available at www.deter.com/unix/software/ypx.sh.gzx).

In many cases, security through obscurity is an approach to hiding poor secure technologies, but this approach works well in protecting corporate assets against NIS attacks. An obscure NIS domain name should be chosen that is not the same as the Internet domain name and that cannot be easily guessed. To protect against Internet-based attacks, a filtering router should be configured to block traffic from the Internet to the RPC portmapper.

Windows NT-Specific Network Vulnerabilities The networking software on Windows NT systems is called NetBIOS. NetBIOS has been vulnerable to attacks because of the method by which users are authenticated. The need to support compatibility with legacy authentication protocols has proven to be the albatross around Microsoft's neck. Another problem with NetBIOS is the ability of an untrusted user to mount file shares.

This ability gives malicious users the ability to read, erase, and create files on shares mounted from untrusted machines.

Server Message Block (SMB) is an application layer protocol that allows system resources (e.g., files and printers) to be shared across networks. SMB is a decade-old technology developed by Intel and Microsoft jointly. Over that time period, different "dialects" of SMB have emerged, including NTLM 0.12 and, recently, CIFS (Common Internet File System). Because several different dialects of SMB are installed on Windows machines, an SMB client and server must initially negotiate and agree to a common dialect. The necessity for Microsoft to support legacy dialects has made today's NT systems vulnerable to flaws in older dialects. SMB authentication is performed through one of three methods: plaintext, LanMan, and NTLM.

The most basic (and insecure) of these is plaintext authentication. With that method, the user name and password are sent over the network in the clear. Anybody who has installed a network sniffer can grab user names and passwords easily. Although using plaintext authentication is not advised, it is also possible that you may be tricked into using it without your knowledge. An attack called the *Downgrade Attack* can fool an SMB client that normally sends user names and passwords in encrypted form into sending them in plaintext [Ramsbottom 1997]. The attack takes advantage of the fact that NT systems must be downward compatible and fools the client into using plaintext authentication rather than NTLM authentication. Microsoft is addressing this problem by not allowing a server to require an SMB client to authenticate down from a more secure protocol to a less secure protocol.

LanMan and NTLM both use a challenge-response form of authentication. Rather than sending in the password in plaintext, both authentication methods use encryption to obscure the real password. Before the authentication begins, the client and server must agree to the method used to authenticate. Assume for now that LanMan authentication is agreed upon. In a challenge/response system, when a client wishes to authenticate to the server, the server first sends a random eight-character-long challenge called a *nonce*. The client accepts the nonce and encrypts it using three 7-bit DES keys that consist of the user's 16-bit DES encrypted password padded by five null characters. The result is a 24-bit ciphertext that is sent back to the server. The server executes the same algorithm, using its copy of the user's password from its SAM database. If the server generates the same ciphertext as the client, the client is authenticated. It is important to realize that the password itself need not be known by the SMB client. Rather, the client need only have access to the DES-encrypted password hash to perform the authentication. Why point out the distinction? Because if a malicious user were able to obtain the password hashes (from the SAM, for example), a malicious SMB client could be coded from the password hash without actually knowing the password itself. For this reason, it is imperative in NT systems that the password hashes in the SAM database not be compromised.

The NTLM authentication is almost identical to the LanMan authentication except that an additional 24 bits of ciphertext are added to the LanMan-style response. The additional 24 bits are generated from the same information, but with the MD4 algorithm, rather than DES encryption [Ramsbottom 1997]. The result that is sent back to the server is 48 bits rather then 24. The use of MD4, as well as the longer response, makes this authentication scheme more secure to packet sniffing then the LanMan authentication. The security risk with both the LanMan and NTLM authentication processes is that they are also susceptible to sniffing, albeit with more difficulty than the plaintext authentication. Challenge-response systems are generally secure to sniffers and replay attacks. However, Microsoft's implementation of the SMB challenge-response system leaves it vulnerable to a replay attack using sniffers [Ramsbottom 1997].

To compromise the password, the attacker must be able to monitor the network using network sniffers. Recall that the encrypted response for both LanMan and NTLM uses the password hash as its input. If the attacker does not have access to the password hashes (such as from the SAM database), an attack can still determine the password hash. The attacker needs to capture both the nonce and the encrypted response. This pair has the same relationship as a plaintext password and its encrypted hash. With both components, a hacker can either wage a brute-force attack or use a dictionary-based attack to guess the encrypted response. If the password chosen is sufficiently weak, the password hash can be guessed and used to authenticate the hacker to the SMB server.

Another well-known vulnerability with NetBIOS involves the ability to remotely mount unprotected shares. A file share is unprotected if the user does not explicitly require authentication to be performed before accessing a network-shared file or directory. By modifying the code to an SMB client, a malicious user from the Internet can access any network shared files or directories on a computer that is connected to the Internet. Code to modify the SMB client is readily available on the Internet. Because the shares are unprotected, users can do anything they want, including deleting, modifying, copying, or adding files on the network share. The malicious client can even attack protected shares through brute-force authentication attacks. The best defense against mounting from untrusted remote sites is to configure the firewall to filter out all NetBIOS traffic originating from the Internet so that a malicious client cannot get through the firewall.

Denial of Service

Denial-of-service attacks typically attempt to bring down network servers and a site's access to the Internet. Some denial-of-service attacks can be performed on a smaller scale. For example, Java applets can implement denial-of-service attacks that consume all of your computer's memory and CPU resources (see Holes in the Sandbox, Chapter 2). This type of attack can prevent you from getting work done on your machine. The denial-of-service attacks considered in this section are those that can bring down whole sites off the Internet.

Denial-of-service attacks rank among the most malicious Internet-based attacks. Many companies are now as dependent on the Internet as they are on the phone for conducting business. Launching a denial-of-service attack against an Internet service provider or a particular business is tantamount to bringing the phone system down (a physical attack could do both at once). Companies that rely on the Internet for business stand to lose a lot of revenue from denial-of-service attacks. Online trading companies and ISPs are obvious examples. Bringing down an ISP affects not only the ISP, but also all the businesses that rely on the ISP for Internet service. If an ISP is perceived to be unreliable for service, many of its clients will leave it for one of the other many choices of national and local ISPs available. One of the more infamous attacks against an ISP was launched against Public Access Networks (PANIX), a New York ISP. The crackers who attacked PANIX used the TCP/IP SYN flood attack. This attack floods the target site with hundreds of incomplete Internet connections per second, effectively preventing any other network connections from being made to the victim network server. The TCP/IP protocol for Internet connections makes this attack possible. Unfortunately, there are no good defenses against it—leaving many sites vulnerable to denial-of-service attacks. A security expert at Lucent Technologies called this attack "the final Internet security problem" that he has been anticipating [Edupage Editors 1996].

Denial-of-service attacks are commonly staged in two main forms. The first form is an attack that will prevent other users from accessing the computer remotely. The second form will either eat up system resources or crash the target computer. Some of these attacks are platform independent, and others are specific to Windows NT. Two well-known denial-of-service attacks that affect both Windows NT and Unix systems are the SYN flood attack and the Ping O' Death attack. In addition, NT-specific denial-of-service attacks include out-of-band attacks, two types of DNS server attacks, RPC attacks, and a locking attack.

Cross-Platform Attacks: SYN Flood and Ping O' Death The SYN flood attack is one of the most widely known and publicized attacks against systems that use the Internet TCP/IP protocol. This attack affects both Windows NT and Unix platforms. The objective of the SYN flood attack is to deny other users access to the target computer. The attack works fairly simply. The objective is to fill up a buffer of incoming requests on the target machine with incomplete connections. When the buffer is full, the target machine can no longer receive any connection requests. The attacker sends a SYN request—the first stage of a three-stage TCP/IP connection protocol—to the target computer while spoofing the originating address of the request to that of another machine. The other machine has to be routable but not reachable [daemon9 et al. 1996].

After receiving the SYN request, the target machine will acknowledge the connection attempt with a SYN-ACK response—the second stage of the TCP/IP connection protocol. However, because the originating machine address has been spoofed and the spoofed machine is effectively off-line, the target machine will have to wait the full time-out period for the final acknowledgment. Not receiving a reply, the target computer will continue to send SYN-ACK responses for several minutes, holding open the connection and occupying a location in the incoming connection queue. If the attacking computer continues to send distinct SYN messages, the queue for handling requests will fill up quickly. The result will be that no other *legitimate* connections can be made to the target machine. Unfortunately, the source code to an exploit that automates the SYN flood attack against a site of the cracker's choice has been released in an underground newsletter [daemon9 et al. 1996]. The upshot of this information is that anyone one who knows how to download and install software can now launch severe denial-of-service attacks against any other Internet site.

Some security experts have called on the Internet community at large to engage in a war against these types of disabling attacks. How can Internet sites protect themselves and others? One characteristic of the SYN flood attack mentioned above is that a machine's IP address is spoofed. Typically, to draw attention away from the cracker's own site, the spoofed IP address will not be a machine on the cracker's own network. This attribute of SYN flood attacks can be used by Internet service providers and even Internet sites to stop SYN flood attacks at their source. An ISP can drop any outbound packets with originating addresses that do not belong to the domain of addresses the ISP services. Clearly, packets originating from within one of the ISP's domains should not have an originating address with a domain outside the ISP's serviced domains. Although this measure would not stop all SYN flood denial-of-service attacks, it would go a long way toward stopping the majority of SYN flood attacks.

Internet sites can incorporate some defensive measures against the SYN flood attack. On Unix-based systems, some stopgap countermeasures include increasing the size of the queue from about five to several thousand requests. In particular, Solaris systems can dynamically increase the buffer of incoming requests as more SYN requests are received. A Linux fix provides a mechanism that will randomly delete a pending connection entry if the queue becomes full, which stops incoming connection requests from being refused. For Windows NT, Microsoft's security Web page (www.microsoft.com/security) discusses this attack with some possible countermeasures.

The Ping O' Death attack has varying effects on different operating systems. The attack works by sending a series of oversized packets via the ping command. The packets are reassembled at the host machine by the ping server. The result of reassembling the large packets is a very large datagram that will overrun the incoming ping buffer. Depending on which flavor of Unix at which version level, the effects of the attack could hang, crash, or reboot the system. The attack is described and the vulnerable platforms are listed at the Ping O' Death Web page: www.sophist.demon.co.uk/ping/index.html. On Windows NT, the result will depend on whether NT 4.0 or 3.51 is running. NT 4.0 will crash, and NT 3.51 could hang, crash, or reboot the system. Versions of Unix have patches out for this attack, and both versions of NT have patches out.

Windows NT-Specific Denial-of-Service Attacks Several types of denial-of-service attacks are effective against Windows NT systems, in particular. These sites can be found in the NT Security Web sources cited at the back of this chapter. Out Of Band (OOB) attacks have been shown to shut Windows NT systems down with relative ease. Windows NT has also proven to be vulnerable to DNS-based attacks. RPC, the insecure protocol discussed earlier with respect to Unix systems, is also a liability to Windows NT systems, especially with denial-of-service attacks. Finally, an example of an odd attack unique to Windows NT systems that locks out users from using a shared application is described.

Windows NT has proven not to be robust against data-driven attacks to OOB ports. Out Of Band refers to a provision in the TCP/IP protocol implementation that allows certain data to be marked "urgent." Not all operating systems implement this capability in their TCP/IP stacks. An attacker can send OOB data by initiating a connection and sending some data that is specified as OOB. On receiving OOB data, NT can do any number of things, from turning the screen white to causing the computer not to be able to handle any data from the network. In order to secure your machines against these types of attacks, see Microsoft for available patches.

There are two types of Domain Name Service (DNS) attacks Windows NT machines are vulnerable to. In the first attack, a malicious user can crash the DNS server on a Windows NT Server 4.0 machine. The attack exploits a weakness in the DNS server in which a DNS client sends a reply message to a query that was never initiated. Upon receiving the reply packet, the DNS server will crash and cannot be used until the machine is rebooted. To ensure your NT server machine is not vulnerable to this attack, install Service Pack 3.

The second DNS attack creates a temporary spike in the CPU meter. Versions of NT running a DNS server are vulnerable to this attack. The attack works by initiating a telnet connection to port 53 (the DNS port on Windows NT) and entering a single alphabetic character. The result is that the CPU usage will rise to some value between 65 percent and 70 percent for about five minutes (this utilization will vary with each computer. The DNS denial-of-service problems are a result of the inability of the DNS server to handle anomalous or malicious inputs. The server is configured to handle only the inputs it is expecting in the proper sequence. The DNS attacks described here send DNS servers unexpected input that results in a denial-of-service to users of the network server machine.

A similar attack, using unexpected input, against the Remote Procedure Call service running on Windows NT systems can bring an NT server to its knees. The attack is simple to implement, which also makes it dangerous. An attacker need only to telnet to port 135 on an NT machine and type in a string of garbage characters. The RPC service running on port 135 will thrash on the garbage input until the CPU usage reaches 100 percent. Once the utilization meter tops out at 100 percent, the user can do little on the machine. The only recourse the user has is to reboot. Administrators should patch their systems against this flaw.

The final NT-specific attack described here is the *locking attack*. Unlike the other attacks that can bring a machine down, this attack prevents users from accessing and running shared programs such as those found in Microsoft Office. A widely distributed exploit program can be used to lock users—even the administrator—out of programs. Any user of any privilege can run this attack, including the guest user. As an example, a remote user can log onto the guest account, if it is not disabled, run the program continuously to lock users out of using a network shared program such as MS Word. This kind of attack can be employed by a competitor to prevent someone from completing a document on time. Providing this ability to an unprivileged user such as the guest account makes this attack feasible. Earlier in this chapter, the Windows NT Deadly

Default section described how vulnerable Windows NT systems are to guest accounts enabled out of the box. As always, administrators should consult the vendor for patches.

Weak Authentication

One of the weak links in any computer security system is authentication of users. Authentication is used to verify that a user is permitted access to the computer's resources. Everybody is used to authentication in all walks of life. Every time you unlock a door or start a car, you are providing a token of authentication—your key. Most of the time the lock does not know the bearer of the key, but the assumption is that the bearer is authorized for entry or usage. In most computer systems, authentication requires presentation of both identification and password. User IDs, abbreviated forms of identification, are used to inform the computer what level of privilege a particular user is granted. If the password offered with the user ID matches the password on record (in a password database), the user is granted access to the computer with the privilege level assigned to the user's account.

Authentication has proved to be a weak link because of the ease with which authentication can be foiled. The main problem is the selection of passwords. On most systems, users are given the prerogative to select their own passwords. A more secure method is to randomly generate passwords and assign them to users. The problem with this method is that a randomly generated password is much more difficult to remember than one selected by a user. In the interest of usability, most system administrators allow users to select and change their own passwords. Like many other areas in computer security, though, usability and convenience are usually at odds with security. The fallibility of having people select passwords is that people will tend to select passwords that, in addition to being easily remembered, are also easily guessed. For example, dictionary words are easy to guess. So are names, astrology signs, and other personal information. Some people have even published lists of frequently used passwords. All of these lists can be entered in a password cracker's database and used to guess passwords. For this reason, password databases should be obscured from everyone except the administrator, who should periodically inspect them for unauthorized new entries as well as test the strength of passwords using the same tools that crackers use.

Two advances will make user authentication more secure in the future: user certificates on smart cards and biometrics. User certificates work much like the certificates described in the sidebar on Netscape's Communicator 4.0 deadly default. The basic idea is that users generate a public/private key pair. The public key is vouched for by a certification authority who signs the user's certificate. To authenticate to a site, users present their certificates via the smart card or other token. If the protocol for presenting the certificate is secure, a user will be required to enter either the private key passphrase that serves as the user's signature or a PIN that authenticates the user to the smart card, which subsequently presents the certificate to the site. The overhead for this technique is high right now. The authenticating site needs to maintain a list of users and their public keys in order to authenticate users.

Biometrics Recent advances in biometrics are making authentication more reliable and less likely to be foiled. Biometric devices use some measurable property of people that is unique for each person in order to authenticate identities. For example, devices are now being commercialized that allow users to be identified and authenticated through only their fingerprints. Some fingerprint scanning devices will be built right into mouses to be as nonintrusive and transparent as possible [Pieper 1997]. Another form of authentication using biometrics is iris scanning. The human eye's iris has visible properties that are unique to each person. These properties can be recorded and used for positive identification in the future [Williams 1997].

Biometric devices can be used to authenticate identities in two ways. They can authenticate a presented form of identification or directly identify the person. In the former scenario, the user presents a form of identification such as a smart card or magnetic stripe card that is read by a card reader. The biometric is then read by a sensor. If the biometric read by the sensor matches the information stored on the card, authorization is given to the user. The advantage of this system is the low cost of processing. All the information necessary to authenticate resides on the smart card or token that the user carries. This system alleviates the necessity to maintain centralized databases of user identities and biometric signatures.

The second type of biometric authentication does not require a token to authenticate. In this case, users are not presenting any form of identification except their own biometric. This system can capture the biometric then perform a search on an existing database of biometric signatures. When a match is found, the identity of the user will be known, and the authentication and privilege will be given according to the information stored in the database for the user's identity. This system requires more server-side processing to maintain databases and perform searches to authenticate individuals.

Not all biometrics can be used for both types of identification. The recent advances in biometrics will likely drive biometric authentication outside the highly secret defense and nuclear industries into commercial applications such as e-commerce transactions. The rest of this section shifts focus to the form of authentication commonly practiced today: user IDs and passwords entered in a computer terminal.

Unix and Windows NT Authentication User names and passwords represent the information required for "front-door" access to Unix and NT platforms. The importance of secure, difficult-to-guess passwords cannot be overemphasized. Both Windows NT and Unix platforms do not store the user's actual password in plaintext for security reasons. If the actual plaintext password were stored and the system were compromised such that the file containing the passwords could be viewed, full access to every account on the system could be achieved. Instead, they store a hash of the password, which is the result of using the password as the input to a one-way hash function. A one-way hash function is a theoretically irreversible procedure that maps the text password onto a unique, random-looking string of characters. Theoretically, a user's password cannot be determined from the hash value; however, if a password guess hashes to the same string as a user's stored password hash value, it can be determined with a high degree of certainty that the guess is, in fact, the same as the user's true password.

Password authentication under NT and Unix is performed precisely in this manner—a password entered in a login attempt is first run through the secure hash function, and the result is compared with the particular user's stored hash value. If the two values match, the password is correct, and the user is allowed to proceed; if they do not, the user is denied access.

Unix and Windows NT differ in the method that is used to create the password hash values. Unix uses an algorithm derived from the Digital Encryption Standard (DES) with a maximum password length of 8 characters. The maximum password length for Windows NT is 14 characters. Windows NT actually computes and stores two different hash values for the same password [Ramsbottom 1997]. One is used for the NT login and the other is used in authentication for shared network resources—the SMB password. The NT login hash is computed through use of the MD4 algorithm developed by Ron Rivest of RSA Data Security, which is considered to be secure for this purpose. For the second hash for the SMB password, the password is split in half and the parts are independently encrypted with "magic" constants using the DES algorithm [Ramsbottom 1997]. This process introduces a great deal of weakness into the system because the plaintext for the each smaller piece can be found in much less computational time than if the password were encrypted as a single piece. The argument is simple: if the key space is exhaustively searched for one half of the password (seven characters), the searcher is guaranteed to recover keys for both halves of the SMB password (because the two key spaces are identical). To make matters worse, the SMB password is identical to the login password, except for the alphabetic case. This means the strong MD4 algorithm used for the NT login password is rendered useless if the SMB password is captured and cracked. It takes a trivial amount of extra computational time to recover the NT login password if the SMB password is found.

An additional weakness in the Windows NT password storage scheme is the lack of *salt*. In Unix, a two-character salt is added to the password hash, basically defining a permutation on the hash. This permutation process prevents identical passwords from having identical hashes (it is unlikely that the randomly chosen salt value will be the same). Windows NT provides no such provision. The upshot of not using salt is that if the password hashes are found, and two users have the same password, these two stored hash values will be the same, thus breaking two passwords for the price of one.

Accessing the Password Database The strength—that is, the irreversibility—of the password hashes is a moot point if the hashes themselves are completely and undeniably protected from prying eyes. If this were the case, one could simply store the plaintext password in a file for authentication purposes without going to the lengths of obscuring it through the hashing process. Keeping the password file hidden is not truly possible in case of either Unix or Windows NT. The password file in Unix can be read by any user on the system in many cases. A method called shadowing passwords can be employed in some Unix implementations to hide the actual hash values from public view. The administrator, commonly referred to as the super user, can still peruse the file containing the password hashes, though.

Windows NT utilizes a scheme much like shadow passwords in Unix. Password hash values are stored in the SAM (Security Accounts Manager) portion of the system registry. This part of the registry is accessible only to the system administrator. Microsoft employs a "security through obscurity" approach to the storage of the password hashes by encrypting the hashes using DES with a key derived from the Relative Domain ID (RID) [Ramsbottom 1997]. When this was discovered, password hashes could be easily be unobfuscated. Microsoft has purportedly made this process much more difficult in Service Pack 3 for Windows NT 4.0, which adds 128-bit encryption to the obfuscation process.

Although obfuscating the password database can be a good security measure (a better one is to ensure that the passwords are strong, even if the database is found), security of the system should not rely on the obfuscation. This point was underscored by a program called PWDump. PWDump, written by Jeremy Allison <jra@cygnus.com>, is able to extract user information and password hashes by first changing access permissions of the SAM, then unobfuscating the password hashes and writing the result to a file. The SAM access permissions are then restored. This process requires system administrator permissions to execute, but these hashes are necessarily entirely secure. This program could potentially be executed as a Trojan horse or even as a malicious ActiveX control. More likely, though, an unprotected copy of the SAM may reside elsewhere on the machine. This occurs when an Emergency Restore Disk (ERD) is created, and the SAM is backed up. Because Unix password hashes are most commonly world readable, the gymnastics required to access NT password hashes are not necessary under Unix.

Assuming that the password hashes for both platforms can be obtained, one might ask what can be done with them? As stated above, the reversal of a one-way hash function is theoretically impossible. However, a method known as a dictionary attack can be employed to find the plaintext password. In a dictionary attack a guess of the password is made, and this guess is then hashed. The hash of the guessed password and the true password are then compared. If the two match, the guess is correct and the attacker now knows the victim's password. If the two hash values do not match, the guess is deemed to be incorrect, and the entire process is then repeated until the correct password is found. As the name of the attack implies, a dictionary is often used as a basis for generating guesses. Although this may sound like a tedious process, modern CPUs can accomplish the task extremely quickly. There are many very effective password-cracking utilities—including Crack written by Alec Muffett, which operates on both Unix and NT platforms, and L0pht Crack written by L0pht Heavy Industries—that run under the NT platform.

Clearly, passwords are weak links in the security of any system. Until user certificates or secure biometrics are widely employed in commercial systems, the best defense against authentication attacks is to enforce long passwords (at least eight characters with mixed case and numbers), ensure that users do not choose passwords that are based on dictionary words, their names, or user IDs, and routinely run password crackers to find weak passwords before the crackers do.

Operating System Holes

A whole range of software, typically called system software, provides services to the operating system. Because system software performs a number of functions in support of system services, the software often needs special privileges, such as super user access. Vulnerabilities in the system software can be exploited to escalate privilege for unauthorized users. Unlike software described in the other categories in this chapter, much of the system software is not available to untrusted outside users if the machines are protected behind a properly configured firewall.

To get an appreciation of how much system software is vulnerable to malicious exploits, you really need look at the Bugtraq newsgroup or Web archive (www.geek-girl.com/bugtraq/index.html). Security-related problems in OS software come out nearly every day across all kinds of operating systems. Given the range of programs that could be covered, this section focuses on two types of attacks relevant to Unix and NT systems: buffer overflows and system registry attacks.

Buffer Overflows A vast majority of Unix-specific OS software problems are related to buffer overflows, also called buffer overruns and stack smashing. A buffer overflow is caused by errors in C programs that fail to check the length of the input before writing it to a fixed length buffer. A buffer is simply a contiguous section of memory assigned to data of a particular type. C programmers typically call buffers arrays. When arrays are dynamically allocated during runtime, a certain section of memory (the buffers) is set aside for variables when functions are called. Problems can occur when the variables are filled with values that exceed the amount of memory allocated for their corresponding buffers. If the called function is filling an array with data read in from user input, for example, and function fails to check the length of the input, it may be possible to over-flow the buffer with user-inputted data. In the best case, overrunning the buffer has no discernible effect on the program. In the worst case, the user has figured out exactly how to manipulate the data that is overrunning the buffer to execute instructions contained in the input data. In most cases, overrunning the buffer will result in a *segmentation fault*, generally followed by the much-hated *core dump*—the Unix equivalent of choking on bad input.

How can users manipulate the program to execute instructions of their choosing? The user must know specific details of the machine processor architecture such as how data is stored on the program stack in relation to other reference points for called functions, including the stack pointer and return instruction pointer. If the end user knows these reference points and relations precisely, and the program is vulnerable to buffer overflows, an attack can be launched that overwrites the stack frame with enough data to reach the return instruction pointer, which is then replaced with an address of the user's choice. This address usually points to an address within the overwritten stack frame that contains a series of assembly language instructions implementing the commands of the user's choice. Coming up with an exploit attack is quite complex, but buffer overflow errors are common. Once a buffer overflow error is found, sophisticated crackers (and even research scientists) can manipulate the data structures to demonstrate the ability to execute arbitrary code.

All of this information would not be very useful if it were not for the fact that the system software that is vulnerable to buffer overflows typically has a high level of system privileges. Many system software programs can run with the privileges of the super user even when called by a nonprivileged user. These programs are called set user-ID (SUID) utility programs. In Unix, the user ID of a process determines the privileges that it is given on the system. Many utilities need super user privileges in order to work, but non-privileged users need the ability to run them. A program that executes under super user privileges that can be called by a nonprivileged user is called a SUID root program. An example is the passwd command in Unix. The passwd command allows users to change their passwords by altering the system password file. However, because this file is writable only by the super user, the utility would normally need to be run by an administrator in order to work. The passwd utility is available to nonprivileged users through SUID, which allows the utility to run with full super user privileges, even when invoked by a nonprivileged user. If utilities that run using the SUID root mechanism are exploited, the attacker may obtain super user access.

Consider an SUID root program that has a buffer overflow vulnerability. Regardless of what function the program is *supposed* to perform, simply by exploiting a buffer overflow vulnerability, malicious users can instruct the program to perform any instructions of their choice with the privilege of the super user. The most common exploitation is to manipulate the buffer overflow vulnerability to create a command shell with super user privileges. From the command shell, the malicious user can execute any system commands with the rank and privileges of the super user. This means that attackers can create or delete user accounts and execute virtually any instruction on the machines without restriction. The Unix utility programs vulnerable to buffer overflows are too numerous to list, but examples such as umount, xlock, and recently lpr have suffered from such vulnerabilities. Additional attacks on SUID root programs rely on poorly written code that does not adequately filter "escape" characters from user input. If such a program constructs operating system commands directly from this input, the malicious user may be permitted to run arbitrary commands as a privileged user. Such attacks are very similar to those used to exploit vulnerable CGI applications.

Currently, the best solution to ensure that your organization's operating systems are not at risk to buffer overflow attacks is to stay on top of security lists such as Bugtraq, monitor incident response lists such as CERT (www.cert.org), and apply OS vendor patches as they become available.

Windows NT programs are not free from buffer overflow problems. A recent bug in Microsoft IIS Web server suffers from a buffer overflow problem that will crash the server when it is exercised (see the Flaws in the NT IIS Web Server section earlier in this chapter).

Windows NT System Registry Attacks Buffer overflow problems are found in programs that execute on both Unix and NT platforms, but Windows NT platforms suffer from attacks unique to this platform: the system registry attacks. The NT system registry contains the system configuration information and keeps track of all program executables. Corrupting this file can result in complete system failures. Knowing the contents of the registry also provides attackers with valuable information that can be used to compromise the system. For this reason, the system registry is a common target for hackers. Unless certain steps are taken, it is trivial to break in and modify the registry. Types of attacks include those that examine the registry, alter the registry, and destroy the registry.

The default settings for the registry make it readable by the everyone group. Assuming that the guest account is enabled, any user can log in and view the registry in the attack scenario described in Windows NT Deadly Defaults section. The security risk is that the entire system configuration is then viewable to the remote user. Information contained within can be used to aid in a break-in attempt. The best defense against this type of attack is to restrict the access permissions for the everyone group and to disable the guest account.

As well as being readable by the everyone group, parts of the registry are writable by members of the everyone group. For example, the administrator, who is also a member of the everyone group, has a high level of access privilege to the system registry. This level of privilege could be used to compromise the system registry. For example, files ending in .reg will automatically write to the registry when it is opened. The privilege that a .reg file assumes is that of the user who executes it. For example, consider a Trojan horse .reg file placed on the system. A curious administrator may open the file. Opening the file gives the .reg file the privileges of the administrator (effectively SUID root), which can then be used to alter any part of the registry.

The final types of attack against the system registry are attempts to destroy the registry. Included with some installs of NT is a program called rollback.exe. This program destroys the NT registry, and the result is that the entire system has to be reinstalled. This program can be used to destroy the registry of target computers when used as a Trojan horse. For example, the program can be renamed a common executable program. Subsequently, when a user executes the Trojan horse, the result will be the wiping of the system registry file. The only way to avoid this is to be careful about what programs you download and execute.

Defending the Server

Clearly, the security of the network server operating system software is as critical to the security of e-commerce as are the other components described in this book. This chapter began with a discussion of firewalls' inadequacy for protecting the network server against data-driven attacks. The second section of this chapter, The Network Server Vulnerabilities, classified common vulnerabilities in network servers into seven categories, many of which can be exploited even through well-configured firewalls. Furthermore, the preceding section considered the vulnerabilities as they pertained to the two most common desktop platforms today: Windows NT and Unix systems. Many of the vulnerabilities apply across both platforms; some are specific to either Windows NT or Unix.

What we can glean from this study is that since the introduction of Windows NT, a number of vulnerabilities have been reported and demonstrated in practice that do not apply to other platforms. This observation should not be surprising. Windows NT is a new operating system that is still technologically immature, especially compared with the relatively old Unix. Unix has never been short on security bugs, but the method by which bugs are reported and corrected is different for developers of the two systems. Since the development of Linux and the GNU utilities, Unix-based operating system code has been freely available. Users are encouraged to find and correct flaws in the applications, utilities, and operating system kernels for freely distributed software. Over the years, this availability has led to more robust implementations of Unix systems. A note of caution, however: a quick look at any Unix bug track list will dismiss any idea that Unix is secure out of the box.

Perhaps the biggest problem that Microsoft is having is not with its security but with its marketing spin. Microsoft has marketed Windows NT as more secure than Unix in an effort to play on the fears of corporate MIS officers and consumers. The vulnerabilities found in Windows NT 4.0 in its first year of introduction should be enough to debunk this claim. Rather than arguing over bragging rights of which operating system is more secure, it is more instructive to work at securing the network server regardless of the platform—neither Windows NT nor Unix is secure out of the box.

One dominant theme throughout this chapter is that the system administrator must heed bug track lists (such as Bugtraq), incident response centers (such as CERT CC, FIRST, and CIAC), and the vendor notices of security problems. Unless system administrators are aware of flaws in the software, they will be unaware of attacks against these vulnerabilities—let alone able to defend against them. Checking with the vendor site often is the best defense against known vulnerabilities. For obvious reasons, vendors usually will not make much fanfare out of vulnerabilities that are found. For this reason, if you do not visit your platform vendor's appropriate site, you may not even be aware that the vendor has released a patch or Service Pack to fix security problems found "in the wild."

Aside from regularly updating and properly configuring the OS software, it is imperative to implement a program for regularly monitoring system logs and firewall logs. Log files record all kinds of system events from regular logins to attempted break-ins. Unless the log files are monitored and audited on a regular and frequent basis, you will not know who is rattling the doorknob and who may have already penetrated your system. A number of free and commercial packages are available to provide some intelligent monitoring of log files. Some packages provide auditing facilities for filtering out common events from logs and highlighting anomalous events that could represent attempted break-ins (see www.cs.purdue.edu/coast/coast-tools.html for some of the publicly available tools). Other packages also provide real-time intrusion-detection software. This software monitors system activities around the clock to detect system attacks. System events are compared with those in a database of known attack patterns or signatures to determine if an attack is in progress. If one is detected, an alert is sent to the system administrator, sometimes over a pager. Even without expensive commercial packages, the vast majority of system attacks can be detected through regular vigilance of system and firewall log files.

References

CERT Advisory 93:06. "wuarchive ftpd Vulnerability." Online. CERT Coordination Center. April 9, 1993. Available: ftp://info.cert.org/pub/cert_advisories.

CERT Advisory 95:16. "wu-ftp Misconfiguration Vulnerability." Online. CERT Coordination Center. November 30, 1995. Available: ftp://info.cert.org/pub/cert_advisories.

CERT Advisory 96:06. "Vulnerability in NCSA/Apache CGI Example Code." Online. CERT Coordination Center. March 20, 1996. Available: ftp://info.cert.org/pub/cert_advisories.

CERT Advisory 97:07. "Vulnerability in the httpd nph-test-cgi Script." Online. CERT Coordination Center. February 18, 1997. Available: ftp://info.cert.org/pub/cert_advisories.

Danckaert, P. "SNMP Information." Bugtraq, Second Quarter archives (Mar–Jun) 1997. Available: geek-girl.com/bugtraq/1997_2/0059.html.

daemon9, route, and infinity. "Project Neptune." Online. *Phrack Online*, 7:48, file 13 of 18. Available: www.fc.net/phrack/files/p48/p48-13.html.

Edupage Editors. "Cracker Attack Paralyzes PANIX." *RISKS Digest*, 18:45, September 13, 1996.

Garfinkel, S. and G. Spafford, *Practical Unix and Internet Security*, Second Edition. O'Reilly & Associates, 1996, 497.

Lange, L. "As Yet Another Hack Slashes at NT, Software Giant Sits Down with the Enemy — Microsoft Opens Dialogue with NT-Security Hackers." *EE Times*. July 14, 1997, Issue 962.CERTCC. "Vulnerability in NCSA/Apache CGI Example Code." CERT Advisory CA-96:06, March 1996.

Microsoft. "Microsoft FrontPage Modification Security Issue." Online. Available: www.microsoft.com/frontpage/documents/bugQA.htm.

Microsoft. "Predictable Query IDs Pose Security Risks for DNS Servers." Online. Available: ftp://ftp.microsoft.com/bussys/winnt/winnt-public/fixes/usa/hotfixes-postSP3/dns-fix/Q167629.txt.

Microsoft. "Securing Your Site Against Intruders." Chapter 5, *Microsoft IIS 2.0 Documentation*, 1997.

Pieper, O. "User Authentication for the Electronic Payment Environment." *Proceedings of the Electronic Commerce Security Conference,* August 4–5, 1997, Arlington, VA, A3-3 to A3-9.

Ramsbottom, A. *FAQ: NT Cryptographic Password Attacks and Defences*. Online. July 17, 1997. Available: ntbugtraq.rc.on.ca./samfaq.htm.

Wall, L., T. Chriastiansen, and R. Schwartz. *Programming Perl*, Second Edition. O'Reilly. 1996.

Williams, G. "Iris Recognition Technology." in *Proceedings of the Electronic Commerce Security Conference,* August 4–5, 1997, Arlington, VA, A3–11 to A3–34.

Referenced Web Sites

| Bugtraq | www.geek-girl.com/ bugtraq/index.html | The premier site for archiving security flaws in software. |
| CERT Coordination Center | www.cert.org | The original Computer Emergency Response Team that warehouses security alerts. |

COAST Tools Archive	www.cs.purdue.edu/ coast/coast-tools.html	The Purdue University COAST security tools archive. A great place to find free security tools.
Deter.com	www.deter.com/unix/ index.html	An online resource for Unix security links and security software.
Hack NT	www.ilinks.net/ ~486578/hack_NT/ hacknt.html	A list of NT vulnerabilities and exploits.
ISS's NT Vulnerabilities list	www.iss.net/vd/ nt_vulnerabilities.html	Internet Security Systems vulnerability list for Windows NT. Comprehensive and well organized.
Microsoft Security	www.microsoft.com/ security	The official source of Microsoft security flaws.
NT Bugtraq	ntbugtraq.rc.on.ca	Archive of flaws in Windows NT, moderated by Russ Cooper.
NT Security	www.ntsecurity.net.	Source of NT security information.
Phrack Online	www.fc.net/phrack/	The original underground hacker's journal.
Ping O' Death Web page	www.sophist.demon.co .uk/ping/index.html	This Web page will tell you if your machine is vulnerable to the Ping O' Death denial-of-service attack.
PW Dump	www .masteringcomputers .com/util/nt/pwdump .htm	Jeremy Allison's utility for cracking NT password hashes.

Chapter 6

Securing the Future
of E-Commerce

Certifying Components for Security

The preceding five chapters laid out in detail problems in security in the major components of e-commerce: the Web client software, the data transaction protocols, the Web server software, and the network server operating system software. The premise for highlighting the vulnerabilities in each of these major components is that a weakness in any single major component can compromise the security of the whole e-commerce transaction—and ultimately undermine confidence in e-commerce. It is important to note that the root causes that underlie most of the security vulnerabilities found in practice are flaws in the design, implementation, and configuration of software. One need only look at the archives of Bugtraq (www.geek-girl.com/bugtraq/index.html) to see the software flaws underlying the laundry list of infamous security bugs.

This chapter looks to the future by looking back to the underlying causes of security problems in the past. If the future of e-commerce is to be secure, the software components themselves must first be secured. The battle over the form software will assume in the future is being fought by competing camps with banners whose names read CORBA, DCOM, DCE, JavaBeans, and ActiveX. All of these technologies, sometimes called frameworks, provide a way to distribute self-contained pieces of software in forms called objects, or more generally, components, over distributed networks such as the

253

Internet. Because the software components that execute in these frameworks will be deployed in enterprise-critical applications such as e-commerce, the security required of these components will be paramount to the applications in which they execute. This chapter introduces the concept of *certifying software components for security*.

Before beginning a discussion about how to certify a component for security, it is first useful to define what we mean by *software component*. The next section addresses this issue and discusses the role of component-based software in building high-quality software systems. The main thrust of this chapter, however, is the future of securing e-commerce components through certification. Today, an infrastructure exists for certifying components through certification authorities (CAs). However, CAs do not currently certify behavioral attributes of software such as security, malicious behavior, or tolerance to malicious attack. Rather, CAs verify the identity of a software publisher or individual with an associated public key. This chapter, however, asserts that future software certification will be similar to certification we now see in electrical devices certified by the Underwriters Laboratory (UL) to meet some threshold of electrical safety. Currently, certification of software for behavioral attributes is an open research problem. However, this chapter gives a preview of the possible mechanisms for certifying software for security now being researched.

What Is a Software Component?

The infancy of e-commerce and its software components can be likened to the preindustrial era in the United States. Before parts became standardized, master craftsmen would custom-design and build each hammer, each saw, each chair, and each wheel. As a result, devices, equipment, and appliances built from these parts were one-of-a-kind systems. The industrial era brought standardization of parts so that devices could be reliably constructed from parts engineered to precise specifications. A bicycle manufacturer could buy standard bolts, wheels, seats, frames, and handlebars in wholesale quantities and be assured that the parts would fit together reliably to build bikes of consistent quality. The quality of a bike is no longer judged so much by who constructs it (after all, many of us assemble bikes at home now) but by the components that make up the bike. The higher the quality of the components, the higher the resulting quality of the bike, and the higher the cost.

Software today is often written in monolithic entities called programs. A single program may contain in some cases millions of lines of code. Understanding the complex interactions of objects or functions in a complex program is well beyond the grasp of the human mind. Out of complexity arise errors. Monolithic programs are also difficult to maintain and manage over time. As errors are discovered, patching them with correct code becomes increasingly difficult. Roughly 30 percent of the time a bug is fixed, a new bug is introduced with the fix. Writing correct small programs is a tractable problem. Writing correct large programs is a near impossibility. The demands placed on software in both general-purpose applications (such as desktop software) and special-purpose applications (such as telephone switching software) make coding small provable programs infeasible.

Today, we are still struggling to bootstrap software into its industrial era. The first necessary step to "industrialize" is to standardize on interfaces between software components. The second step is to build and verify the quality of the components that compose the systems. This latter step is addressed later in this chapter in certifying software components for security. Standardizing the interfaces between software types allows components to "fit" with other components. Developing standard interfaces also allows a software component to be reused in several different systems. For example, the interface of the bike frame to the bike wheel is standard enough to allow wheels of many different brand names to fit the same type of bike (e.g., a road bike). The CORBA, DCOM, and other frameworks mentioned in the introductory paragraph are tackling exactly this problem of standardizing interfaces. Software components that execute within these frameworks must have standard interfaces defined by these frameworks. Unfortunately, because these frameworks are competing in many different application domains, a component meeting one framework's standard interface may not be able to interface with another framework. Some frameworks are now developing interfaces that are generic enough to encompass components designed to other frameworks.

Aside from standardizing interfaces, one goal of some component frameworks is to create "open" systems. Open systems are designed to allow interoperability of software components written in different programming languages, compiled on different vendors' compilers, and executed on heterogeneous platforms. Open systems generally break down barriers between vendors to allow interoperability of components written by different software publishers.

In each of the major components of e-commerce transactions exist myriad and incompatible software. For example, consider the number of protocols currently available to end users and commerce Web servers for secure communications. Users can choose SSL, PCT, SET, S-HTTP, S/MIME, CyberCash, First Virtual, and DigiCash, to name a few. Because most of these protocols are competing and incompatible, users must choose one protocol over another. In reality, this choice is made by the merchant with whom the consumer is engaging in business, so merchants are put in the uncomfortable position of deciding which of these protocols to support for their servers, all the while hoping that the client-side browsers will support the protocols in the future. The market will ultimately decide the winners and losers in de facto protocols; however, the necessity for interoperable, cross-platform software components (which underlie protocol implementations) will not diminish.

For the purposes of this chapter, a component is a piece of software that is encapsulated (wrapped) in a standard interface that can interoperate with other similarly encapsulated components over an open framework. The future of software will embrace software components in order to make software development economical (e.g., through large-scale reuse), much as standardization of parts made the industrial era possible. When software components and their corresponding frameworks become more pervasive, market forces will shape the survival of some components over others. Those components that prove to be most secure, reliable, and robust in application after application will beat out competitors of similar components. Economic models will also emerge that will reward developers of components based on licensing or even more radically, based on component usage. Each use of a component corresponds to a financial transaction, with the "usage fee" being billed to the component's client. The more a component is used, the more financial rewards are reaped by the component's developer.

What makes this model appealing is that industrial-strength applications can be created by interconnecting components, many of which will be produced by several different vendors. This means that specialists will emerge to produce the best kind of widget for a particular task. In the bike example, for instance, some vendors will emerge that are better at creating bike frames then they are at producing wheels. Similarly, in software, some applications will require a graphics plotter, a spreadsheet, and a back-end processing engine. Company A that is building such an application may have the expertise to build a great back-end processing engine but lack the skills to build a good graphics plotter or a spreadsheet. This company will be able to use a spreadsheet component produced by company B and a graphics plotter component developed by company C. Because all of these components were built to a standard interface over an open systems framework, company A will be able to "plug and play" the components in a single application.

Many software programs facilitate a typical electronic session between two parties to an e-commerce transaction. On the client side of the transaction, a user interacts with a Web browser, browser plug-ins, active content, a mailer, and news reading clients. On the server side of the transaction, the software programs include Web servers, mail servers, FTP servers, news servers, database programs, CGI scripts, and other server-side applications that handle client requests. Remember, too, all the protocol software in between, such as the secure communication protocols first mentioned in this section. All of these programs will in the future be componentized, if they are not already. Componentization of these software programs will allow interoperability of different protocols and different clients and servers. For example, an ActiveX control, which currently executes on only Wintel machines, can execute on Unix machines if it is encapsulated in an open systems framework component wrapper such as CORBA. Not that this goal by itself is worthy of componentization. Rather, the ability to reuse components and build industrial-strength applications from components written by other people (such as specialists) will usher software into its industrial era. Nowhere is this more important than in e-commerce applications.

E-commerce transactions cannot afford the failures in security that have marked the last decade of software development. Consider the Internet Worm launched by Robert T. Morris Jr., in 1988 [Garfinkel and Spafford 1996]. A single bug in a network server program allowed a variant of a virus (called a worm) to spread to thousands of computers in a matter of hours and cripple the Internet while still in its infancy. The worm took advantage of a buffer overflow vulnerability in the `fingerd` network server program to insert and execute its own code on the network server host machine. The rogue code replicated itself by launching similar attacks on other network server machines. Because most servers were running the same version of the server program, hosts across the Internet were infected and shut down. As e-commerce emerges from its infancy, vulnerabilities in the software that make up the infrastructure of e-commerce can effectively bring the Internet-dependent business world to its knees. The losses in the Internet Worm incident of 1988 would pale in comparison with those in an equivalent attack on the modern-day Internet. Certifying software components that compose the e-commerce infrastructure is the most promising approach to preventing large-scale security failures that can undermine the future of e-commerce.

The Status Quo

To determine the future of e-commerce security, it is best to establish its current status. Existing security assessment techniques, called penetrate-and-patch, have to date been unsuccessful. A discussion about the current practice of certifying software components focuses specifically on what certification means to end users.

Penetrate-and-Patch

Most computer security analysis today is performed with penetrate-and-patch tactics. Security is assessed at the *network level* by specialists attempting to break into systems through *well-known* security holes. Teams of specialists, sometimes called tiger teams or red teams in the government and consultants in industry, will use a bag of tricks learned or passed down from experience to break into systems. In recent years, the experience of tiger teams has been captured in automated security analysis tools such as SATAN or commercial security scanners. These tools frequently require only that the user know the IP addresses or the domain of the networked site to be assessed. From there, the tools check the visible hosts for known vulnerabilities. If they are successful, the specific vulnerabilities discovered are patched. What is actually patched is either configuration files of software or the software itself. This kind of assessment is effective because of the great number of networked systems that are insecurely configured or whose software has not been patched or upgraded to the current release version. The penetrate-and-patch approach is an important part of assessing and maintaining systemwide security; however, it is far from a good solution to securing e-commerce systems.

The problem with penetrate-and-patch is that it occurs too late—*after* software has been developed, released, and installed on end-user systems. This means that if a vulnerability is discovered in a given software application or default software configuration, every site in which the software is installed will be vulnerable. If the software is popularly used, such as sendmail on Unix systems or Microsoft's IIS server, the number of sites that will be vulnerable could be staggering. To make matters even worse, once a vulnerability is known, an exploit script, which can be used to compromise the systems through the software vulnerability, is usually distributed widely through underground networks. Exploit scripts allow users who know little or nothing about the software vulnerability to take advantage of it for malicious purposes. The availability of exploit scripts on the Internet is one reason businesses are fearful of teenagers with little or no formal education in software development. The problem of penetrate-and-patch occurring too late in the software life-cycle can be addressed if software components are certified for security *before* being released. This topic is taken up later in this chapter.

The second problem with penetrate-and-patch is that the "good guys" are always behind the "bad guys." Penetrate-and-patch is a *reactive* approach to security. What happens in practice is that expert software crackers spend their time attempting to break into systems by finding flaws in software. If they are successful, the exploitation script is distributed widely in underground networks. Once it is distributed, crackers worldwide begin to use it to break into vulnerable systems. After a certain threshold of cracker activity is reached, enough astute system administrators in the field will notice and send reports to one of the incident response centers such as the CERT Coordination Center (www.cert.org). CERT then traces the flaw to its origin, contacts the vendor, codes a patch, and then releases an alert to the Internet. By this time, if the flaw is significant, it will have been widely exploited by crackers who have known of its existence for some time.

System administrators who monitor the security alerts from incident response centers and their vendors will now have the opportunity to patch the flaws well after the underground community has had its crack at your system. Compounding the problem is that most administrators do not patch their vulnerable software for two reasons. First, most administrators think their system won't be compromised. This is the "it won't happen to me" syndrome. The second reason is that they often fall victim to the "why fix it if it ain't broke" syndrome. As a result, most vulnerable software that has a patch available is not ever patched in practice. The best hope against this problem is that the bug will be fixed in the next release version (though that is not always true), which will take effect when the software is upgraded.

Another consideration is that sometimes patches contain flaws that introduce new security vulnerabilities. It's hard to believe, but it is true for two supporting reasons. First, patches are often coded very quickly by vendors to react to a "hot" situation. Some patches can be thousands of lines of code that are produced in as little as 48 hours. The patch is now known as a hack or a kludge—a quick fix to a pressing problem. Vendors patching software this way are much like the little Dutch boy who stuck his finger in the dike to stop the water from flooding the town. Patching one flaw may prevent its exploitation, but it may also introduce other flaws, much as plugging one hole in the dike can cause water to flow from new holes. The second reason is a side effect of the first. Because patches must be coded very quickly, most software engineering practices are thrown out the window. One result is that little testing or analysis is performed on the newly patched software before the patch is released.

Remember that penetrate-and-patch attempts to analyze systems for known vulnerabilities. Because penetrate-and-patch is now performed with automated software analysis tools, there is an additional delay (on the order of weeks or months) between the time vulnerabilities are released through incident response teams and the time they are incorporated in software penetrate-and-patch tools. Be aware, then, that penetrate-and-patch occurs too late in the life cycle of software to adequately address the problems of e-commerce security. To begin to address the problems of security that will affect e-commerce systems, security analysis must occur before software is released, through established models of certification to make the approach commercially viable.

Certifying Identity

The current model of certification on the Internet is being widely touted as the solution to Internet security problems. Certification authorities (CAs) are used to vouch for identities in digital certificates. The idea behind having CAs is to allow two or more people who do not know each other to be able to trust each other's asserted identities. Exchanging public keys is not sufficient to ensure that the name associated with the public key is legitimate. This is where CAs play their role. Individuals or organizations can submit their signed public key certificate to a CA for verification. The CA will perform some identity check, from the trivial, such as checking that an e-mail address is valid, to the elaborate, such as running Dun & Bradstreet checks for registered companies. If the identity asserted by the applicant checks out, and the public key matches the applicant's signed certificate, the CA will digitally sign the certificate. This endorsement means that the CA has vouched that the public key presented by the certificate legitimately belongs to the identity named on the certificate. When a certificate signed by a trusted CA is presented the first time to an unfamiliar party, the unfamiliar party can, with a high degree of confidence, download a copy of the certificate and associate the certificate's public key with the asserted identity. Subsequently, the party presenting the certificate can be authenticated by digitally signing any electronic document, whether it's an e-mail, a Word document, or an active content component. The signature is created through use of the private key half of the public/private key encryption pair. The authenticating party will have positive assurance as to the identity of the signer if the signature is successfully decrypted by the public key.

The process of obtaining certification and being authenticated is not unlike what we encounter in our daily lives with driver's licenses. The driver's license is a certificate of identity widely recognized in the United States. The state's seal is an endorsement by the state that the identity and other personal information listed on the license are undeniably bound to the picture. When the license is presented to an unfamiliar party, the party need only match the picture with the applicant to verify the associated information. In this case, rather than using public/private keys for authentication, the party uses the picture as the "public key" to bind the applicant with the other identity information. The authentication step does not necessarily consist of checking a signature as much as matching the person's face with the picture on the driver's license. If a visual match is made, the authenticating party will assume that the other identification information on the license is correct because it has been vouched for by the state.

CAs currently verify only the *identity* associated with public keys. In the future, this model of certification will be drastically changed to incorporate certification of secure properties of software components as well as the identity of the one who is publishing the component.

Certifying Software

The current system of assessing security through penetrate-and-patch places the odds of successfully violating computer security clearly in favor of computer criminals. Rather than being approached from a reactive stance, security must be built into the software components that make up e-commerce systems and ensured through rigorous certification processes.

E-commerce is still in its infancy. Tools and applications that will enable e-commerce on a large scale are still being invented, and security issues in Internet-based software are now significant barriers to the growth of e-commerce. The estimates for the size of the e-commerce market in the year 2000 vary wildly from $10 billion to $200 billion. The expected growth of e-commerce to date has been impeded by a key technical barrier—software security—with sociological implications. *Lack of assurance about security* is the greatest barrier currently restraining the growth of e-commerce. Consumers must have confidence that their electronic transactions will remain private and unaltered. In addition, consumers must trust that the system will prevent fraud and that merchant systems will keep their transactions private. Merchants require assurance that their systems and digital assets will remain safe from security intrusions, sabotage, and fraud. For e-commerce to reach its potential market size of over $100 billion in the next three years, confidence in the security of the system must be assured.

For security assurance to be marketable, it must be delivered in the form of certification. If software components can be certified to demonstrate secure properties, the larger banks, credit card companies, Fortune 500 businesses, investors, and consumers will have the proof of security they require before investing their money in e-commerce applications. Drawing in major commercial players will also raise confidence in the business and consumer communities that will serve to further stimulate growth in the e-commerce market. The size of the expected market for e-commerce in the 21st century will be affected in large part by the assurance that certification technology can provide. If the components of e-commerce applications can be certified for security, we may well see a market that burgeons significantly close to its expected upper-bound potential size.

In the preceding section, the role that certification authorities play in security today was discussed. Currently, CAs verify only the identity of a person or organization with an associated public key. There are reasons, however, for certifying secure behavior of software components rather than simply the identity of an individual or organization. Fortunately, the certification of components for secure behavior can leverage the infrastructure that currently exists for certification authorities. As long as CAs are in the business of third-party certification, certifying software components for security is a natural extension of the current model. In order to certify software components for security, CAs or other independent verification and validation (IV&V) laboratories will need the software analysis techniques and, more important, the tools to certify software components for behavioral attributes rather than a static one such as identity. In the following section, the types of components that are ripe for certification and the nature of these certification processes are discussed.

To Be Stamped

The initial success of Java applets and ActiveX components in penetrating the marketplace onto users' desktop machines is a strong indicator of how pervasive software components distributed over the Internet will be. As the applications in which Internet-ready components are used mature from the "razzle-dazzle" variety to business applications, the security issues already apparent will become leading concerns for businesses and consumers.

In Chapter 2, the security models for Java applets and ActiveX controls were discussed in some detail. Java applets run in a security sandbox that prevents applets from behaving maliciously, such as writing to the disk, reading files from disk, or making arbitrary network connections. The implementation of the Java security model is complex, and as a result, flaws in the security model have been found that have been demonstrated to leverage a complete system penetration. Each flaw has been subsequently patched, but this by no means indicates that the Java security model is robust against all future attacks. The sheer complexity of the language implementation practically precludes a secure implementation. The question that remains is not *if* more security flaws are present, but *when* they will be discovered, *by whom* (crackers or researchers), and *in which type of application* (experimental or enterprise critical).

Java Components

Since the Java Developers Kit started supporting signed applets, the sandbox has metaphorically been opened up to permit potentially dangerous behavior on the part of Java applets. Signing applets is a way to assign trust to an applet to have greater privileges.

For example, applets that are developed in-house or those acquired from trusted vendors may be assigned a high level of privilege on internal computer systems. Allowing Java applets to roam outside the sandbox, in turn, gives Java applet developers the ability to program them to perform a richer variety of functions that were previously prohibited by the sandbox. For example, assigning a Java applet a trust level that permits file I/O will give the applet the ability to perform word processing functions that require file access. Although opening up the sandbox in many cases is necessary to support business functions, it also opens up the possibility that a Java applet will behave maliciously. The current model for signing applets does not incorporate any testing or certification of security. Rather, if an applet is trusted (usually because of its supplier), it can be signed and given full rein of internal system resources.

The model for signed applets is placing at risk digital assets based on the best judgment of the person signing the Java applet and the corresponding configuration of the Web clients. Because the sandbox will be opened up to permit possibly malicious Java applet behavior, signed Java applets are ripe for *security certification*. Certifying Java applets for security would use exactly the same infrastructure built in for signing and executing signed applets. Instead of signing an applet based on its publisher, the signing would be performed by a certification authority or IV&V center that has subjected the applet to rigorous testing for insecure behavior. If the applet passes the testing processes, it will be certified (using a digital signature) as safe for execution in a trusted environment.

JavaBeans define an application programming interface (API) for software components written in the Java programming language. Because Java is a cross-platform language, Java components are inherently suited to building Internet-ready components. E-commerce applications form a class of Internet-based applications that must run on a variety of platforms in a full-featured language. JavaBeans leverage the rich cross-platform features of the Java programming language into a component framework—which provides the features, such as software reuse, described in the What Is a Component? section. One key area in which e-commerce applications differ from other Internet-based applications is the magnitude of losses resulting from security breaches. When money is involved in an application and a tangible loss (or gain for a thief) is apparent, the stakes for security escalate very quickly. JavaBeans are no exception. The Java security model (the sandbox) is a good starting point for building secure systems out of components. However, as noted with Java applets, this model is being opened up for signed applets.

The same concerns ring true for JavaBeans. JavaBeans downloaded as Web objects will be subjected to the Java sandbox, unless they are given explicit privileges through signing. On the other hand, for applications built from JavaBeans, the Java security model provides no assurance against insecure behavior. In this respect, applications built from JavaBeans suffer from the same types vulnerabilities as applications designed in other type-safe languages. This point is particularly relevant again to e-commerce applications, such as client/server intranet applications built from JavaBeans components. Applications built out of JavaBeans components have no means for enforcing security constraints. Without any oversight from the Java Security Manager, applications built from vulnerable JavaBeans can fall victim to malicious attacks. As with signed Java applets, JavaBeans are ripe for *certification of security*.

ActiveX Components

The other major competing component model for Internet applications is ActiveX. The security model for ActiveX controls is based solely on trust and human judgment. If the end user trusts an ActiveX control, it is allowed to download and execute, no holds barred. This means that the ActiveX control is given the full privileges of any other program on a Win32 machine. The trust enforcement mechanism is Authenticode, which will display the identity of the publisher of the software control if it is signed. If the control is not signed, the end user has the right to refuse execution of the component, or the component can still be permitted to execute. The same rights apply to signed components, although depending on which security policy is selected in the end user's Internet Explorer Web client, executing a signed component is made easier than executing an unsigned component. Regardless, the purpose served by Authenticode is to give the end user the opportunity to inspect the names of those who signed the component, if it was signed at all, prior to executing the component.

If the user elects to execute the ActiveX control, all bets are off about security. Because no security model is used to constrain the behavior of an ActiveX control once it is permitted to execute, ActiveX controls are good candidates for certification of security. As with signed Java applets, the existing infrastructure for signing and approving execution of ActiveX controls can be used for approving execution of certified controls. ActiveX controls can be tested and evaluated for insecure properties based on structural and behavioral attributes of the components. If the ActiveX components pass the rigorous certification requirements (which are dynamic in nature themselves), the components can be stamped with the seal of approval from the certifying agent, which could be an established CA or an IV&V laboratory. When the component is downloaded to the end user's Web client, provided that the component is stamped with a trusted CA's *security certification signature*, it can run unimpeded with the full privilege necessary for a given e-commerce application.

The Rest of the Bunch

Although Java applets and ActiveX controls are the components widely used today, e-commerce applications are in fact built from many software programs that will likely be componentized in the near future. Component frameworks such as CORBA allow software programs to be compontentized regardless of the programming language in which the component is written. This means that a component written in Java will be able to interoperate with a component written in C. Similarly, CORBA will provide the ability to encompass other frameworks such that ActiveX components can interoperate with JavaBeans components. Regardless of which framework or programming language implementation is used, the security concerns for e-commerce components are paramount. The software products involved in e-commerce transactions include Web browsers, plug-ins, active content, Web servers, other network servers, databases, server-side applications, and protocol implementations. A vulnerability *in any one of these components* can leave a gap in the security of the whole system from which a perpetrator can steal data, corrupt files, or commit fraud. The smallest of holes can often be leveraged into the largest of penetrations. For this reason, software certification technology that will certify security will be an essential part of developing and executing future e-commerce applications.

The technology for certifying software components for security is an open research topic. One of the fundamental research questions asks what constitutes a sufficient condition for certifying a software component as "secure." Are there necessary conditions that can be imposed on developers of software components? Developing security certification technology for software components will provide the cornerstone technology necessary to provide confidence and assurance in the security of e-commerce applications built in component-based frameworks. The next section provides a glimpse into the types of technologies that may provide the necessary and sufficient conditions for component security certification.

Certifying Technologies

Certification has long been used in electrical devices to provide safety assurance to consumers. Manufacturers of electrical devices will place the Underwriters Laboratory (UL) approved seal on their devices to demonstrate that the device meets an industry-accepted standard for safety. More recently, models for certification have emerged for computer and software systems. In industries where software is running on safety-critical systems, the appropriate government regulatory agencies are reaching for techniques to certify these systems as safe. The U.S. Food and Drug Administration (FDA) has issued a report for manufacturers of computer-controlled medical devices that involves premarket notification requirements in order to obtain FDA approval [FDA 1991]. Seeking approval from the FDA is often called certification; however, the guidelines do not dictate a particular approach to developing safe software, nor do they dictate a required software quality assurance measure or development procedures. The onus is on the medical device manufacturer to demonstrate due diligence to safety engineering. Until a means for evaluating the safety of software-controlled medical devices is more universally accepted, the current approach for showing due diligence using industry best practices suffices for FDA certification.

The U.S. Nuclear Regulatory Commission (NRC) also has a vested interest in certifiably safe software. Many nuclear reactors are controlled by software processes. A failure in software could have catastrophic consequences. A technical position document from the NRC provides guidelines for manufacturers to analyze software against known failure modes [NRC 1994]. The guidelines state that the applicant shall use best-estimate methods for analyzing the safety of the system against known and postulated failure modes. However, there is no mention of an analytical technique that is mandated to assure the safety of the end product.

Probably the strictest requirements for safe software in a government regulatory agency come from the Federal Aviation Administration (FAA). The FAA requires flight control software to undergo advanced levels of software testing. For example, the FAA requires Multiple Condition Decision Coverage (MCDC) testing for highly critical code. This requirement forces the applicant to extensively test each of the possible states of the conditional expression in a branch statement. The idea is to force the applicant to test each branch condition to ensure that the program will behave safely in the event of unexpected inputs.

The regulatory agencies have a responsibility to the public to ensure that dangerous software is not executing on safety-critical devices. However, the agencies are struggling as much as the manufacturers with ways to evaluate and certify the safety of critical systems. As new techniques to assess the quality of software, such as fault-injection analysis, become more widely accepted, manufacturers will have more tools at their disposal, and regulatory agencies will have more solid ground on which to rate and certify systems [Voas and McGraw 1997].

More closely related to e-commerce are certification guidelines for different products that some organizations are pushing. For example, JavaSoft is pushing 100 percent Pure

Java certification to ensure that Java programs written and compiled on different vendors' Java Virtual Machines (JVMs) conform to the Java language specified by JavaSoft. The idea is that if you are writing Java programs that use special nonstandard features of one vendor's JVM implementation, the program will not be cross platform (i.e., it will not execute on different vendors' JVMs) and will not pass the 100 percent Pure Java tests. Differences in JVMs can cause a program compiled successfully to one JVM to crash on another. Java applications and applets that meet the 100 percent Pure Java certification should in theory be able to run on any JVM and platform. Critics of the 100 percent Pure Java certification effort call it a protectionist marketing drive to prevent domination of Java by other vendors. Regardless of its motivation, the certification provides a model for testing Java software against a minimal standard of conformance.

The National Computer Security Association (NCSA) (www.ncsa.com) is also heavily involved in certifying security products. The NCSA certifies antivirus software products, firewall products, and Web sites. The goal is to establish some minimum threshold by which every vendor of an antivirus product or firewall product can be tested. For example, vendors of antiviral software products should be able to detect 100 percent of all viruses that are currently in the wild and 90 percent of those known to exist in the NCSA virus laboratory. Firewalls are certified by penetration testing of sample installations against known attacks. Network scanning tools such as SATAN and ISS are used in the certification tests. As long as the firewall demonstrates the ability to thwart the penetration attempts at an acceptable level, the firewall will be certified. If the firewall is installed differently from the configuration in which it was tested, the firewall may be vulnerable to one of the attacks that it thwarted during certification. Chapter 5 also highlights reasons that even well-configured and certified firewalls are still vulnerable to data-driven attacks.

Clearly, the problems with evaluating software for quality attributes are not new. The regulatory agencies described earlier are concerned with identifying flaws in software that have potentially unsafe consequences. Waiting for the first nuclear reactor to melt down as a result of a software flaw and then patching it is not considered an acceptable practice. Therefore, the manufacturers and their regulatory agencies do their best to make sure the software is safe the first time it is released.

The problem is similar in security, but different in terms of approaches. Software running on corporate network servers can certainly be considered security critical. If a flaw exists in a network server that later permits a successful malicious attack, the problem is found and the software is patched. Although lives are not usually at stake because of a malicious attack, the cost of a break-in in terms of the labor required to track the intrusion and recover the system can be staggeringly high. Furthermore, if digital assets have been corrupted or stolen, the costs escalate very quickly. Even though companies face losses every year due to security intrusions, the penetrate-and-patch model is still alive and well. That is, those in the industry are still willing to take losses and then patch software to ensure that the same flaw is not exploited again on their site. Unfortunately, there is no assurance that an organization's site will not be violated by another security flaw in the same software or other software.

The goal of software component certification is to analyze software components for security before components are released and installed on sites. Security analysis technologies currently available are geared mostly toward networked site assessment. In order to prevent security flaws in software from being installed on networked sites in the first place, however, it is important to focus security assessment at the software component level. Technologies for assessing security of software applications and/or software components are currently being developed in research laboratories, including the author's own (www.rst-corp.com/project_summaries.html). Because this technology is still being researched and developed, commercial tools are currently not on the market. However, in the span of two to three years, when component-based software is expected to become integral to not only e-commerce applications, but to software applications in general, we can expect to see commercial software analysis tools that analyze software components for security.

What types of analysis are we talking about? Software analysis is generally performed through *white-box* or *black-box* analysis techniques. White-box analysis involves using the source code for a software component in order to perform analysis. Black-box analysis presumes that the source code is not available and instead uses only the input/output behavior of the software and/or the binary object of the compiled program. Because white-box analysis can also use the structure of a program, more sophisticated types of analysis can be performed in general with white-box analysis. For example, static analysis of a program can be used to evaluate complexity metrics. The more complex a program, the more likely it is to contain flaws. White-box dynamic analysis uses both the structure of the program and the ability to exercise it. Dynamic analysis is useful for studying the behavior of a program. Inspecting source code can be useful for detecting insecure function calls and poor programming practices; however, without dynamic analysis of a program, there could be many potentially insecure events that cannot be detected through static analysis.

An example of dynamic analysis is evaluating code coverage for testing. Usually a program is run against selected inputs to determine if the program produces acceptable outputs. Testing is necessary to find flaws that may be embedded in different portions of the program code. The more extensive the testing, the less likely it is that flaws will be discovered in the program once it is released. Most software applications today are too complex for testers to exhaustively test every input to determine its behavior under all circumstances. As a result, testers sample only a portion of the input space for each input to a program and gauge the quality of the program based on the sampled inputs. A key criterion for evaluating the effectiveness of testing is the proportion of the code covered by the sampled inputs. For example, if after all the testing only 8 out of 10 functions were tested, the function coverage of the testing would be rated at 80 percent. The same types of metrics can be applied to statement coverage, branch condition coverage, and other coverage metrics. The idea is to give the tester an estimate for how well the code has been tested. The more code that is covered, the better the testing. By completely covering the code, the tester has the highest probability for flushing out flaws in the code. Code coverage is a useful metric for security analysis of software components, too. The idea is to determine which parts of a program have not been tested to determine where potential security-related flaws may lurk. White-box analysis lends itself well to code coverage because the source code can be instrumented to determine which portions of the code were "hit" by the testing.

Another class of techniques used in dynamic white-box analysis is fault-injection-based techniques [Voas and McGraw 1997]. The idea behind fault-injection analysis is to simulate the effect of flaws within a program to determine their effect on the program's observable behavior. Why is fault injection necessary? Because we don't know the location of flaws in the program. If we knew where flaws were in the program, we could easily debug and fix programs before releasing them. Instead, we can use fault injection techniques to simulate the effect of flaws everywhere within a program to determine the consequences of buggy code. Rather than simulating the effect of many simultaneous flaws (which would be a harrowing experience) at once, faults are injected singly. Assertions for *unacceptable program behavior* are coded and evaluated while the program is tested. If the assertions are "tripped" while the program is being exercised, an unacceptable program state or output has been reached. Using assertions is a way of codifying a program's security policy. If the security policy of the program is violated while it is being analyzed through fault injection, the specific program location where the fault was injected, as well as the nature of the fault that violated security, will be known. This information will tell the analyst which portions of the program are sensitive to faults—effectively which portions are "security critical."

Armed with this information, software developers will be able to isolate and fortify sections of the code that could potentially cause failures in security of the application and its environment *before* the software is released. Knowing the specific location of the fault injection and the nature of the injected fault may be enough to exploit the fault via the program inputs without fault injection. Developing the exploit through the program inputs that re-create the simulated fault demonstrates the severity of the fault. If the simulated fault can be demonstrated to be exploitable from program inputs, the nature of the flaw is severe and must be fixed. Finding an exploit effectively closes the loop from when software is developed, hacked, penetrated, and patched. By employing this technology in the laboratory, testers can effectively code patches before software is released—for a radical departure from the status quo! Although software-based fault injection provides powerful techniques for analyzing software for security flaws, new classes of techniques for software analysis will no doubt be developed in the future in this still maturing field.

Software components can be certified through different software analysis techniques, both black box and white box, dynamic and static. Virus scanners that have already been extensively used in software certification will also play a role in detecting viruses that may have been maliciously planted in software before distribution. Advanced software analysis techniques can also be used to detect the presence of Trojan horses in software. Certification processes will emerge through both advanced research and agreement through industry consortia. Once a component has been subjected to a rigorous process using several analysis techniques, the component can be certified as free from malicious content and robust to malicious attack. A digital signature will be stamped by the certifying authority whose stamp of approval will certify not only the identity of the publisher, but also the security of the component.

How Safe Is It?

Throughout this book, the dangers of various technologies used in e-commerce have been described, together with techniques for mitigating the dangers. In Chapter 1, several real-life anecdotal examples of security and privacy violations in applications of e-commerce were presented. These examples underscore the point that e-commerce security problems are not theoretical, but they actually occur in practice. Since information on these incidents was published, several more security incidents have made the front pages in newspapers and business magazines. To continue to follow security incidents that are observed in practice, one of the best archives to monitor is the *RISKS Digest* (catless.ncl.ac.uk/Risks). Expect to see new and more innovative attacks against the security of e-commerce systems as more and more business is transacted over the Internet.

Chapter 2 describes the client-side vulnerabilities in many types of e-commerce applications. The major focus of this section is to enlighten the reader about the dangers of active content on the Internet. The significance of active content is that it overcomes the limitations of HTML in surfing the Web to make the Web a viable medium for all ranges of business and entertainment applications. Active content is being embedded in Web pages everywhere, often without the end user's awareness of its presence. What makes active content dangerous is that anyone who puts up a Web page has the ability to run programs on your machine. This means that someone else may be able to access your personal files, corrupt your files, send data back over network connections, or deposit Trojan horses, all without your knowledge. The chapter also discusses other problems with Web clients as evidenced in several release versions of the Netscape Navigator/Communicator and Microsoft's Internet Explorer. The future of Web clients appears to be complete desktop integration, wherein the desktop is simply an extension of the Internet. A host of potential security problems can certainly arise from flawed implementations, already demonstrated in practice and detailed in Chapter 2.

One of the most significant paradigm shifts in Web technology—push technology—is described in Chapter 2. Push technology is changing the way we receive our information from the Web. Rather than requesting data from the Web, we have it pushed to our machines. Push technology can be an extremely efficient way of receiving updates from favorite Web sites or channels, customized through personalized filters. Furthermore, push technology is tackling a large problem in site maintenance—software upgrades. That is, push technology can be used to automatically upgrade or patch software applications with the latest and greatest versions to introduce new features and patch previous flaws, including security-related flaws.

Although push technology promises to deliver content in new and innovative approaches, it also holds the potential for abuse of end-user security and privacy. Push technology is currently used to distribute active content such as Java applets, JavaScript, and digital images to the end user's machine. The use of push technology to deliver active content and software upgrades (essentially program executables) now makes downloading of potentially malicious programs completely transparent. That is, end users will have little control or knowledge over which types of programs are downloaded to their machines because it is prescheduled. The best technological solution—not widely practiced today—to address this problem is to incorporate digital signatures in active content applications downloaded from push sites. The use of digital signatures will at least assure the end user that the active content has been downloaded from a trusted site rather than a perpetrator who may have hijacked the link. However, digital signatures will not provide any assurance as to whether the active content is safe.

Chapter 3 describes several protocols now used to secure the data transaction in e-commerce applications. Currently, end users and merchants have a variety of options to use in securing the data from client to server. What is important to remember is that data transaction security simply protects the data from being observed in transit by unauthorized third parties. That is, the data cannot be read and interpreted by someone who has no business observing the data sent over the Internet. This is important to provide privacy of transactions. But secure transaction protocols will not provide security for the systems on either end of the transaction protocol. The security provided by these protocols can be completely circumvented if either end of the transaction is insecure.

Chapter 4 provides an in-depth treatment of the security of the Web or commerce server used to handle e-commerce transactions over the Internet. This software is typically an insecure link in the chain of software that handles e-commerce transactions. If the security of the data transaction protocol is significantly stronger than the security provided by the Web server software, an attacker will simply target the Web server software to grab the sensitive data. Chapter 4 describes the vulnerabilities in Web server configuration that plague many Web sites today.

Chapter 5 addresses the security of the Web server machine itself. The Web server machine is usually in fact a network server offering a host of network services to the Internet at large. Vulnerabilities in the network services, including and beyond the Web server itself, can be ports of entry for nefarious Internet users. Underlying the server software is a bunch of supporting operating system software. Vulnerabilities in this software can be used to bypass the secure mechanisms (such as access control in network services) and secure configurations of Web server software to violate the security of the commerce server. In most sites offering commercial transactions over the Web, the valuable data is stored on databases that reside behind the firewalls and the network server machine. Data-driven attacks can exploit weaknesses in the network server software to access the valuable database server machine. Chapter 5 classifies network server machine vulnerabilities into seven broad categories that have been demonstrated in practice. The chapter shows how the two most popular network server platforms found on desktops today, Unix and Windows NT, stacked up against vulnerabilities found in practice according to the seven categories.

Finally, in this chapter, a preview of the future of secure e-commerce is given. Software used in e-commerce applications will likely follow the component-based software paradigm now being actively promoted and developed by software companies today. The future of e-commerce applications will be secured more readily when security is considered during development and before release. Promising techniques for analyzing software for secure properties before release are introduced. Furthermore, the notion of certifying software for security using an existing infrastructure of certification authorities is described as a commercially viable approach for software development companies to produce and market secure software.

Now that the potential hazards of e-commerce have been laid out, the most pressing question remains: How safe is it? The answer will vary with the way that each person participates in e-commerce. The intent of this book is not to impede the growth of e-commerce but rather to present the risks of e-commerce resident in the underlying technology. Each user or company must assess the risks involved with participating in e-commerce. If you are using the Internet today, you are a participant knowingly or not in e-commerce. Knowing the risks in e-commerce will allow end users to make appropriate judgments of where to do business and from which machines. If the machine from which you surf the Internet is an enterprise-critical machine for your business (i.e., the loss of data or breach of security on the machine or trusted machines can result in crippling losses to the organization), you would do well not to engage in risky Internet activities from it. On the other hand, if you are surfing the Net from a home machine wherein the penalties for loss of data or breach of privacy are not severe, engaging in e-commerce may be the best way to take advantage of this new paradigm of computing.

Ultimately, the user must carefully weigh the risks of surfing from a particular machine against the benefits of e-commerce over the Internet. Likewise, businesses must be aware of the risks in providing Internet services to their employees. Certainly, securing the server machines, software, and firewalls in addition to engaging in ethical Internet practices will make the Internet a safer medium for all to use in its myriad applications.

References

Garfinkel, S. and E. Spafford. *Practical Unix and Internet Security*. Sebastopol, O'Reilly Associates Inc. 1996.

U.S. Food and Drug Administration. *Reviewer Guidance for Computer Controlled Medical Devices Undergoing 510(k) Review*. 1991.

U.S. Nuclear Regulatory Commission, *Draft Branch Technical Position*. 1994.

Voas, J. and G. McGraw. *Software Fault Injection: Inoculating Programs against Errors*. John Wiley & Sons. 1997.

Referenced Web Sites

Bugtraq	www.geek-girl.com/bugtraq/index.html	The premier site for archiving security flaws in software.
CERT Coordination Center	www.cert.org	The original Computer Emergency Response Team that warehouses security alerts.
National Computer Security Association	www.ncsa.com	An organization that promotes computer security through awareness training and certification.
Reliable Software Technologies	www.rstcorp.com	The author's company, which engages in security research and consulting.
RISKS Digest	catless.ncl.ac.uk/Risks	The *RISKS Digest* archives. Moderated forum on risks to the public in computers and related systems. Peter G. Neumann is the group moderator.

Index

A

Access control, 224. *See also* Documents; Fine-grained access control
list(s) (ACL(s)), 169–171, 174
file, 172–174
mechanisms, 186
Access permissions. *See* File access permissions
Access-control mechanisms, 212
Access-controlled documents, 114
Access-controlled Web pages, 150, 169
Account user ID, 226
Accountability, 98
Accutrade, 5
ACH transactions, 147
costs, 146
ACL(s). *See* Access Control List(s)
ACM, 11
Active channels, 89–92
Active content. *See* Client-side
Active Server Pages (ASP) file. *See* Unprocessed ASP file flaw, 229
ActiveX, 32, 33, 37, 253
component publisher, 45
components, 50, 264
containers, 38–39
framework, 38
insecurity, 38–66
scripting, 39–41
security, 38–66
Software Developer Kit (SDK), 42
trust, establishment, 41–63
wrapper, 38
ActiveX controls, 3, 15, 17, 18, 22, 32, 38–40, 45–48, 50, 51, 54, 55, 57–67, 72, 76, 77, 83, 84, 91, 243, 257, 262, 264, 265
methods, 50–51
scripting, 47–50
ActiveX Exploder Control, 51, 64–65
Address restrictions. *See* Internet Protocol
Administrative functions. *See* Back-office administrative functions
AIX, 208, 230
America Online (AOL), 19, 20
Anonymizer Web site, 111, 112
Anupam, Vinod, 86
AOL. *See* America Online
Apache, 223
servers, 164. *See also* NCSA/Apache server
Web servers, 222
APIs. *See* Application programming interfaces

Applet Class Loader, 70–71
Applets, 54. *See also* Java applets; JavaSoft; Trusted applets; Untrusted applets
signing, 72–77
security, 77
Application programming interfaces (APIs), 149
Windows API functions, 64
Application-level attack, 160
Application-level security, 218
ASCII characters, 198
ASCII mail readers, 88
ASP. *See* Active Server Pages
Assertions, 201
Asymmetric encryption, 114, 115, 140
Asymmetric key encryption technique, 140
ATMs. *See* Automated teller machines
AT&T, 8, 208
Attachments, 88–89
Attacker organization, 112, 113
Authentication, 123, 200, 218, 224. *See also* Client; Digital certificates; Host-based authentication; Market authentication; Password; Unix; User authentication; Weak authentication; Windows NT
file, 187

Authentication, *(Continued)*
protocols, 139
Authenticode, 41–63, 68, 76, 77
1.0, 44
2.0, 44, 54
process, 42–45
security enforcement. *See*
Microsoft
security flaws, 45–54
Auto-By-Tel, 8
AUTOEXEC.BAT, 80
Automated teller machines
(ATMs), 4, 108, 113, 137
Automatic directory listing,
167, 224
Automation. *See* Back-office
automation

B

Back-end
credit card
infrastructure, 127
databases, 24, 158, 159,
161, 185
financial infrastructure, 151
financial settlement
systems, 155
processing engine, 256
settlement system
infrastructure, 134
transaction processing
infrastructure, 8
Back-office
administrative functions, 7
automation, 7
Backticks, 198, 199
Banking. *See* Internet banking
.BAT file, 80
Batch cycles, 134
Batch file, 82
BAT/CMD flaw, 228
BBSs, 82, 83
Behavior, 200, 201. *See also*
Program
Bell Labs, 86, 208
Biometrics, 241
Black-and-white model, 76, 77
Black-box analysis, 268

Blinding, 100, 143, 144
paradigm, 151, 152
Breaking News Network, 13
Brokerage firm, 6
Brokers. *See* Full-service
brokers
Browsers, 22, 44, 48, 60. *See also*
Client; Internet Explorer;
Netscape Navigator; World
Wide Web
plug-ins, 37
vendors, 130
Buffer. *See* Program
overflows, 191–197, 245–246
Bugtraq, 248, 253
newsgroup, 244
Built-in classes, 70, 71
Business
paradigm dangers, 1–29
transactions. *See* Internet
Business-to-business
commerce, 2
Business-to-business
e-commerce, 32
ByteCatcherX control, 50, 51
Bytecode, 68. *See also* Java
bytecode
verifier, 68–71

C

C, 32, 38, 67, 183, 184, 196,
199, 265
C-language routine, 222
function, 182
programmers, 245
C++, 32, 38, 67
CA. *See* Certification
Authority
CAFE. *See* Conditional Access
for Europe
CardJava, 67
Caronni, Germano, 14
Cash. *See* CyberCash; e-cash;
Electronic cash; Visa
Cash-based systems, 142
Castanet, 90, 91
client, 92
CCC. *See* Computer Chaos
Club

Central Intelligence Agency
(CIA), Web site, 11, 12
Central processing unit
(CPU), 148, 152, 239
meter, 239
resources, 236
CERT Coordination Center
(CC), 46, 72, 84, 227,
246, 248, 258
Certificate deadly default. *See*
Communicator 4.0
Certificates. *See* Digital
certificates
Certification Authority (CA),
41–46, 53, 62, 117, 120,
176, 178, 254, 260–262,
265. *See also* Trusted CAs
role, 106–109
CGI. *See* Common Gateway
Interface
Challenge/response system,
234, 235
Channels. *See* Active channels;
Secure channels
Chaos Computer Club, 17
Check-summing
functions, 231
Chemical Bank, 108
Chief information officer
(CIO), 206, 210
CIA. *See* Central Intelligence
Agency
CIAC, 248
CIO. *See* Chief information
officer
Cipher-cracking code, 35
Ciphertext, 114. *See also* RC5
48-bit ciphertext
Citibank, 107, 108
Web request, 113
Class Loader. *See* Applet Class
Loader
Client. *See* Castanet
authentication, 132–133, 178
database, 185
browser, 110, 120, 176
hostname restrictions,
168–171

privilege, escalation, 165–166
security, 22
software. *See* World Wide Web
Client/server
computing, 32
intranet applications, 265
paradigm. *See* World Wide
Web
Client-side
active content, 15
browsers, 256
security risks, 21
systems, 78
vulnerabilities, 31–95
Code-cracking applet, 35
Code-signing flaw, 77
COMMAND.COM, 65,
80, 82
Commerce. *See* E-commerce
Commerce server. *See* World
Wide Web
securing, 157–203
summary, 202
Commerce-oriented Web
sites, 10
Commission on Critical
Infrastructure
Protection, 21
Common Gateway Interface
(CGI)
application, 231, 246
bin directories, 182
binary executables, 181
cgi-bin directories, 181,
182, 184
CGI-related security issues,
230
cgi-src directories, 181
directories, 223, 224
executable directories, 231
executables, 182, 230
exploits, guarding, 230–232
file permissions, 225
input stripping, 230
program sources, 165, 167
programs, 24, 180, 182,
197–200, 224, 231
script sources, 184, 188

scripts, 24, 36, 158, 161,
165–167, 179–185, 188,
189, 216, 218, 222, 223,
231, 232, 256. *See also*
Custom-grown CGI
scripts; Default CGI
scripts
dangers, mitigation, 179–185
flaws, 229–232
security problems. *See*
Windows NT
software, 24
source directories, 182
sources, 188
utilities, 181
Communications Decency
Act, 11
Communicator
4.0, 220–221, 240
certificate deadly default,
220–221
4.01, 62
4.01a, 220–221
Component-based software,
25, 268
Computer Chaos Club (CCC)
ActiveX Control, 65–66
Computer Security Institute
(CSI), 10
Conditional Access for Europe
(CAFE), 100, 151–152
Confidentiality, 132
breach, 12–16
CONFIG.SYS, 80
Consumer, 133–135
transaction request, 133
Containers. *See* ActiveX
Control. *See* ActiveX control;
ActiveX Exploder
Control; Computer
Chaos Club ActiveX
Control; Deadly controls
Cookies, 34, 175, 178
distribution, 224
CORBA, 253, 255, 257, 265
Core dump, 245
Corporate LAN, 214

Cost/benefit trade-off
analysis, 180
Counterpane Systems, 15
CPU. *See* Central Processing
Unit
Cracker, 184, 185
community, 197
Credit card
number, 134
encryption, 134
transactions, 134, 135, 151
Cross-platform
attacks, 237–238
language, 263
portability, 67
software components, 256
vulnerabilities, 232
Crypto API, 76
Cryptographic coin systems,
141. *See also* Stored-value
cryptographic coin system
Cryptographic coins, 141–143
Cryptographic keys, 153
CSI. *See* Computer Security
Institute
Custom-grown CGI
scripts, 230
Cyber malls, 8
Cybercash, Inc., 9
CyberCash, 99, 125, 127–131,
135, 154, 255
firewall, 130
Wallets, 147
CyberCoin, 100, 146–147
Cybersleuths, 79
Cybersnot
bug, 82
Industries, 79–81
problem, 79–81

D

Data Encryption Standard
(DES), 114
Data integrity, 123, 132
violations, 19–20
Data transaction, securing,
97–156
summary, 154–155

Databases, 160–161. *See also* Object-oriented databases; Relational databases
access. *See* Password
administrator (DBA), 187
programs, 256
vulnerabilities, 185–189
Data-driven attacks, 208, 211, 214–216, 238, 247
DBA. *See* Database administrator, 187
DBM, 185
DCE, 253
DCOM, 253, 255
Deadly controls, 46, 50, 63–66
Deadly defaults, 186. *See also* Communicator 4.0; Network; Windows NT
Deadly Web Server configurations, 223–225
Dean Witter, 5
Debit card payments, 135
DEC. *See* Digital Equipment Corporation
Default CGI scripts, 222–223
Defense-in-depth strategies, 187
Deloitte & Touche, 17
Delphi, 38
Denial of Service, 20–21, 236–240
attacks, 158, 192, 236–240. *See also* Windows NT-specific denial-of-service attacks
problems, 239
programs, 159
vulnerabilities, 218
Department of Justice (DOJ), Web site, 11, 12
DES. *See* Data Encryption Standard; Digital Encryption Standard
Desktop integration problems, 78–82
deVitry, David, 16

Dialog boxes, 44, 48, 53, 59–62
Dial-up access, 214
Dial-up modem connections, 138
Dictionary-based attack, 235
DigiCash, 143, 147, 151, 152, 154, 255
software, 145
Digital certificates, 132, 133, 150, 168, 224
authentication, 175–178
Digital Encryption Standard (DES), 172, 242, 243
algorithm, 242
encryption, 207, 233
keys, 234
Digital Equipment Corporation (DEC), 6
Digital signatures, 120, 140
Directories. *See* Common Gateway Interface
Directory listing. *See* Automatic directory listing
Dirty dozen, 32, 34, 36, 82–92
commands, 80, 228
Distribution. *See* Cookie distribution
DNS. *See* Domain Name Service
DNS-based attacks, 238
Document permissions, 225
Document root, 165
Documents, access control, 168–178
DOJ. *See* Department of Justice
Domain Name Service (DNS), 168, 232, 239
look-up, 171
server, 92, 169
server attacks, 236
DOS, 65
Dot dot /..\.. flaw, 228–229
Double-reverse client look-up, 169
Dow Jones & Company, 109

Drop-in replacements, 183
Dun & Bradstreet, 42, 260
Dynamic analysis, 200, 268
techniques, 201
Dynamic HTMLs, 4
pages, 4
Dynamic routing algorithms, 101
Dynamic white-box analysis, 269
techniques, 201

E

8K URL bug, 229
E-broker, 5
e-cash, 142–146
liability, 144
E-commerce. *See* Electronic commerce
EDI. *See* Electronic Data Interchange
EEPROM. *See* Electrically Erasable Programmable Read Only Memory
EFT. *See* Electronic funds transfer
Electrically Erasable Programmable Read Only Memory (EEPROM), 149
Electronic cash (E-cash/ e-cash), 23, 99, 135
cards, 153
industry, 9
process, 137–138
protocols, 100
representing, 140–142
securing, 138–140
transactions, 3, 4
transfers, 100
Electronic coins, 140
Electronic commerce (E-commerce). *See* Business-to-business e-commerce
applications, 24, 26, 160, 263, 265, 273

future, securing, 253–274
market, 125
payment systems, 100
security, 3, 21–26, 157,
270–273
future, 25–26
status quo, 257–261
services, 21, 24
systems, 11, 13, 24, 258,
259, 261
threats, 9–21
transactions, 100, 227,
241, 272
Electronic Data Interchange
(EDI) systems, 2, 7
Electronic funds transfer
(EFT), 18
Electronic mail (E-mail), 83
address, 111, 260
attachments, 37, 72, 84, 89
message, 109
Electronic transactions, 98. *See
also* Secure electronic
transaction
Electronic wallet, 128
E-mail. *See* Electronic mail
Emergency Restore Disk
(ERD), 243
directory, 226
Encryption. *See* Credit card
number
algorithm, 158
End-to-end encryption, 103
End-to-end service, 102
End-user protection, 44
Enterprise Integration
Technologies, 119
Enterprise-critical
applications, 179, 193
data, 59
machine, 92, 273
operation, 23
ERD. *See* Emergency Restore
Disk
E-Schwab, 5
E★trade, 5
European Commission, 17
European Currency Units, 17

European Union, 17
exec SSI command, 167
Execution privilege, 223
Extranets, 7

F
FAA. *See* Federal Aviation
Administration
FBI. *See* Federal Bureau
of Investigation
FDA. *See* U.S. Food and Drug
Administration
Federal Aviation Administration
(FAA), 266
Federal Bureau of
Investigation (FBI), 10
Federal Reserve, 98, 100
Fedwire system, 98, 100
File access permissions,
164–165
File input/output (I/O),
75, 263
access, 77
functions, 68
File Transfer Protocol (FTP),
83, 103, 126, 162, 208,
212
protocols, 232
server, 157, 213, 256
sessions, 47
Fine-grained access control, 54
Firewall, 47, 160, 210–212,
235, 248. *See also*
CyberCash
insecurity, 210–216
locking, 213–214
log, 248
log files, 248
FIRST, 248
First Virtual (FV), 99,
125–127, 255
Flat-file format, 171, 185
Frameworks, 255
Fraud. *See* Internet
Front-end server software, 162
Front-end software, 226
Front-end Web, 8
servers, 24

FTP. *See* File Transfer
Protocol
Full-service brokers, 5
Full-service retail
brokerages, 5
FV. *See* First Virtual

G
GAO. *See* Government
Accounting Office
GE. *See* General Electric
General Electric (GE), 6, 12
General-purpose
computing, 213
General-purpose
machines, 213
Get ../.. flaw, 229
GET method, 227
Ghostscript users, 87
GIF, 22
Gingrich, Newt, 13
GNU utilities, 248
Goldberg, Ian, 14
Government Accounting
Office (GAO), 161
Graphics files, 87–88
GTE, 131

H
Hard-currency systems, 136
Hashing algorithm, 178
Heterogeneous platforms, 102
Holes. *See* Java Sandbox;
Operating system;
Security
Host-based authentication, 178
Hosting machine. *See* World
Wide Web
HP-UX, 208, 230
HTML. *See* HyperText
Markup Language
HTTP. *See* Secure HyperText
Transfer Protocol
HyperText Markup Language
(HTML), 3, 31, 32, 165,
271. *See also* Dynamic
HTMLs; Parsed HTML
documents, 67–68, 167, 224

HyperText Transfer Protocol
(HTTP), 119, 215. *See
also* Secure HyperText
Transfer Protocol
daemon, 166, 216
GET method, 36, 86, 105
network daemon, 162
network protocol, 105
port, 164
protocol, 36, 126, 227
request, 34, 229, 230
Secure HyperText Transfer
Protocol (S-HTTP), 23,
100–101, 125, 255
usage. *See* World Wide Web
server, 166, 222, 225, 231.
See also NCSA HTTP
servers
Web protocol, 226

I

IBM, 131
ICMP. *See* Internet Control
Message Protocol, 192
Identity, certification, 260–261
IE. *See* Internet Explorer
IEAK. *See* Internet Explorer
IIS, 228
IIS server, 229, 258
ILF. *See* Internet Liberation
Front
Independent verification
and validation (IV&V),
262, 264
center, 263
Industrial-strength
applications, 256
Input stream, 193, 194
Input stripping. *See* Common
Gateway Interface
Insecurity. *See* ActiveX;
Firewall; Network
software insecurity
Instruction pointer, 193
Integration problems. *See* Data
integration problems
Integrity. *See* Data integrity

Intelligent agent
applications, 5
Inter-business commerce, 2
Inter-business functions, 6
Interface software, 159
Internal LAN, 210
Internal Revenue Service
(IRS), 161
Internet
banking, 3–4
business transactions, 6–9
commerce providers, 10
connection downtime, 51
fraud, 17–19
investing, 4–6
sabotage, 11–12
security violations, 11
sessions, 122, 124
theft, 17–19
users, 82
vandalism, 11–12
Internet Control Message
Protocol (ICMP), 192
Internet Explorer (IE), 59, 64,
71, 107, 206, 271
3.x (IE 3.x), 48, 53, 56, 59, 86
3.0 (IE 3.0), 53, 56, 62, 78
browser, 86
cache, 80
3.02 (IE 3.02), 79, 81, 82
4.x (IE 4.x / MSIE 4.x), 33,
48, 78
Web browser, 52
4.0 (IE 4.0), 52, 53, 55, 59,
62, 81, 86, 90, 91, 178
Administration Kit
(IEAK), 53
Administrators Kit, 59
protocols, 7, 36
users, 85
Web applications, 179
Web client, 264
Web site, 6
Worm, 195, 196, 257
Internet Liberation Front
(ILF), 12

Internet Payment System, 99,
126, 127
Internet Protocol (IP), 20,
101, 103. *See also*
Transport Control
Protocol/Internet
Protocol
address, 92, 111, 165,
168–171, 175, 188, 232,
258. *See also* Network;
Return IP address
spoofing, 174, 176, 237
address ranges, 168
address restrictions,
168–171, 174
memory location. *See*
Return IP memory
location
packet, 192
spoofing, 178
Internet Service Provider
(ISP), 19, 50, 82, 104,
158, 214, 236, 237
servers, 237
Internet-based
attacks, 226, 233
commerce, 9
company, 8
credit card orders, 131
denial of service attacks, 21
software, 261
transaction, 132
Internet-dependent
business, 257
Internet-safe clients, 218
Intra-business functions, 6
Intranet Web applications, 179
Intrusion-detection software.
See Real-time intrusion-
detection software
Investing. *See* Internet
investing
I/O. *See* File input/output
IP. *See* Internet Protocol;
Return instruction
pointer
IRIX, 208, 230

IRS. *See* Internal Revenue Service
ISAAC, 14
ISP. *See* Internet Service Provider
ISS, 228, 257
IV&V. *See* Independent verification and validation

J

Java, 32, 33, 37, 38, 57, 189, 205, 236. *See also* CardJava
applets, 3, 15, 22, 32, 35, 38, 45, 54, 58, 63, 66–68, 70–72, 75, 76, 80, 91, 189, 262–265, 271
application, 54, 67
bytecode, 69
classes, 71
components, 262–264
developers, 75
Developers Kit, 262
Developers Kit 1.1 (JDK 1.1), 54, 76
language, 67
library, 70, 71
security, 66–77
model, 76
policies, 71
Java Sandbox, 68–71, 76
holes, 72
security model, 54
Java Security, 45, 63
Java Security Manager, 264
Java Virtual Machine (JVM), 68–71, 267
JavaBeans, 253, 263
JavaScript, 15, 31, 32, 39, 49, 57, 80, 84–87, 112, 271
code, 84
vulnerabilities, 85
JavaSoft, 67, 68, 72, 266, 267
applet, 76
JDK 1.1. *See* Java Developers Kit 1.1
JIT. *See* Just-in-time
JPEG, 22

JPEG graphic file, 88
JScript, 39, 84
Just-in-time (JIT) service, 186
JVM. *See* Java Virtual Machine

K

Kimera, 70
Kludge, 34, 259

L

LanMan, 234, 235
authentication, 235
LANs. *See* Local area networks
Large-scale security failures, 257
Link following. *See* Symbolic link following
Linux, 208, 230, 238
LiveConnect, 87
.LNK files, 79, 80, 81
Local area networks (LANs), 7, 53, 67, 104, 174, 211. *See also* Corporate LAN; Internal LAN
Locking attack, 236, 239
LoVerso, John Robert, 84, 85
Lower-level representation, 182
Lowest common denominator, 220
Lucent Technologies, 86, 236

M

Machine-specific object code, 38
Macintosh, 67
system, 205
Macromedia, 16
Mail server, 157, 162, 216
Malware, execution, 35–37
Marimba, 90, 91
Market authentication, 133
Massachusetts Institute of Technology (MIT) bug, 82
MasterCard, 100, 131
credit card, 126
MasterCard International, 152, 153

MCDC. *See* Multiple Condition Decision Coverage
McLain, Fred, 64, 65
MD4, 235
algorithm, 242
MD5, 182
Memphis, 78
Mercantec, 16
Merchant, 133–135
request acknowledgement, 133
Merrill Lynch, 5
Message digest. *See* Order
Meta-characters, 198
Microsoft, 18, 131
Authenticode security enforcement, 76
FrontPage Server Extensions, 230
IIS Web server, 246
Mail/News, 78
MS Word, 239
application, 89
documents, 89, 260
macros, 22, 89
Office, 239
MIDS, 82
MIS manager, 206
MIS officers, 248
Mission-critical machine, 92
MIT. *See* Massachusetts Institute of Technology
Mondex, 152–153
cards, 151
smart cards, 152
Monolithic programs, 254
Morgan Stanley, 5, 7
Morris, Jr., Robert T., 195
MSIE 4.x. *See* Internet Explorer
MSNBC, 72
Multiple Condition Decision Coverage (MCDC), 266

N

NASA. *See* National Aeronautics and Space Administration

NASDAQ stock quotes, 4
National Aeronautics and
    Space Administration
    (NASA),Web site, 11, 12
National Computer Security
    Administration (NCSA),
    222, 223
    NCSA HTTP servers,
        164, 174
    NCSA HTTPd server,
        227, 230
    NCSA/Apache server, 182
National Westminster Bank
    PLC, 152
NCSA. See National
    Computer Security
    Administration
Need-to-know, 9
NetBIOS, 226, 233, 235
Netscape
    2.0 users, 85
    2.01 users, 85
    3.0, 85
    application, 220
    Commerce server, 164, 223
    Communicator, 90
        4.x, 33
        4.0, 78, 178, 220
    mail agent, 78
    Mailer, 88
Netscape Navigator, 59, 71,
    85, 88, 206
    2.x, 86
    3.*, 57
    3.x, 86
    3.0, 16
        browser, 36
    4.x, 106, 107, 109
    4.0, 86
Netscape users, 85
Network
    information system (NIS),
        207, 218, 232, 233
    IP address, 232
    level, 257
    operating systems
        (NOSs), 232
    platform, 205

server vulnerabilities,
    216–247
    caveats, 218–219
    deadly defaults, burying,
        219–226
    software vulnerabilities. See
        Unix-specific network
        software vulnerabilities
Network of Workstations. See
    University of California
Networking software
    insecurity, 232–235
News server, 157, 162, 256
NeXTmail, 89
NeXTStep, 89
NIS. See Network
NNTP, 103
Non-Java compiler, 69
Non-Java-compliant
    compilers, 70
Nonrepudiation, 121, 132
NOSs. See Network
NRC. See U.S. Nuclear
    Regulatory Commission
NTLM authentication,
    234, 235
NYSE stock quotes, 4

O

Object-oriented (OO)
    databases, 24, 160–161
    extensions, 66
Off-line
    accounts, 137
    payment systems, 151
    transaction, 137
OO. See Object-oriented
OOB. See Out Of Band
Open Group Research
    Institute, 84
Operating system (OS), 192,
    209, 218, 233, 244. See
    also DOS
    control, 206–208
    foundation, 210
    holes, 244–247
    OS-level access controls, 225
    OS-related software, 233

securing, 205–206
    security, 25
    software, 207, 229, 244, 248
    vendor patches, 246
Order, message digest, 134
OS. See Operating system
Out Of Band (OOB), 238
Overflows. See Buffer
    overflows

P

Packet, 101
Pages. See Dynamic HTML
    pages;World Wide Web
PANIX. See Public Access
    Networks
Paper-based transactions, 98
Paradigm dangers. See
    Business
Parsed HTML, 230
Password, 175
    authentication, 168, 171–175
    database, access, 243–244
    hash values, 243
Password-cracking
    access, 187
    software, 187
    utilities, 244
    Web page, 172
Payment confirmation, 135
Payment information, 132
Payment request, 135
Payment systems; Stored-
    account payment systems;
    Stored-value payment
    systems
PCT, 255
PEBES. See Personal Earnings
    and Benefits Estimate
    Statements
Penetrate-and-Patch, 257–259
    tools, 259
Perl, 40, 161, 199, 231
    interpreter, 230, 231
    scripts, 181
    shell interpreter, 184
    system, 198

Permissions. *See* Document permissions; Common Gateway Interface; File access permissions
Personal Earnings and Benefits Estimate Statements (PEBES), 160
Personal identification number (PIN), 66, 108, 148, 149, 220, 241. *See also* VirtualPIN
PGP, 88
phf, 182
phf script, 230
PIN. *See* Personal identification number
Ping O' Death, 236–238
Ping program, 192
PKE. *See* Public key
Playboy Web site, 11
Plug and play, 256
Plug-ins, 72, 87–88. *See also* RealAudio plug-in; Shockwave
PointCast, 5, 90, 91
Network, 33, 90
Point-of-sale (POS)
credit card purchases, 154
credit card transactions, 128
purchase, 135
transactions, 130, 131
POS. *See* Point-of-sale
POST method, 105
Postscript, 22
files, 87, 89
interpreter, 32
Princeton Secure Internet Programming team, 113
Princeton University Safe Internet Programming, 72
Privacy, breach, 12–16
Private key encryption, 114, 116
Privilege. *See* Client privilege; Execution privilege
Program
behavior, 269
buffer, 191

stacks, 196
vulnerabilities, 200
Protocol stack, 104
Protocol-based attack, 139
Public Access Networks (PANIX), 236
Public encryption keys, 196
Public key
certificate, 260
cryptography, 115, 116, 121, 122
algorithms, 132
encryption (PKE), 114, 140
Public/private key encryption pair, 260
Public/private key pair, 220, 240
Public/private keys, 150, 260
Pull technology, 5
Purchase amount, 134
approval/denial, 134
Purchase confirmation, 134
Purchase status inquiry, 134–135
Push technology, 5, 37, 89–92, 206, 271
PWDump, 226, 243

Q
QFN. *See* Quicken Financial Network
Query IDs, 232
Quicken, 18, 66
Quicken Financial Network (QFN), 110, 111

R
RAM. *See* Read/write random access memory
RC2, 117
RC4, 117
RC5 48-bit cipher, 14
RC5 48-bit ciphertext, 35
RC5 encryption algorithm, 14
Read-only memory (ROM), 148, 149. *See also* Electrically Erasable Programmable Read Only Memory

Read/write
permission, 225
privileges, 226
random access memory (RAM), 148
RealAudio plug-in, 87
Real-time intrusion-detection software, 219
Referenced Web sites, 28–29, 94–95, 156, 250–251, 274
References, 26–28, 92–94, 155–156, 202, 249–250, 273
REGEDIT program, 80
Register-based cash systems, 141
Registry attacks. *See* Windows NT
Relational databases, 160–161
Relative Domain ID (RID), 243
Remote login
capability, 213
servers, 157, 162
Remote procedure call (RPC), 207, 208, 233, 239
attacks, 236
Request acknowledgement. *See* Merchant
Restrictions. *See* Client hostname; Internet Protocol
Retail brokerages. *See* Full-service retail brokerages
Return instruction pointer (IP), 194
Return IP address, 194
Return IP memory location, 194
RID. *See* Relative Domain ID
RISKS, 11, 270
archive, 21
rlogin, 103
Root, 163. *See also* Document root; Server root; User ID
privilege, 190
Routers, 213

RPC. *See* Remote procedure call
RSA 48-bit cipher, 35
RSA Data Security Corp., 14, 109, 132, 135, 242
RSA encryption, 109
  technology, 130
rsh, 103

S

Sacrificial lamb, 160
SAIC, 131
SAM. *See* Security Accounts Managers
Sandbox, 45. *See also* Java Sandbox
SATAN, 211, 258, 267
  network scanning tool, 10
Schneier, Bruce, 15
Schwab, Charles, 19. *See also* E-Schwab
SCO, 208
Scripting. *See* ActiveX; ActiveX controls
Scripts, 37. *See also* Common Gateway Interface; Default CGI scripts; Server-side scripts
SDK. *See* ActiveX Software Developer Kit
Secure channels, 101–124
Secure Electronic Transaction (SET), 99, 125, 131–135, 138, 206, 255
  protocol, 150
Secure Internet Payment System (SIPS), 99, 125, 127, 128, 131, 146, 147
Secure sessions
  confidential data leak, 105
  establishment, SSL usage, 103–106
Secure Sockets Layer (SSL), 23, 59, 100, 113, 121, 125, 127, 132, 154, 175–177, 206, 255
  connections, 164

process, 114–119
protocol, 149
session, 106, 117, 178
usage. *See* Secure sessions
Secure software, design, 189–197
Secure transport, 23
Security. *See* ActiveX; Client security; Electronic commerce security; Java security; Operating system security; Server-side security; World Wide Web; World Wide Web Server
analysis. *See* Software
certification, 263
  signature, 264
components, certification, 253–254
decisions, making, 62–63
flaws. *See* Authenticode
holes, 257. *See also* University of Maryland
manager, 71–72
policy, setting, 55–63
risks. *See* Client-side; Server-side security risks
zones, 52–55
Security Accounts Manager (SAM), 209, 243
access permissions, 243
database, 234, 235
file, 225, 226
password file, 226
Security-assurance techniques, 186
Security-critical
  flaws, 201
  sections, 202
Security/privacy problem, 224
Security-related
  bugs, 215
  flaws, 197, 227, 271
  problems, 244
Segmentation fault, 193, 245

Server. *See* Commerce server; World Wide Web Server
defending, 247–249
root, 165, 180
security. *See* World Wide Web
software. *See* Front-end server software
vulnerabilities. *See* Network
Server Message Block (SMB), 234
client, 235
password, 242
server, 235
Server Side Includes (SSIs), 167, 224, 230. *See also* exec SSI command
Server-side
applications, 34, 36, 256
processing, 241
programs, 36, 79, 189, 218, 229
scripts, 161–162
security, 24, 202
security risks, 21
Server-write key, 118
Service, denial, 20–21
Service Packs, 229
Sessions. *See* Secure sessions; World Wide Web
SET. *See* Secure Electronic Transaction
SFP. *See* Stack frame pointer
Shades-of-gray model, 77
Shell interpreter, 184, 230
Shell scripts, 181
Shockwave, 15, 16
  plug-in, 88
Shopping cart, 39
S-HTTP. *See* Secure HyperText Transfer Protocol; World Wide Web
Signal-to-noise ratio, 33
Signature algorithms, 144
Signatures. *See* Digital signatures
Singapore Privacy Bug, 87

SIPS. *See* Secure Internet
    Payment System
Site-specific information, 226
Small-value
    purchases, 150, 153
    systems, 99
    transactions, 146, 151, 155
    market, 100
Smart cards, 147–148, 240,
    241. *See also* Mondex;
    Stored-value smart cards
    applications, 148–150
    value, storage, 150–151
Smartcards, 23
SMB. *See* Server Message
    Block
S/MIME, 15, 220, 255
    e-mail, 220
    encryption, 220
SNMP, 214
Software. *See* Common
    Gateway Interface;
    Component-based
    software; Front-end server
    software; Interface
    software; World Wide
    Web; World Wide Web
    Server
    certification, 261–262
    component, definition,
        254–257
    design. *See* Secure software
    flaws, 46–47
    insecurity. *See* Network
    patch, 182
    security analysis, 197–202
    vulnerabilities. *See* Unix-
        specific network
        software vulnerabilities
Software Publisher Certificate
    (SPC), 41–44, 46, 64
Software-based fault
    injection, 270
Solaris, 208, 230
Source-code-level
    instrumentation
    techniques, 201
S&P. *See* Standard & Poor

S/PAY, 135
SPC. *See* Software Publisher
    Certificate
Special-purpose applications,
    255
Spoofing, 169. *See also*
    Internet Protocol; World
    Wide Web
SRI, 11
SSA. *See* U.S. Social Security
    Administration
SSIs. *See* Server Side Includes
SSL. *See* Secure Sockets Layer
    SSL-enabled server, 103
    SSL-protected session, 104
    SSL-secured session, 105, 112
Stack frame, 193
    pointer (SFP), 194
Stack smashing, 194
Stacks. *See* Program
Stamping, 262–265
Stand-alone machines, 205
Standard & Poor (S&P), 20
Static analysis, 199, 200
Static check, 68
Static type checking, 69
Static Web pages, 161
Status inquiry, 134
Status quo. *See* Electronic
    commerce security
Sting operations, 146
Stored account, 97
Stored value, 97
Stored-account
    payment systems, 98,
        124–135, 142, 143, 154
    payments, 138
    systems, 99, 100, 142
    transactions, 155
Stored-value
    cards, 150
    cryptographic coin
        system, 142
    e-cash systems, 138
    payment systems, 98,
        135–154
    pros/cons, 136–137
    register, 152

smart cards, 151
    systems, 99, 100, 136–137,
        152, 153
Stress testing, 197
Sub-shell, 231
SUID. *See* User ID
Sun Microsystems, 67, 72,
    207, 218, 233
SunOS, 208, 230
Super user, 184
    privileges, 163
Swiss Federal Institute of
    Technology, 14
Symbolic link following, 167
Symmetric cryptographic
    key, 139
Symmetric cryptography, 122
Symmetric decryption,
    114–116
Symmetric key
    approach, 139
    pair, 118
SYN flood, 237–238
SYN flood attack, 238. *See
    also* Transport Control
    Protocol/Internet Protocol
SYN-ACK response, 237
System registry attacks, 245.
    See also Windows NT

T

Tainting, 231
Take-home message, 175
Tamper-evident devices, 141
Tamper-resistant devices, 141
TCB. *See* Trusted computing
    base
TCP. *See* Transport Control
    Protocol
TCP/IP. *See* Transport Control
    Protocol/Internet
    Protocol
Technologies, certification,
    265–270
Technology-based system, 81
Telebroker, 19
Telecommunications
    infrastructure, 151

Telnet to Port 103, 229
Telnet, 83, 103, 208, 229, 232
  sessions, 47
Telnet-based attack, 229
Terisa Systems, 119, 131
test-cgi script, 223
Theft. *See* Internet
Time Of Check To Time Of
  Use (TOCTOU), 199
  flaws, 200
TOCTOU. *See* Time Of
  Check To Time Of Use
Traceability, 98, 138
Transaction. *See* Data
  transaction; Electronic
  cash; Electronic
  commerce transactions;
  Internet; Secure
  electronic transaction
  processing infrastructures.
    See Back-end
    transaction processing
    infrastructure
  request. *See* Consumer
Transport. *See* Secure
  transport
Transport Control Protocol
  (TCP), 102, 103
Transport Control Protocol/
  Internet Protocol
  (TCP/IP), 102, 103, 113,
  125
  connection protocol, 237
  protocol implementation, 238
  protocols, 206, 236, 237
  sessions, 192
  SYN flood attack, 236
Tripwire, 231
Trojan Horse, 18, 19, 51, 59,
  206, 225, 247, 270
Truncate flaw, 228
Trust
  establishment. *See* ActiveX
  manipulation, 46
Trust-based model, 53
Trusted applets, 76

Trusted CAs, 43, 140,
  178, 221
Trusted computing base
  (TCB), 231
Trusted zone, 54
TRW, 42

U

UL. *See* Underwriters
  Laboratory
Ultrix, 208
UMD. *See* University of
  Maryland
Underwriters Laboratory
  (UL), 26, 254, 265
Uniform Resource Locator
  (URL), 103, 107,
  109–111
  address, 108, 112
  bug. *See* 8K URL bug
  command, 228
  links, 79
  request, 105, 174
  .URL files, 79, 80, 81
  window, 112
University of California
  (Berkeley), 14
  Network of Workstations, 14
University of California
  (Davis), 199, 200
University of Maryland
  (UMD), security hole,
  81–82
University of Washington, 70
Unix, 67, 208–210, 217, 218,
  221, 231, 238. *See also*
  Vanilla Unix
  authentication, 242–243
  bug traq, 248
  crypt algorithm, 172
  file systems, 225
  implementation, 243
  machine, 207, 215
  market, 227
  network server machines, 216
  password, 244
  platforms, 24, 212, 216, 232,
  237

shell, 184, 199
  systems, 163, 164, 193, 205,
  207, 210, 222, 223, 227,
  233, 258
  utility programs, 246
  Web server software, 277
  workstations, 207, 208, 233
Unix-based operating
  system, 248
Unix-based systems, 238
Unix-flavored systems, 223
Unix-specific network software
  vulnerabilities, 233
Unix-specific OS software, 245
Unprocessed ASP file, 229
Untrusted applets, 76
Untrusted Web clients, 179
U.S. Air Force, Web site,
  11, 12
U.S. Food and Drug
  Administration
  (FDA), 266
U.S. Nuclear Regulatory
  Commission (NRC), 266
U.S. Social Security
  Administration (SSA),
  Web site, 160, 161
Usage fee, 256
User authentication, 168,
  171–175
User ID (SUID), 173–175,
  188, 190, 194, 196, 230,
  240, 241, 244–246. *See*
  Account user ID
  root, 194, 247
  root program, 246
User-inputted data, 245

V

Value added networks
  (VANs), 2, 7
Vanilla Unix, 210
VANs. *See* Value added
  networks
VBScript, 15, 31, 39, 49, 80,
  83, 84
Verifier. *See* Bytecode verifier
VeriSign, 41, 46, 62

VirtualPIN, 126, 127
Visa, 131
  Cash, 100, 153–154
  credit card, 126
  International, 100, 150
VisualBasic, 38, 40
Vulnerabilities. *See* Client-
    side; Cross-platform;
    Database vulnerabilities;
    Network; Unix-specific
    network software
    vulnerabilities; Windows
    NT-specific network
    vulnerabilities

W
Walk-throughs, 198
Wall Street Journal Interactive
    Edition Web page, 109
Weak authentication, 240–244
Web. *See* World Wide Web
Web sites. *See* World Wide
    Web
Web-based
  applications, 149
  attacks, 159
  enterprises, 186
  environment, 186
  form, 8, 32
  products, 149
  session, 124
  transactions, 100, 101
White House Communications
    Agency, 13
White-box analysis, 201, 268
  techniques. *See* Dynamic
    white-box analysis
    techniques
Win32 machines, 38, 59
Windows 95, 16, 56, 79, 220
  platform, 18
Windows NT, 16, 79, 208–210,
    216, 218, 221, 237
  authentication, 242–243
  CGI security problems, 230
  deadly defaults, 225–226
  platform, 18, 24
  Deadly Defaults, 247

file server, 225
IIS Web Server, flaws,
    228–229
login password, 242
OS, 209
platforms, 246
Server 4.0, 225
system registry attacks,
    246–247
Windows NT-specific denial-
    of-service attacks,
    238–240
Windows NT-specific
    network vulnerabilities,
    233–235
Windows system, 205
Wintel machines, 38, 80, 257
Worcester Polytechnic
    Institute, 79
Word. *See* MS Word
World Wide Web (WWW/
    Web), 3, 7. *See also* Front-
    end Web
  access, 212
  applications, 19, 39, 67, 162,
    179, 189, 198. *See also*
    Internet Web
    applications; Intranet
    Web applications
  security-critical area, 197
  archive, 244
  browser, 15, 32, 35–38, 59,
    68, 78, 89, 90, 106, 111,
    193, 224, 256. *See also*
    Internet Explorer
browser interface, 78
client machine, 104
client requests, 179
client software, 22, 253
clients, 32–34, 103, 106, 108,
    113, 176, 198, 271. *See
    also* Untrusted Web
    clients
client/server paradigm, 89
commerce servers, 25
document, 170
forms, 31, 84, 105
host, 167, 224

hosting machine, 12
interface, 187
link, 112
objects, 263
page developer, 79
page requests, 36, 169
pages, 4, 5, 12, 17–19, 31, 32,
    35–38, 40, 49–51, 59,
    64, 66, 67, 78–80, 88,
    109, 110, 113, 119, 162,
    165, 167, 168, 170, 173,
    175, 179, 181, 185, 187,
    199, 224, 238. *See also*
    Access-controlled Web
    pages; Password-
    protected Web page;
    Static Web pages
protocol, 34, 127, 208, 215
requests, 159, 160, 162, 165,
    169–171, 184, 188, 216,
    224, 227. *See also*
    Citibank
search engines, 31, 33
security, 163
service, 227
sessions, 31–33, 37, 103, 110,
    112–114, 175, 177, 206
securing, S-HTTP usage,
    119–124
shopper, 117
site address, 111
sites, 5, 11, 12, 16–19, 22,
    34–36, 49–54, 68, 78,
    84–90, 105, 109, 119,
    146, 178, 185, 228,
    267, 272. *See also*
    Central Intelligence
    Agency; Commerce-
    oriented Web sites;
    Internet; National
    Aeronautics and Space
    Administration; Playboy
    Web site; Referenced
    Web sites; U.S. Air
    Force; U.S. Social
    Security Administration
spoofing, 109–114
surfers, 32, 35, 162

World Wide Web (WWW/
  Web) *(Continued)*
surfing, 111
systems, 2
technology, 271
user accounts, 171
World Wide Web (WWW/
  Web) Server, 2, 12, 32,
  34, 103, 104, 106, 108,
  110, 124, 128, 150,
  157–160, 179–182,
  185–189, 192, 199, 213,
  216, 217, 223, 224, 227,
  232. *See* Apache; Front-
  end Web servers;
  Microsoft

authentication, 150
configurations, 166, 272. *See
  also* Deadly Web Server
  configurations
files, 163
flaws, 226–229. *See also*
  Windows NT
host machine, 222
installation, 163–164
machine, 272
options acceptance risk,
  166–167
requests, 165
root directory, 229
security, 21, 23–25, 162–178

software, 3, 157, 162, 210,
  218, 222, 227, 253, 272
trust, 176
vulnerability, 182
Worm. *See* Worm
WWW. *See* World Wide Web

X

X.509 certificates, 42, 120

Y

Yankee Group, 6

Z

Zones. *See* Security; Trusted
  zone